THE MEXICAN WAR

THE MEXICAN WAR

By the Editors of

TIME-LIFE BOOKS

with text by

David Nevin

TIME-LIFE BOOKS / ALEXANDRIA, VIRGINIA

Time-Life Books Inc.
is a wholly owned subsidiary of
TIME INCORPORATED

Founder: Henry R. Luce 1898-1967

Editor-in-Chief: Hedley Donovan
Chairman of the Board: Andrew Heiskell
President: James R. Shepley
Vice Chairmen: Roy E. Larsen, Arthur Temple
Corporate Editors: Ralph Graves,
Henry Anatole Grunwald

TIME-LIFE BOOKS INC.

Managing Editor: Jerry Korn
Executive Editor: David Maness
Assistant Managing Editors: Dale M. Brown,
Martin Mann, John Paul Porter
Art Director: Tom Suzuki
Chief of Research: David L. Harrison
Director of Photography: Robert G. Mason
Senior Text Editor: Diana Hirsh
Assistant Art Director: Arnold C. Holeywell
Assistant Chief of Research: Carolyn L. Sackett
Assistant Director of Photography:
Dolores A. Littles

Chairman: Joan D. Manley
President: John D. McSweeney
Executive Vice Presidents: Carl G. Jaeger,
John Steven Maxwell, David J. Walsh
Vice Presidents: Peter G. Barnes (Comptroller),
Nicholas Benton (Public Relations),
John L. Canova (Sales), Herbert Sorkin
(Production), Paul R. Stewart (Promotion)
Personnel Director: Beatrice T. Dobie
Consumer Affairs Director: Carol Flaumenhaft

THE OLD WEST

EDITORIAL STAFF FOR "THE MEXICAN WAR"
Editor: Thomas H. Flaherty Jr.
Deputy Editor: Gerald Simons
Picture Editor: Robert G. Mason
Text Editors: Bobbie Conlan-Moore, Lee Hassig
Designer: Edward Frank
Staff Writers: Susan Feller, Margaret Fogarty,
David Johnson
Chief Researcher: Lois Gilman
Researchers: Karen M. Bates, Mindy A. Daniels,
Pat Good, Deborah Heineman, Richard Kenin,
Sara Mark, Carol Forsyth Mickey
Art Assistants: Van W. Carney, Lorraine D. Rivard
Editorial Assistants: Diane Bohrer, Barbara Brownell

EDITORIAL PRODUCTION
Production Editor: Douglas B. Graham
Operations Manager: Gennaro C. Esposito
Assistant Production Editor: Feliciano Madrid
Quality Control: Robert L. Young (director),
James J. Cox (assistant), Michael G. Wight
(associate)
Art Coordinator: Anne B. Landry
Copy Staff: Susan B. Galloway (chief),
Margery duMond, Patricia Graber, Florence Keith,
Celia Beattie
Picture Department: Linda Hensel
Traffic: Jeanne Potter

THE AUTHOR: David Nevin is a veteran journalist and a long-time student of the American West. He began his writing career as a Texas newspaperman and later spent 10 years on the staff of LIFE magazine. He is the author of eight books, including three other volumes in the TIME-LIFE Old West series: *The Soldiers, The Expressmen* and *The Texans.*

THE COVER: Attacking at Buena Vista in February 1847, Kentucky cavalrymen of General Zachary Taylor's army charge headlong into the Mexican ranks. The bloody victory at Buena Vista was one of the 10 major battles in the Mexican War, which won California and a vast territory called New Mexico for the United States and ushered in the great age of Western migration. Major General Winfield Scott, Taylor's successor as the chief American commander, brought the war to its triumphant conclusion with a full-scale invasion of the Mexican heartland. Scott's achievements were honored by a gold medal, authorized by the United States Congress and shown on the frontispiece. A bust of Scott appears on the face of the medal, while the names of his victorious battles are encircled with laurel leaves on the reverse side.

CORRESPONDENTS: Elisabeth Kraemer (Bonn); Margot Hapgood, Dorothy Bacon (London); Susan Jonas, Lucy T. Voulgaris (New York); Maria Vincenza Aloisi, Josephine du Brusle (Paris); Ann Natanson (Rome). Valuable assistance was also provided by: Bernard Diederich, James Budd (Mexico City); Carolyn T. Chubet, Miriam Hsia (New York); Traudl Lessing (Vienna).

The editors are indebted to David S. Thomson, text editor, and David Murray, writer, for their help with this book.

Library of Congress Cataloging in Publication Data
Time-Life Books.
    The Mexican War.
    (The Old West)
    Bibliography: p.
    Includes index.
    1. United States—History—War with
Mexico, 1845-1848—Campaigns and battles. 2.
Southwest, New—History—To 1848. I. Nevin,
David, 1927-II. Title. III. Series: The Old West
(New York)
E405.T55   1978   973.6'23
            77-95212
ISBN 0-8094-2302-2
ISBN 0-8094-2301-4 lib. bdg.

Other Publications:

THE GOOD COOK
THE SEAFARERS
THE ENCYCLOPEDIA OF COLLECTIBLES
THE GREAT CITIES
WORLD WAR II
HOME REPAIR AND IMPROVEMENT
THE WORLD'S WILD PLACES
THE TIME-LIFE LIBRARY OF BOATING
HUMAN BEHAVIOR
THE ART OF SEWING
THE EMERGENCE OF MAN
THE AMERICAN WILDERNESS
THE TIME-LIFE ENCYCLOPEDIA OF GARDENING
LIFE LIBRARY OF PHOTOGRAPHY
THIS FABULOUS CENTURY
FOODS OF THE WORLD
TIME-LIFE LIBRARY OF AMERICA
TIME-LIFE LIBRARY OF ART
GREAT AGES OF MAN
LIFE SCIENCE LIBRARY
THE LIFE HISTORY OF THE UNITED STATES
TIME READING PROGRAM
LIFE NATURE LIBRARY
LIFE WORLD LIBRARY
FAMILY LIBRARY:
    HOW THINGS WORK IN YOUR HOME
    THE TIME-LIFE BOOK OF THE FAMILY CAR
    THE TIME-LIFE FAMILY LEGAL GUIDE
    THE TIME-LIFE BOOK OF FAMILY FINANCE

CONTENTS

1 | A bucolic land on the eve of war

Mexico early in the 1840s, as painted by artist Daniel Egerton, had an idyllic air. Though a fortress guarded its port city of Veracruz *(below)*, there was little in the bucolic scenes of prancing horses and trudging burros to reflect the turmoil of Mexico's recent past, much less warn of the disastrous war that soon would turn these same sites into bloody battlegrounds.

Independent from Spain for barely two decades, Mexico had already lost Texas. With that territory about to join the Union, Mexicans sensed that their expansionist neighbors to the north hungered for New Mexico and California as well. Mexican newspapers cried out for a preventive war, predicting that American conquerors would wipe out the Catholic religion and turn Mexicans into slaves.

But Mexico was ill-prepared for war. Her generals fought each other for the presidency; her army bulged with untrained officers commanding underfed, underequipped Indian conscripts.

Yet war fever forced one president out of office when he attempted to negotiate with Washington. In the spring of 1846, with Texas annexed to the United States and American troops raising a fort on disputed land above the Rio Grande, a new Mexican president declared war. The countryside woke up to the sounds of soldiers, horses and cannon thundering north.

6

Castle San Juan de Ulúa *(left)* guards the harbor and travelers skirt the shore at Veracruz, the target of an American invasion in 1847.

Mexican cavalrymen escort a peacetime shipment of money along the road from Veracruz to Mexico City. From the steep hills above the road the Mexicans would later try in vain to stop the American advance on their capital.

9

Caballeros work and romp in the hills above Mexico City. At left center is the castle of Chapultepec, the formidable guardian of the route the Americans would take to assault the walled city in the climactic battle of the war.

POLK

AND

DALLAS.

A provocative march toward a showdown on the Rio Grande

Spring had come to south Texas in March 1846, and wild flowers blazed in the bright sun as Brigadier General Zachary Taylor's army moved out of its winter camp at Corpus Christi. Ordered by President James K. Polk to "defend the Rio Grande," the army marched southwestward across a rolling stretch of wilderness that was claimed by both Mexico and the United States. For a dozen years the two young republics had been increasingly abrasive neighbors; now it seemed that only arms could settle the disputes between them.

Yet a tenuous peace still prevailed as Taylor's army of 3,000 men moved toward the Rio Grande in four sections, each separated by a day's march. Dragoons led the way, 378 of them in a broad column of four, the horses blowing and snorting, saddle leather creaking and bridles jingling. Behind them came Major Sam Ringgold's "flying artillery," a highly mobile unit equipped with little bronze guns slung low between oversize wheels. The guns, much lighter than conventional artillery, were a new, as yet untested weapon of Ringgold's devising that he was convinced would change the nature of warfare. A day behind them came the 8th Infantry with a second Ringgold-trained battery and, farther back, two more regiments of infantry, the 5th and the 7th. Beside the 5th Infantry rode Captain Ephraim Kirby Smith, a company commander from West Point who, in a letter to his wife, eloquently observed that the Nueces River wound through the prairie they were crossing "like a blue ribbon carelessly thrown on a green robe."

The 1844 campaign banner of James K. Polk and his running mate, George Mifflin Dallas, shows Polk encircled by 26 stars, one for each state. A lone blue star symbolized Polk's promise to annex Texas.

The procession continued with the 3rd and 4th Infantry Regiments and the last of the light-artillery batteries that Ringgold had trained. With the 4th Infantry rode slender, 23-year-old Lieutenant Sam Grant (as Ulysses S. Grant had become known to his West Point classmates). Grant was astride a newly broken mustang that he had frequent disagreements with "as to which way we should go and sometimes whether we should go at all." Behind Grant came the heavy cannon, big 18-pounders, so-called because the cannon balls they fired weighed that much. Bringing up the rear were some 300 supply wagons, grinding along on iron-tired wheels.

The general of this small army moved rapidly up the line on his favorite horse, Old Whitey. Zachary Taylor was 61 years old; he was solid and powerful, a veteran frontiersman and Indian fighter who had never before been in command of a force anywhere near this large. Yet Taylor's courage was legendary; he became calmer as battle neared and his troops were devoted to him because his manner instilled confidence in them all.

For 20 days the army marched across sun-baked Texas plains. "The troops are in excellent condition," Taylor reported. But this judgment might have surprised some of the troops. More than 800 of their number had been left behind in Corpus Christi, too weak to travel after a pestilential winter of dysentery, fever and even snake bite. Now they were frequently tortured by thirst as the water holes became smaller, farther apart and often spoiled by salt. "The sun streamed down on us like living fire," Kirby Smith wrote, and the blue woolen uniforms were suffocating. The soldiers' caps offered little protection, and their faces and necks were baked by the sun until blisters cracked and ran. The road turned into loose sand that Captain William S. Henry, a perceptive diarist, said was "like hot ashes, and when you stepped upon it you sank up to the ankles."

Taylor's advance patrols began sighting Mexican cavalry units, which fell back cautiously. Once the Mexicans set fire to the prairie grass, and the nervous Americans found themselves riding through the flames and worrying about their ammunition. They began to encounter the infamous chaparral that covers much of south Texas and northern Mexico. The open prairie gave way here and there to masses of thorny trees and bushes — live oak, mesquite, thornbush and cactus, bent and twisted in their search for water in the dry soil — so intermingled in spots as to be impenetrable.

About 30 miles from the Rio Grande the troops reached the Arroyo Colorado, a salty tidal stream about 100 yards across and four feet deep with steep banks. On the far side a Mexican officer in brilliant uniform sat his horse, watching the Americans draw up. Mexican bugles sounded in the chaparral, and it appeared that a strong enemy force awaited Taylor and his 3,000. In formal Spanish the Mexican officer informed Taylor that war would commence if he attempted to cross the stream. Taylor grunted and ordered his men to ford the arroyo immediately. "If a single man of you shows his face after my men enter the river," Taylor told the Mexican, "I will open an artillery fire on him." The men liked that. They had come a long way and, Kirby Smith said, were "cheerful and apparently eager for the game to begin."

Four companies of infantry marched in single file toward the water while Ringgold's artillerymen lighted their slow-burning matches, ready to touch off their cannon and rake the opposite bank with metal. The troopers splashed into the water, muskets and cartridge boxes held overhead. There was no motion on the other side. The wading troops passed the halfway point, reached the shore and scrambled up the far bank. They began to cheer. The Mexicans had gone, the last lancer drifting down the trail as the Americans came dripping from the crossing. The band struck up "Yankee Doodle Dandy," and some of the soldiers decided the Mexicans would never fight.

Taylor's men moved on toward the Rio Grande. They arrived on March 28, 1846, and looked across the 100-yard width of the river at the Mexican city of Matamoros. It had been a difficult trek across some

200 miles of prairie and desert and what they now saw struck them, said Captain Henry, the diarist who had reported what the hot sand felt like, as "a fairy vision before our enraptured eyes." The city, said Lieutenant Sam French, was "embowered in green foliage with tropical plants around the white houses." The Americans would have been less enraptured had they been aware that the Mexican Army of the North awaiting them had at least as many men as they did and twice as many cannon.

Mexicans climbed onto their roofs to see the American troops. Presently a number of pretty young women came down to the river, took off their clothes and began to bathe. The troops cheered, Kirby Smith wrote, and "some of our young officers were in the water opposite and soon swam toward them." The Mexican guards called the women back and the Americans returned "after kissing their hands to the tawny damsels, which was laughingly returned."

The scene was pretty, but the practical Taylor wasted little time admiring the view. He raised the Stars and Stripes on a 30-foot staff by the riverbank and looked for a spot to build a fort. The ground he selected overlooked an exposed horseshoe bend of the river, from which the American guns could rake Matamoros in two directions. It was an act of calculated boldness, for the fort also would be vulnerable to fire from Mexican guns emplaced on the two southern sides of the river's bend. As work on the fort progressed, Taylor sat, daring the Mexicans to move.

Thus two armies — and two nations — paused on the brink of war. In many respects the two young nations seemed evenly matched. Indeed, many European observers believed, perhaps wishfully, that the Mexicans might give the opportunistic United States a severe comeuppance. Mexico's Spanish heritage included a deep streak of militarism; its army was larger and more experienced in formal warfare. The U.S. Army, except for a successful but undistinguished campaign against the Seminole Indians of Florida in the 1830s, had for a generation known almost no activity beyond peace-keeping duty in widely scattered frontier garrisons.

The 17 months of hectic combat that lay ahead would change the Army — and the course of American history. The Mexican War vastly enlarged the

Pennsylvania Avenue, stretching to the White House *(rear)*, was the heart of prewar Washington, a city of about 40,000 people.

Beyond the Capitol, as it looked in 1850, rises the unfinished Washington Monument, begun at the height of the war with Mexico.

Carried into office on a wave of renascent nationalism, President James K. Polk envisaged a United States that was destined to expand westward—by peaceful means, if possible—all the way to the Pacific.

American West. It assured the United States control of Texas and it added half a million square miles of new territory: New Mexico, California and all of the vast wilderness from the Rocky Mountains to the Pacific Ocean. Except for minor adjustments later, the national boundary was established.

It was a controversial war that in some ways marked the nation's coming of age. For the first time the United States engaged in a major conflict on foreign soil. The war also brought new weapons into wider military use—the rifle, previously only a specialty weapon, and that pearl of the armorer's art, Sam Colt's repeating six-shooter. Ringgold's fast-firing mobile artillery proved such a potent weapon that guns like it were later adopted by many of the world's armies.

For the first time, too, much of the American junior officer corps was professional, the product of the military academy up the Hudson River at West Point that was beginning to thrive under the direction of a tough, intelligent commandant named Sylvanus Thayer. Grant and French and Ringgold and William Henry and Kirby Smith were all graduates, as was Robert E. Lee, who eventually would join Taylor's force. More than 200 officers serving in the Mexican War became Union and Confederate generals in the Civil War, 15 years later.

This was also a war of daring and of great surprises. Major General Winfield Scott, who later took the chief command from Taylor, engineered a bold amphibious landing on Mexico's Gulf Coast; then, without a dependable line of supply, he led 11,000 men into mountains more than two miles high against a defending army of 30,000. Military experts in other countries were sure he was doomed. But Scott and his men came down the mountain passes and stormed through the gates of Mexico City in one of the most brilliant campaigns in U.S. military history.

The war produced other epic efforts. Led by Alexander Doniphan, a Missouri lawyer with no mili-

tary experience, 800 men marched 3,000 miles from Fort Leavenworth, in what is now Kansas, through the deserts of northern Mexico to the mouth of the Rio Grande; they fought two battles, lived off the land and functioned without help and without—as the men complained sharply—even one payday. A young officer by the name of John Charles Frémont rode across the Rocky Mountains with a few dozen men and came out of the snows of the Sierras to help shake California loose from Mexican rule—only to be court-martialed for refusing to acknowledge the authority of an Army superior who arrived later. When Zachary Taylor's line broke under a Mexican assault one terrible morning, he appealed to his once-hated son-in-law, Jefferson Davis, the future president of the Confederacy. Davis threw the Mississippi Rifles into the breach and broke the Mexican charge.

The war was marked by incidents of individual courage and resourcefulness, especially on the part of the U.S. Infantry, which was always outnumbered although usually better equipped than the foe. At Monterrey, infantrymen fought their way up precipitous Federación hill, captured the fort on top and turned its guns on the Mexican batteries on nearby Independencia hill. Phil Kearny and Robert E. Lee opened the route to Mexico City by finding a path through terrain the Mexicans considered impassable and thus not worth guarding. Attacking the seemingly impregnable castle of Chapultepec near Mexico City, infantrymen threw ladders against the high walls and scaled them through a storm of musket fire.

Epic though it was, the war caused a wide, sometimes violent, division in American public opinion. Much of the young nation was infected by war fever. In the massacre 10 years before of the defenders of the Alamo during Texas' revolt against Mexican rule, Mexican troops had committed a string of atrocities in Texas that had outraged the Texans and aroused

American sympathies. Once war was declared against Mexico, so many men flocked to join the Army that recruiting offices were swamped. Quotas filled quickly and a majority had to be turned away. More than 73,000 of the 116,000 men who served on the U.S. side were state-raised volunteers.

At the same time many Americans rightly perceived that Mexico was a weak nation riven by an almost uninterrupted series of revolts that had started in 1821 when the nation had won independence from Spain. A substantial minority in the United States felt the war was little more than a huge land grab by politicians who were single-mindedly determined to expand the nation, regardless of the cost in blood and treasure; antiwar riots broke out in a number of cities. Zachary Taylor himself was opposed to the war until campaign fever took hold.

The Mexican War was never the simple land grab that some critics saw, but there is no doubt that the United States was inexorably thrusting westward in the 1840s. The nation's fast-growing population hungered for new land and new opportunities. A vanguard of 700 American settlers had already arrived in Mexican California; in 1842 the first wagon trains of pioneers had reached Oregon, and the Willamette Valley had begun to fill. This thirst for Western territory was fueled by the almost irresistible idea that the United States was fated to control the continent from the Atlantic to the Pacific. A newly coined phrase, Manifest Destiny, was on everyone's lips. There seemed to be no stopping this westward movement. "They might as well try to stop Niagara," cried James E. Belser of Alabama in the U.S. Congress.

Inevitably, the impulse to move West collided with the interests of Mexico, which claimed not only California but also a vast territory called New Mexico that included the present states of New Mexico, Arizona, Utah and Nevada and part of western Colorado. Although these areas were so distant from Mexico City that the Mexican government ruled them in name only, Mexico was still determined to resist U.S. encroachments. The Americans' inability—or unwillingness—to understand Mexico's determination was a major factor contributing to the war.

Mexico's problems in dealing with its northern neighbor were compounded by its chronic revolution-

SIMPLICITY OF OLD ZACK'S HABITS.

ary turmoil. In 1810 a village priest named Hidalgo had raised the cry for independence from Spain. The Spanish tracked Hidalgo down and beheaded him the next year, but there was no extinguishing the fire he had lighted. Ten years later the wealthy people and landowners in Mexico struck a momentary deal with the rebels and together they ejected the Spanish.

Thereafter the politics and national life of Mexico were dominated by clashes between the two groups that had joined so briefly against Spain. One group, the original rebels, was liberal, democratic and appealed directly to the people. They called themselves federalists because they wanted a loose federation of states. The other group was conservative, autocratic and favored a centralized government that would serve the interests of the wealthy, the landowners and the Church. Its followers called themselves centralists.

The man most adroit at moving between these factions—and who thus became the dominant figure

Camped in precise rows on the Gulf shore north of Corpus Christi, in Texas, a United States "army of occupation" under Zachary

Taylor waits for orders in October of 1845. The following spring the Americans—3,000 strong—marched south against Mexico.

in Mexico—was Antonio López de Santa Anna, who liked to call himself the Napoleon of the West. Born in 1795, Santa Anna gained his first fame while fighting the Spanish. He was a tall, handsome scoundrel, with broad shoulders and slender hips, who loved fine uniforms, women and money and spent much of his enormous energy in their pursuit. He was often a competent general, but his real skill lay in seizing power. Repeatedly it slipped from his grasp, but such was his capacity to charm the crowd that he made amazing recoveries and emerged again and again as the nation's president.

Mexico's instability helped ignite the war in 1846. Its people resented the muscle-flexing of the young United States, especially American moves to take over Texas, which the Mexicans with some reason still considered theirs. It was the U.S. annexation of Texas in 1845—with the resulting dispatch of Taylor's army to protect the disputed border on the Rio Grande—that brought the conflict to a head.

Texas had achieved its independence in 1836 when its rebel army of 783 men under Sam Houston demolished a Mexican force almost twice its size commanded by Santa Anna at the Battle of San Jacinto. Santa Anna was captured and the canny Houston, himself half dead with a leg wound, struck a bargain: Santa Anna could live if he would send his troops home and surrender all Mexican claims to Texas. Santa Anna agreed, but he soon was forced from power. His successors repudiated his agreement with Houston, and for years the Mexican government insisted that Texas was simply a wayward province, in revolt but still part of the Mexican nation.

Texas walked alone for 10 years as an independent republic, constantly alarmed by Mexico's threats to invade and eager to be protected by the United States. Moves to annex Texas were stalled, however, by the growing furor in Washington over slavery, an increasingly sensitive political issue; Northern anti-slavery forces feared that admitting Texas would give the South a big, new, proslavery state. This impasse was overcome in 1844 when Democrat James K. Polk won the U.S. Presidential election as an ardent expansionist. This was a clear signal that the American people—even some who detested the spread of slavery—would back the annexation of Texas. Con-

gress quickly passed a joint resolution inviting Texas to join the Union. On July 4, 1845, Texas accepted and in December it became a state.

Polk was indeed an expansionist. He wanted Texas and, even more, he meant to have the big coastal province the Mexicans called Upper California. But he hoped to acquire them without going to war. As Polk saw it, both California and the even larger province called New Mexico were sure to draw settlers and eventually, like Texas, to declare independence. To Polk, it seemed only reasonable that Mexico should sell them rather than wait for them to be taken. He dispatched an emissary, John Slidell, to Mexico City with an offer to pay $5 million if Mexico would be sensible about Texas, another $5 million for New Mexico and up to $25 million for California.

But neither Polk nor anyone in Washington had a clear grasp of what had been going on in Mexico. News of Congress' invitation to annex Texas had outraged the Mexican people, who were already inflamed by years of anti-American rhetoric. The current Mexican president, José Herrera, dared not even discuss Polk's proposition. Instead, he ordered General Mariano Paredes y Arrillaga to form an army and subdue the rebellious Texans. Paredes, a rabid anti-American, promptly turned the army against Herrera, marched into Mexico City and, as 1846 began, installed himself as president. All hope for compromise vanished when Paredes rejected Polk's emissary. Polk took the failure of Slidell's mission as an augury of war and ordered Taylor, already encamped at Corpus Christi, to march for the Rio Grande, though he was cautioned not to fire first. Paredes moved to reinforce the border and ordered his army to attack at the first opportunity. Now war was inevitable.

President Polk chose Zachary Taylor to command the expedition partly because Taylor was already on the scene but mostly because Polk detested the Army's top general, Winfield Scott. Polk's choice was in some ways a wise one. If Taylor was weak on tactics and strategy—in future battles he would twice miss the opportunity to annihilate the Mexican army facing him—he was a tough, courageous old regular who commanded the respect and even the affection of the soldiers he led. They called him Old Rough and

"Depend on it," wrote U.S. envoy John Slidell after the Mexicans refused to see him, "we can never get along with them until we have given them a drubbing."

Ready, and he was always prepared to saddle and ride, to sleep on wet ground, to dine on salt pork cooked over a tiny flame, solacing himself with chewing tobacco. There was usually a quid tucked in his jaw, and he spat with an accuracy that amazed the young West Pointers and delighted his soldiers.

Taylor was born to a Virginia plantation family and reared in frontier Kentucky where his only formal schooling came from a part-time tutor. When in 1808 the Army was enlarged in the face of a British threat, Taylor was commissioned a lieutenant. Winfield Scott entered the Army the same year. But while the more polished Scott served in the cities of the East and even abroad, Taylor spent his military life on one frontier post after another. His attitude toward command was shaped in countless frontier actions against marauding Indians. They taught him that there is no substitute for action, that the solution to a dangerous situation is to go ahead and that there is almost nothing men cannot accomplish if they are determined and their leader resolute.

Taylor had also learned to master his own fear. He sat his horse placidly under heavy fire. Once when he was exposed to a particularly dangerous cannonade, a colonel suggested that they retire just a bit for the sake of prudence. "Let us ride a little nearer," Taylor said,

"and the balls will fall behind us." Men were made strong by a commander who shared their risks with such calm and confidence and this was one reason Taylor had great rapport with his troops.

Another was his distaste for military pomp and ceremony. A frustrated farmer, Taylor enjoyed talking about crops wherever he went, often with soldiers who were themselves fresh from the farm. And he looked the part. Invited by Taylor for a visit, an infantry captain wrote that "he looks more like an old farmer going to market with eggs to sell than anything I can now think of." An Illinois lieutenant described Taylor as "short and very heavy, with pronounced face lines and gray hair, wears an old oil cloth cap, a dusty green coat, a frightful pair of trousers and on horseback looks like a toad." Green soldiers frequently mistook him for a camp hanger-on. On one occasion a recently arrived lieutenant spotted an old man in back of the general's tent cleaning a sword. "A dollar to clean mine too?" he asked brightly. "Sure thing," came the response. The young lieutenant learned of his mistake an hour later when he formally reported to the general.

Taylor's living style was equally plain. He enjoyed being in the field and operated from a single tent pitched under a convenient shade tree. This was home, office and headquarters, and he sat before it in a chair cut from an ammunition box and padded with a blanket. He cocked his feet on another box that served also as a dining table and desk.

But if Taylor was a good leader he was a less effective general. He knew nothing of sanitation or diet and did little to assure his troops' health. He was irritated and bored by logistics and made impulsive mistakes that cost lives. "He would chat with his soldiers one minute and send them to their deaths the next with hardly a thought," a contemporary wrote.

General Scott, the Army's commander in chief, considered Taylor to be "slow of thought, of hesitancy in speech and unused to the pen." He had purposely supplied Taylor with an unusually brilliant and articulate staff officer. The young adjutant took no such derogatory view of his commander. Captain William Bliss, who was so meticulous that friends nicknamed him "Perfect" Bliss and so charming and generous that they liked him anyway, became devoted

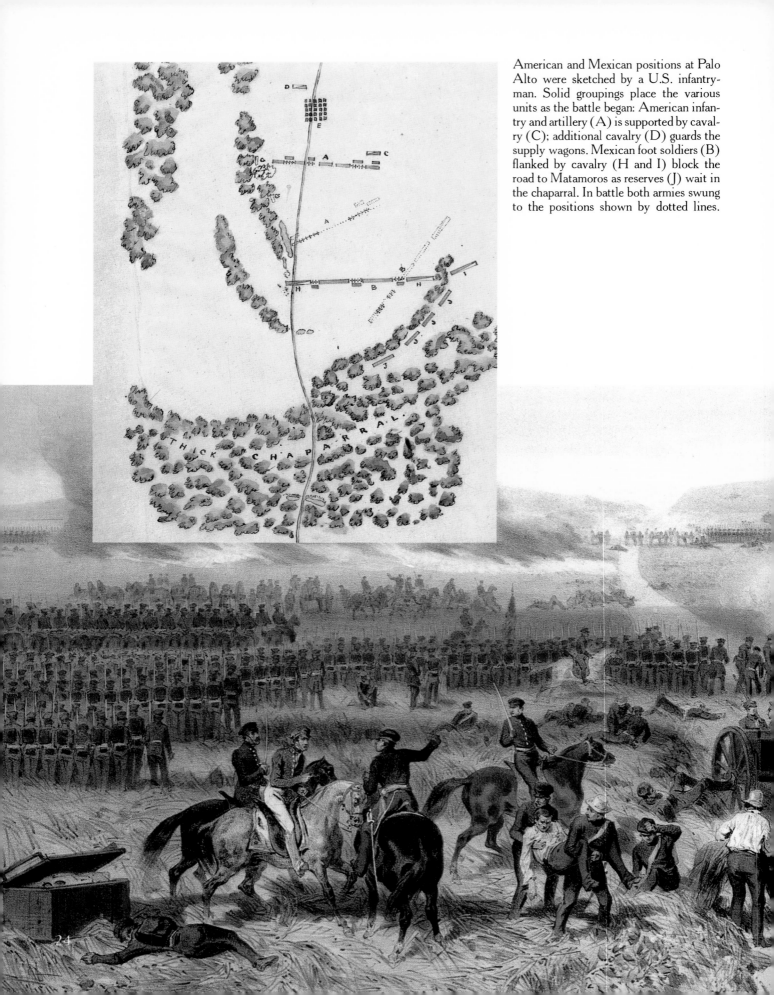

American and Mexican positions at Palo Alto were sketched by a U.S. infantryman. Solid groupings place the various units as the battle began: American infantry and artillery (A) is supported by cavalry (C); additional cavalry (D) guards the supply wagons. Mexican foot soldiers (B) flanked by cavalry (H and I) block the road to Matamoros as reserves (J) wait in the chaparral. In battle both armies swung to the positions shown by dotted lines.

Major Sam Ringgold spills from his saddle, fatally wounded in both of his thighs by Mexican cannon fire. Ringgold, whose superbly drilled "flying artillery" proved itself at Palo Alto, was one of the five Americans who died in the engagement.

Astride "Old Whitey" behind the American line, General Taylor (*at right, below*) confers with his staff. Ox-drawn guns near the line's center and "flying artillery" at left and right sweep the Mexican ranks. A planned bayonet charge was not needed.

25

to Taylor. Eventually he married Taylor's youngest daughter and continued his staff role in the White House when Taylor became President in 1849.

Taylor's command, although small, included more than half of the Regular U.S. Army, then at its lowest ebb in years. The Army's strength was about 5,300 men, spread paper-thin among some 100 posts, mostly along the frontier. Regiments were so fragmented that some had never marched together. Few of the officers had handled large numbers of men in combat, or even on parade.

The Army was understrength in part because the American public, still mindful that the Revolution had been fought to rid the country of the hated British army, had little use for regular soldiers. This negative attitude had been made clear to Sam Grant the first day he donned his new officer's uniform in 1843. Strolling in Cincinnati, near his hometown of Bethel, Ohio, Grant was accosted by a ragged urchin who jeered at him with a popular street saying that characterized all soldiers as loafers. "Soldier, will you work? No sir-ee; I'll sell my shirt first!" Grant said he never really enjoyed wearing his uniform again.

Sharing the urchin's contemptuous attitude, the American public refused to vote funds to support an adequate Regular Army—or even to make duty attractive in the small Army it had. Privates lived hard, dangerous, monotonous lives on rough frontier posts. It is little wonder that the Army attracted mostly immigrants who had trouble finding jobs in a nation that seemed prejudiced against them. About 47 per cent of Taylor's army consisted of immigrants; 24 per cent of his men were from Ireland alone.

Yet professional officers had welded these men into a strong force. Albert Sidney Johnston, another Mexican War veteran who became a Confederate general, observed of them, "When called upon for duty, they do not count the cost." They were brave, Grant said, adding that "a more efficient army for its numbers and armament, I do not believe ever fought a battle."

The army's gallantry was inspired in part by pride. Taylor had asked Louisiana and Texas to raise five regiments of reinforcements, but the regulars were determined to meet, and whip, the Mexicans on their own. A battle must be fought "before the arrival of the volunteers," Captain Philip N. Barbour wrote to his wife, "or the the army will be disgraced."

To the chagrin of this eager Army, its arrival at Matamoros at first produced nothing. The Mexicans made no attempt to cross the Rio Grande or to interfere with the threatening fort that the Americans had begun to build. The fort had five sides made of earthen walls nine feet high and 15 feet thick. A bastion at each corner could hold a battery of cannon. Day by day it rose, an arrogant gesture before the Mexicans' eyes. Taylor also established a supply depot at Point Isabel, a tiny Mexican village on the Gulf Coast about 26 miles east of Matamoros. The road linking Point Isabel and the fort was Taylor's lifeline.

The odd quiet lasted several weeks. Work on the fort went on continuously, but the men found time to hunt for wild horses and to swim in the river. The bands of both armies played in the afternoon, and Grant wrote to his fiancée, a young St. Louis woman named Julia Dent, "I believe there will be no fight."

Naturally, Sam Ringgold turned his light artillery batteries out to drill. Ringgold had revolutionized light artillery in the American Army. The changes, which dated to 1838, were based on two main innovations. One was the introduction of light guns riding on carriages built to move rapidly. The other was a

standardized drill of loading and firing that Ringgold's men practiced incessantly.

The guns were a far cry from the long, iron cannon on cumbersome carriages that were then standard in most armies, including the Mexican. The new U.S. guns had graceful bronze barrels about four feet long with a range of up to 1,523 yards, capable of hurling a six-pound iron ball almost three inches in diameter or a powder-packed exploding shell or a deadly hail of round bullets. Each gun rested on a stout wooden carriage, or caisson, that was slung low between two large wheels. The caisson was attached to a two-wheeled limber that carried ammunition and was drawn by a fast and well-trained team of six horses. Part of the gun crew rode the horses while the rest clung to the caisson, their weight helping to hold down the gun as they galloped into action.

Precision was the key. A battery of four guns rode up and wheeled on command. As the horses turned, the men dropped off the caisson, unlimbered it and broke out rams, swabs, powder and shot. An officer laid the gun for direction and elevation while men rammed home powder sewn in bags of flannel that had been boiled in oil. Next came the ball, the exploding shell or a bagful of lead bullets called canister. The fuselike quick match, ignited by a slow-burning torch, flashed into the powder. Flames gushed from the muzzle and the gun leaped into the air like a terrier, but the men relaid it, swabbed its smoking barrel and rammed home another charge. In 10 seconds the gun was ready to fire again. Older officers trained in heavy artillery could not grasp the mobile firepower Ringgold's cannon would give an army.

Taylor's army on the Rio Grande had both heavy artillery and three of the U.S. Army's total of five batteries of flying artillery. Ringgold commanded his own Battery C. A second battery was led by Lieutenant Braxton Bragg—another future Confederate—and a third by Captain James Duncan. Taylor admired Ringgold's enthusiasm, but Old Rough and Ready really believed in the bayonet. Ringgold was determined to change his mind in the battle ahead.

Infantry training was much simpler. Soldiers were armed, Sam Grant wrote, "with flintlock muskets and paper cartridges charged with powder, buck shot and ball. At the distance of a few hundred yards a man

might fire at you all day without your finding it out." But accuracy was not important because muskets were fired by masses of men in volleys and up close the huge .69-caliber balls were deadly. Rifles, though common in civilian hands, were generally reserved for sharpshooters in the Regular Army. Lucky was the soldier who got his hands on the Model 1841, a .54-caliber muzzle-loader that was the most accurate round-bullet rifle ever made. Later many volunteers were supplied primarily with rifles, but most of the regulars were forced to make do with the Model 1822 flintlock. The Mexican troops they would face used European-made muskets of about the same vintage, and of even shorter effective range.

One Sunday morning during this static period at Matamoros a handsome, red-faced Irishman named John Riley was seized with the desire to go to church. Riley was a big-fisted brawler who had deserted from the British army in Canada, served for a time as a West Point drillmaster and now was a sergeant with the 5th Infantry. He swam the river to Matamoros, went to Mass and did not come back.

Riley was a deserter, one of more than 200 who heeded a Mexican invitation, aimed at immigrants and Catholics, that offered them 320 acres of good Mexican land. Many of the Irishmen in Taylor's army had enlisted as a means of gaining a foothold in a generally hostile American society. Now Mexican propaganda described the American expedition as no less than a crusade against the Church. While Taylor's force shrank, the Mexican army in Matamoros grew steadily. Numbering about 3,000 when Taylor arrived, it had since been strengthened by about 2,000 reinforcements. But the generals in charge appeared to fear Taylor's smaller force. In any case, they did not move against him.

Angrily, President Paredes formally declared a "defensive" war on April 23, 1846, and on the very next day there arrived in Matamoros at the head of still more troops a general who had come to fight. This new leader was Mariano Arista, a tall, muscular man of 43 with a wash of freckles and a head of light sandy hair that were rare in Mexico. Having prospered in the revolution, he had risen to general and acquired land and wealth in northern Mexico. In the early 1830s, however, he had fallen out with Santa Anna and, knowing that Santa Anna was not above having his enemies murdered, he had sought refuge in Cincinnati. There he had learned English and studied American agriculture until Santa Anna's fall from power freed him to return home. Arista was regarded, as an American officer put it, "as a man of great firmness, of good business habits, an excellent judge of character and withal of undoubted courage."

When Arista rode into Matamoros, he took command of more than 5,000 men. Although some of the Mexicans were conscripts and convict soldiers, the army included experienced troops who had fought in Mexico's frequent rebellions: the Tampico Veterans, the 2nd Light Infantry, the 4th and 10th Infantry. Arista also had 1,600 well-mounted lancers under a redoubtable cavalry general, Anastasio Torrejón. Arista sent Taylor a polite note announcing that "hostilities have commenced," and on the day Arista arrived he threw Torrejón and his horsemen across the river, well upstream from Matamoros.

When word of Torrejón's crossing reached him, Taylor sent a cavalry patrol of 65 men to investigate. They galloped off, observed Kirby Smith, "well mounted, well equipped, as gallant a little band as ever struck a blow." At their head on a huge roan horse was Captain Seth Thornton. Aggressive to the point of recklessness, Thornton drove his men hard through the chaparral. Twenty-four miles upstream their Mexican guide refused to go farther. Thornton pushed on, and soon the American patrol was trotting, single file, down a narrow road toward a ranch— several buildings at the far end of a fenced field that was surrounded by chaparral. Beyond lay the river. Thornton's men had crossed the field and were afoot, searching the houses for someone to question, when Torrejón's troopers opened fire from the chaparral.

The Americans mounted and galloped across the field only to find the gates closed. They milled under "galling fire" and fell back toward the ranch buildings. Then a bullet struck Thornton's horse. The big roan, maddened with pain, leaped the fence, threw Thornton to the ground and vanished into the brush. Captain William Hardee rallied the men and led them toward the river. But the ground was marshy, and soon they were surrounded and forced to surrender. Sixteen were dead and several wounded. Thornton, knocked unconscious by his fall, was also captured.

"Hostilities may be considered to have commenced," Taylor wrote to President Polk in the neat language of his flawless adjutant, William Bliss. "American blood has been spilled." Taylor's courier set out posthaste for Washington, 14 days away.

It was 6:30 p.m. on Saturday, May 9, when Taylor's report reached the White House. Polk, seizing on the news of the skirmish, rose from the dinner table and summoned his Cabinet to an emergency session. The Cabinet members quickly arrived at the foregone conclusion: a unanimous recommendation for war.

Polk's message went to Congress at noon on Monday, May 11. The message, cleverly worded to undercut opposition from the Whig minority, did not call on Congress to declare war on Mexico. That would have invited long, soul-searching debate since the Whigs not only opposed war on political and moral grounds but also sensed Presidential infringement on the Constitutional right of Congress alone to declare war. Instead, Polk asked Congress to acknowledge that a state of war already existed, "by the act of Mexico herself," and to provide "the means for prosecuting the war with vigor, and thus hastening the restoration of peace." In effect, the Whigs had two

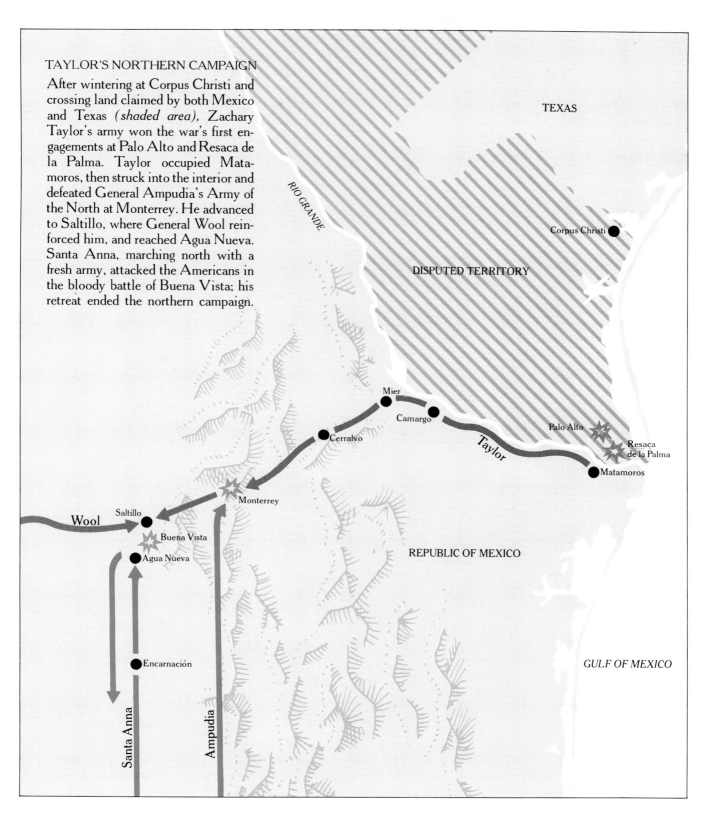

TAYLOR'S NORTHERN CAMPAIGN

After wintering at Corpus Christi and crossing land claimed by both Mexico and Texas *(shaded area)*, Zachary Taylor's army won the war's first engagements at Palo Alto and Resaca de la Palma. Taylor occupied Matamoros, then struck into the interior and defeated General Ampudia's Army of the North at Monterrey. He advanced to Saltillo, where General Wool reinforced him, and reached Agua Nueva. Santa Anna, marching north with a fresh army, attacked the Americans in the bloody battle of Buena Vista; his retreat ended the northern campaign.

TEXAS

RIO GRANDE

Corpus Christi

DISPUTED TERRITORY

Mier

Camargo

Palo Alto

Resaca de la Palma

Cerralvo

Taylor

Monterrey

Matamoros

Wool

Saltillo

Buena Vista

Agua Nueva

REPUBLIC OF MEXICO

Encarnación

GULF OF MEXICO

Santa Anna

Ampudia

choices, both unpleasant: to endorse a war they considered wrong or to argue against backing Taylor's endangered army—a patently untenable position.

In the Senate several Whigs risked their political futures in bitter protests. John M. Clayton of Delaware declared that Polk himself, not Mexico, had provoked the spilling of blood. Sending Taylor into the disputed territory between the Nueces River and the Rio Grande, he said, was "as much an act of aggression on our part as is a man's pointing a pistol at another's breast." But in the House of Representatives, Polk's well-organized Democrats overrode the Whigs with ease. Linn Boyd of Kentucky clinched matters with an amendment to the war bill that proposed to supply the President with 50,000 troops and $10 million for bringing the "existing" war to a "speedy and successful termination." Thereupon a number of Whigs persuaded themselves to support the war, right or wrong. Joining the Democrats, they helped pass the amended bill by wide margins in both houses. Their declaration went to Polk on May 13, and with a stroke of his pen he made the war official.

The declaration produced highly partisan reactions from the nation's press. Whig editor Horace Greeley

American dragoons *(center)* gallop into Mexican cannon fire in this re-creation of the assault on Resaca de la Palma by a U.S. soldier.

shouted hysterically in his *New York Tribune:* "People of the United States! Your Rulers are precipitating you into a fathomless abyss of crime and calamity!" But the prevailing opinion was expressed by poet Walt Whitman, then the editor of the Brooklyn *Eagle:* "Let our arms now be carried with a spirit which shall teach the world that, while we are not forward for a quarrel, America knows how to crush, as well as how to expand!"

In this spirit citizens everywhere staged patriotic demonstrations, and eager young men turned out in droves to enlist at Army recruitment offices. "I have joined the Volunteers Company that's araising," wrote William Dickinson of Shady Grove, Virginia, "to go and slay them Mexicans when caled for." In New York City people paraded with placards emblazoned with the slogan "Mexico or Death," and in Philadelphia 20,000 turned out for a prowar rally. Illinois authorities, asked to raise four regiments, were swamped by enough volunteers to fill 14. Lew Wallace, who later wrote the novel *Ben Hur* while he was governor of the territory of New Mexico, raised a company of volunteers in Indianapolis in just two days. Applicants in Tennessee complained that it was

The dragoons reached the guns, and their headlong charge carried them beyond, leaving the infantry to capture and hold the cannon.

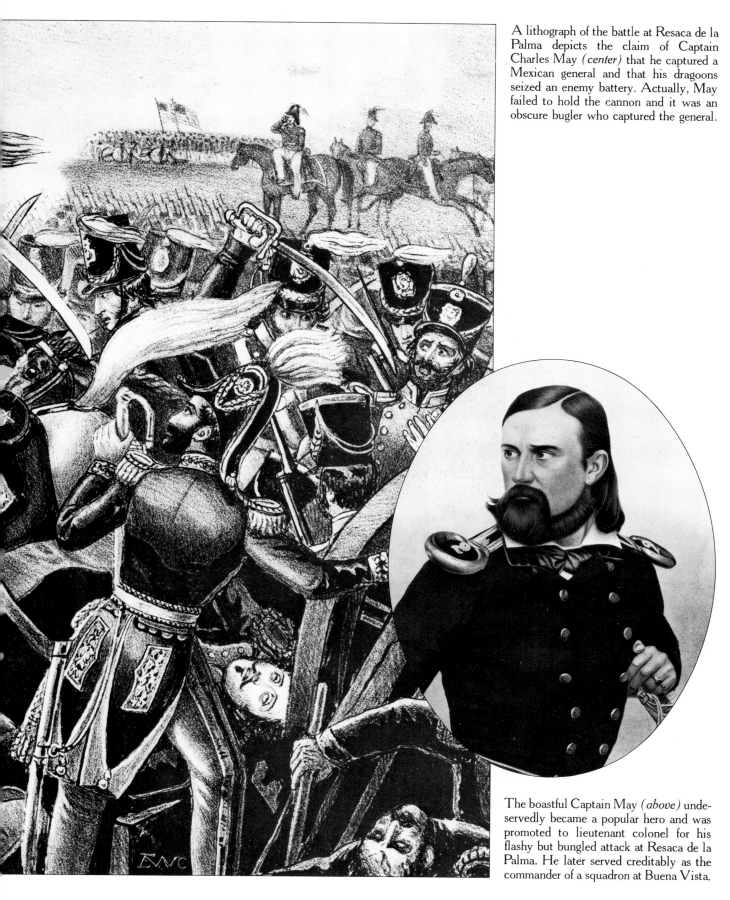

A lithograph of the battle at Resaca de la Palma depicts the claim of Captain Charles May *(center)* that he captured a Mexican general and that his dragoons seized an enemy battery. Actually, May failed to hold the cannon and it was an obscure bugler who captured the general.

The boastful Captain May *(above)* undeservedly became a popular hero and was promoted to lieutenant colonel for his flashy but bungled attack at Resaca de la Palma. He later served creditably as the commander of a squadron at Buena Vista.

BY THE PRESIDENT OF THE UNITED STATES OF AMERICA.

A PROCLAMATION.

Whereas the Congress of the United States, by virtue of the constitutional authority vested in them, have declared by their act, bearing date this day, that, "by the act of the Republic of Mexico, a state of war exists between that Government and the United States:"

Now, therefore, I, JAMES K. POLK, President of the United States of America, do hereby proclaim the same to all whom it may concern; and I do specially enjoin on all persons holding offices, civil or military, under the authority of the United States, that they be vigilant and zealous in discharging the duties respectively incident thereto: and I do moreover exhort all the good people of the United States, as they love their country, as they feel the wrongs which have forced them on the last resort of injured nations, and as they consult the best means, under the blessing of Divine Providence, of abridging its calamities, that they exert themselves in preserving order, in promoting concord, in maintaining the authority and the efficacy of the laws, and in supporting and invigorating all the measures which may be adopted by the constituted authorities for obtaining a speedy, a just, and an honorable peace.

In testimony whereof, I have hereunto set my hand, and caused the seal of the United States to be affixed to these presents. Done at the City of Washington the thirteenth day [L. S.] of May, one thousand eight hundred and forty-six, and of the independence of the United States the seventieth.

JAMES K. POLK.

By the President:
    JAMES BUCHANAN,
        Secretary of State.

The U.S. proclamation of war was signed by Polk on May 13, 1846, four days after Washington learned of a provocative skirmish on the Rio Grande on April 25. News of later battles had not yet arrived.

"difficult even to *purchase* a place in the ranks."

In fact, the rush into war came none too soon. Unknown to Washington, a major battle was in the making. Following orders from Arista, Torrejón and his 1,600 horsemen circled the U.S. position on the Rio Grande, crossed the vital road connecting Point Isabel and Matamoros, and reached the river 10 miles downstream from Taylor's fort. There the cavalry covered Arista as he brought 2,500 infantrymen and some artillery across to the north bank.

Arista's intention was to cut Taylor's lifeline and then to attack and finish off the isolated American force. There was, however, a hitch in the plan. Arista could muster only a few boats and it took his force 24 hours to cross the river. By that time the Americans were moving. Taylor's position suddenly was perilous. He had tarried too long working on the fort, and his army's supplies were dangerously low. Writing to his wife, Kirby Smith said, "Our communication is almost if not entirely cut off with Point Isabel, to which place we must and we will fight our way."

Taylor left 500 men of the 7th Infantry under Major Jacob Brown to hold the fort. Then on the afternoon of May 1, he started the rest of his army at quick pace for Point Isabel. They got there without incident by noon the next day, at about the time Arista's men gained the road. It was obvious to Arista that the Americans had already passed, and he positioned his men near a grove of trees called Palo Alto, or Tall Timber, to await their return.

At the same time, the Mexicans back in Matamoros turned their attention to the fort. All through the 2nd of May the American troops in the fort worked on the last wall, but that evening they heard such a ringing of church bells in Matamoros that they put down their tools and gazed across the river. What they saw was a procession of priests and monks who were moving from one Mexican cannon to the next "blessing gun and shot and shell." Tomorrow would be hot. The Americans slept badly, and the next morning the first Mexican gun sounded, its shot lofting through the sky past a still-gleaming Venus before it burst against the fort.

The American 18-pounders answered, flame and smoke gushing from their muzzles, their iron balls screaming into Matamoros. "It was only 23 minutes after we commenced our fire," a soldier wrote, "before one of our 18-pound shot struck their 12-pound cannon directly in the muzzle. We have not," the soldier added, "heard from their 12-pounder since." Other Mexican guns continued to smash at the fort's walls while mortars lofted exploding shells in lazy arcs that dropped inside the fort. Yet U.S. casualties were very light. One of the first shells blew away part of a sergeant's head. But as the 3rd of May passed into the 4th and 5th, there were no more deaths.

The roaring guns could be heard plainly in Point Isabel, 26 miles away, an angry thunder muted by distance. It was the first time most of the men in the camp had heard hostile cannon. Years later Grant confessed that lying in his tent that morning and listening to the deadly rumble, "I felt sorry that I had enlisted." Wild excitement ran through the camp, but Taylor believed his fort, opposite Matamoros, could hold, and he was unwilling to leave Point Isabel until he had assured its defenses. On the morning of May 6, Mexican cavalry and infantry were in assault positions outside the fort and at dawn a ferocious cannonade began. At precisely 6:30 a.m. Brown ordered his 18-pounders fired, a prearranged signal to Taylor that the assault was near. About 10 a.m., as Brown moved about the fort supervising the construction of shelters, a howitzer shell exploded almost on top of him. He lived in great pain for three more days; later Taylor named the fort in his memory.

The Mexican siege guns continued, eventually pouring more than 2,700 rounds into the fort in a cannonade that lasted five days and nights without a break. By the morning of May 8 the men inside were exhausted by the continued bombardment; outside, the Mexicans were poised for the kill. "I would rather," Captain Henry wrote later, "have fought twenty battles than have passed through the bombardment of Fort Brown." Then, about midafternoon, the Mexican guns paused and the troops outside the fort began to withdraw as the battered defenders heard a different kind of gun cracking in the distance.

The day before, Taylor had issued his orders: the army would march from Point Isabel at 3 p.m. and infantrymen were enjoined that "their main dependence must be upon the bayonet." Old Rough and Ready expected a fight, and he was undaunted by the

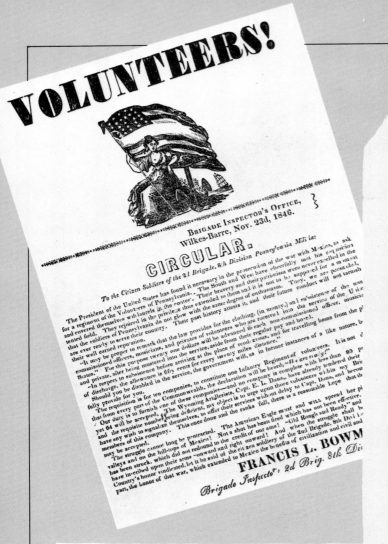

U. S. RECRUITING

RENDEZVOUS

AT THE OFFICE OF

Alphonso Wetmore,

ON PINE STREET.

DIOGONES and T. K. WETMORE will receive the names of recruits for a Company, which each of them are authorized to raise for one of the New Regiments of Infantry of the Army of the United States. The terms of enlistment will be made known at the Head Quarters, where Alphonso Wetmore is authorised to raise a Regiment for the U. S. Service.

ST. LOUIS, January, 29th, 1847.

SOUNDING THE CALL TO ARMS

As news of war spread across the nation, recruiting offices were opened and appeals went out for volunteers. Pennsylvanians were urged to repel "the enemies of our country who have shed American blood on American soil," and Massachusetts men were told that their "glorious successes" would outdo those achieved by "gallant volunteers of the South-West."

The turnout was phenomenal; in Tennessee 30,000 men volunteered. Many of them, said one Bostonian, were "wild, reckless fellows, requiring strict discipline." But all were eager to join the fight.

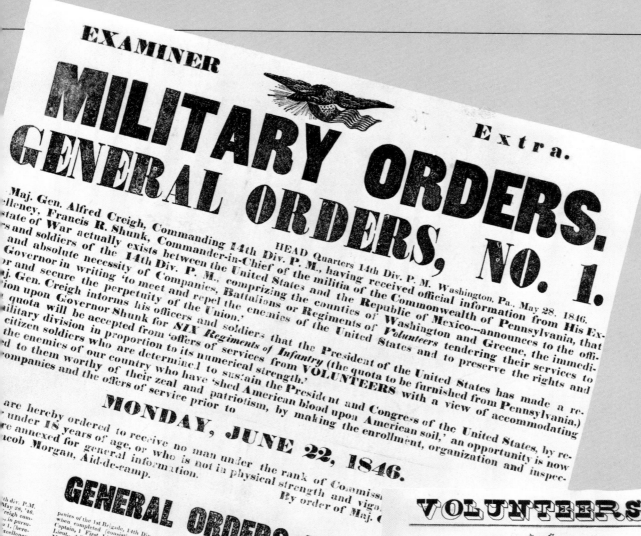

EXAMINER
Extra.

MILITARY ORDERS.
GENERAL ORDERS, NO. 1.

HEAD Quarters 14th Div. P. M. Washington, Pa., May 28, 1846.

Maj. Gen. Alfred Creigh, Commanding 14th Div. P. M., having received official information from His Excellency, Francis R. Shunk, Commander-in-Chief of the militia of the Commonwealth of Pennsylvania, that a state of War actually exists between the United States and the Republic of Mexico---announces to the officers and soldiers of the 14th Div. P. M., comprizing the counties of Washington and Greene, the immediate and absolute necessity of Companies, Battalions or Regiments of Volunteers tendering their services to Governor in writing 'to meet and repel the enemies of the United States and to preserve the rights and to secure the perpetuity of the Union.'

Maj. Gen. Creigh informs his officers and soldiers that the President of the United States has made a requisition upon Governor Shunk for SIX Regiments of Infantry (the quota to be furnished from Pennsylvania.) Military division will be accepted from 'offers of services from VOLUNTEERS with a view of accommodating quota in proportion to its numerical strength.'

citizen soldiers who are determined to sustain the President and Congress of the United States, by repelling the enemies of our country who have 'shed American blood upon American soil,' an opportunity is now offered to them worthy of their zeal and patriotism, by making the enrollment, organization and inspection of companies and the offers of service prior to

MONDAY, JUNE 22, 1846.

are hereby ordered to receive no man under the rank of Commissi... or under 18 years of age, or who is not in physical strength and vigor are annexed for general information. By order of Maj. ...

Jacob Morgan, Aid-de-camp.

GENERAL ORDERS, NO. 2

panies of the 1st Brigade, 14th Div. when completed (consisting of 1 Captain, 1 First Lieut., 1 Second Lieut., 4 Sergeants, 4 corporals, 2 Musicians and 64 privates as established by order of the President) will make the tender of their services to the Governor in writing (prior to the time mentioned in Gene-

ral order No 1) and deliver the original muster roll to Major James Lee, Brigade Inspector of the 1st Brigade, 14th Div., who will deliver the same to Brigadier Gen. Wm. S. Callahan, who is hereby directed to make return to Major General Creigh at Head Quarters Washington, Pa.

Major Gen. Creigh hereby informs the officers and soldiers of the 14th Div. P. M., that the President of the United States has directed that every Regiment of Infantry will consist of 1 Colonel, 1 Lieut. Colonel, 1 Major, 1 Adjutant, (a Lieutenant of one of the companies but not in addition) and the non-

General Orders, No. 3.

HEAD QUARTERS, 14th Division P. M. Washington, Pa., May 28, 1846.

14th Div. P. M., hereby orders that offers of services from Volunteers in General Order No. 2, in the 2d Brigade of said Division, to Maj. R. gade, 14th Division P. M., who will deliver the same to Brig. Gen.

Joseph Garard of the 2d Brigade, who is hereby directed to ... Quarters, Washington, Pa. By order of ...

Major LEWIS ROBERTS, Aid-de-camp.

VOLUNTEERS!

Men of the Granite State!
Men of Old Rockingham!! the

strawberry-bed of patriotism, renowned for bravery and devotion to Country, rally at this call. Santa Anna, reeking with the generous confidence and magnanimity of your countrymen, is in arms, eager to plunge his traitor-dagger in their bosoms. To arms, then, and rush to the standard of the fearless and gallant CUSHING----put to the blush the dastardly meanness and rank toryism of Massachusetts. Let the half civilized Mexicans hear the crack of the unerring New Hampshire rifleman, and illustrate on the plains of San Luis Potosi, the fierce, determined, and undaunted bravery that has always characterized her sons.

Col. THEODORE F. ROWE, at No. 31 Daniel-street, is authorized and will enlist men this week for the Massachusetts Regiment of Volunteers. The compensation is $10 per month---$30 in advance. Congress will grant a handsome bounty in money and ONE HUNDRED AND SIXTY ACRES OF LAND.

Portsmouth, Feb. 2, 1847.

A child outfitted for war was popular lithographer Nathaniel Currier's way of saying that everyone, even the very young, was anxious to join in the war effort.

fact that his army, reduced by illness, desertions and the 500 men left in the fort, now numbered only 2,228 men, while the Mexicans waiting at Palo Alto numbered almost 4,000. The Americans made seven miles that first afternoon, slept, and moved on over open prairie the next morning. They moved slowly, for they were hauling two 18-pounders, drawn by 20 oxen each, and their supply train of 200 wagons.

The Americans saw the Mexicans when the two armies were more than a mile apart. The Mexican line was a mile in length, infantry anchored on a wooded hillock to the right and extending leftward, interspersed with eight-pound cannon on massive carriages. The experienced Tampico Veterans were in the center; to the left, flung across the road and reaching to an impassable marsh, were Torrejón's lancers. The Americans, drawing up, could see the sun glinting on the Mexican bayonets and on the razor-sharp lances from which bright pennants streamed.

But the Mexicans did not attack. "Arista must have thought he performed his whole duty when he barred the road," French observed. "He had been in line of battle all the morning awaiting our coming, yet he *permitted us to deploy undisturbed.*" In fact, Arista was riding along his lines inspiring his men with a fiery speech punctuated by shouts of "Viva la Republica!" Taylor told his men to fill their canteens from a nearby pool and then laid out his battle lines. As men and horses hurried to position with shouts and curses and cracking whips, Taylor sat placidly on Old Whitey, a picture of casual confidence.

The ground, Grant wrote, was "an open, rolling, treeless prairie," spotted here and there with small fresh-water pools. It was covered with a strong, coarse grass "reaching nearly to the shoulders of the men, and each stock was pointed at the top, and hard and almost as sharp as a darning needle." Men and horses crushed the grass underfoot, but it sprang back and slowed every movement.

The Mexican artillery opened up first, muzzles flashing and thunder rolling over the tall grass, but Taylor knew the range was too great and waved his men forward. Grant, writing years after he himself had been responsible for a much larger army, observed, "I thought what a fearful responsibility General Taylor must feel, commanding such a host and so far away

THE YOUNG VOLUNTEER.

from friends." It was 2:30 in the afternoon and the Americans moved deliberately, legs whipped by the saw grass. "As we got nearer," Grant wrote in his memoirs, "the cannon balls commenced going through the ranks. They hurt no one, however, during this advance, because they would strike the ground long before they reached our line, and ricocheted through the tall grass so slowly that the men would see them and open ranks and let them pass." When Taylor saw that the Mexicans were within range of his own cannon, he gave the signal to halt, the drums rolled, and the men and guns took their positions.

The American line was formed just beyond Mexican musket range, the cannon 20 yards ahead of the massed men. The 18-pounders, loaded with grapeshot, opened up first and the flying batteries followed with shells that burst among the massed Mexican troops. Taylor had ordered bayonets, but the battle became an artillery duel. "The infantry stood at order arms," Grant said, "as spectators, watching the effect of our shots upon the enemy." Arista's powder was weak, but even worse, his artillery tactics were poor. The Mexicans aimed their solid balls at the American guns, while the Americans fired on the massed enemy troops with terrible effect. The guns, said Grant, "cleared a perfect road" through the enemy troops.

On the Mexican side, Arista's men shrieked to charge or to withdraw—anything but to stay in this murderous hail. But it was an hour before Arista, stunned by the barrage's ferocity, ordered the charge. Now from the Mexican left came Torrejón's lancers, their horses thrashing the grass in a dead gallop until a boggy swale slowed their advance. Two eight-pounders followed in their wake, far outdistanced.

Infantrymen of the 5th moved out to meet the lancers and formed a hollow square, the foot soldiers' traditional defense against cavalry, muskets protruding from the square's four sides, ready to deliver deadly volleys. Kirby Smith was in that square. "They rode upon us eight hundred strong," he wrote. "When about a hundred feet from us they delivered their fire and continued their charge. A few of our men fell wounded but not a man wavered. At this moment the fire of our second front was delivered with as much precision as on a drill and with a most withering effect." Torrejón's troops veered, broke and fell back.

The horsemen milled for a moment as Torrejón rallied and reformed them and shouted orders for his cannon to open fire. At this moment Sam French and Lieutenant Randolph Ridgely separated two six-pounders from Ringgold's Battery C and raced them to the 5th's assistance. The little guns turned and the gunners dropped off, unlimbered, loaded, rammed and fired, blowing the Mexican gunners away from their pieces before they could touch off their first shots. They fired again as the newly formed Mexican cavalry hurtled down again on the waiting square of the 5th. Watching, Captain Henry saw a lancer struck by a shell, "which exploded simultaneously with the blow, making one mangled mass of horse and rider." The little guns fired in rhythm as the Mexican lancers rallied again and then fell back, broken and stumbling toward their own lines.

As Torrejón's lancers retreated, Mexican cannon at last found the range of the American center and brought the two 18-pounders and the 4th Infantry under heavy fire. Taylor had posted himself on Old Whitey at the center, too, and it was about this time that a staff officer—as recounted in a story that quick-ly made the rounds—reported to Taylor in alarm that the Mexicans were embarked on a threatening flanking movement. Taylor listened to the officer's report, said serenely, "Well, keep a bright lookout for 'em," and went back to the note he was writing.

The U.S. 18-pounders continued their slow and devastating fire while Ringgold moved his little guns around, probing for advantage in the duel of flying metal. The artilleryman made a striking figure on his big horse, Old Branch, moving quickly among the guns, shouting orders in his parade-ground voice. He was thus, loud and in action, standing in his stirrups, when a Mexican six-pound ball struck him. It smashed Old Branch in the withers and broke his neck, and it tore out the inside of both of Ringgold's thighs. He and the horse fell together. When he went down someone ran to him and he ordered, "Don't stay with me; you have work to do. Go ahead!"

Now the flaming wadding from the hot guns set fire to the saw grass. It blazed for a few minutes, then smouldered and a pall of smoke rose over the battle-field, blotting out each side's view of the other. Under the smoke both sides turned, the American right shifting forward, the Mexican left pulling back. Taylor believed the Mexican left was now weak and threw Captain Charles May's dragoons against it. As the smoke lifted, May and his men came hurtling down, but the Mexican artillery opened a deadly fire that broke May's charge and sent his men tumbling backward. By this time, however, James Duncan had run his flying battery in under the smoke to within musket range of the Mexican infantry, who soon found themselves under the muzzles of Duncan's six-pounders. The Mexicans rallied and counterstruck, but the rapid fire of the American cannon beat them to the left. Henry saw the Mexicans "thrown into the utmost confusion" by this "galling enfilading fire" and believed an American charge then would have destroyed Arista's force for good.

But it was getting dark and Taylor had that huge wagon train to worry about. He ordered no charge and gradually the firing stopped. Cooking fires were kindled and exhausted men emptied their canteens. The wounded were brought in by the flickering light of torches and the surgeons' saws were busy. The Americans had lost only five men killed and 43

Shaking his shako, an elegantly turned-out soldier bids his sweetheart farewell while a comrade waits at a discreet distance.

Waving his bonnet, a departing sailor comforts his tearful lady. Presumably, the rowboat nearby was to ferry him to his ship.

Smartly uniformed infantrymen prepare to march out of Exeter, New Hampshire, on the first leg of their long journey to Mexico. This is the only known photographic image of troops departing for the war.

wounded; Mexican casualties were estimated to be seven times as large. The Americans, who now held the ground the Mexicans had occupied in the morning, picked up Mexican wounded as well and buried their dead. Taylor's tent was set up and he sat writing a preliminary report. Sam Ringgold, shuddering with pain from his torn legs, was lying flat on the bottom of a jolting wagon making for Point Isabel and a naval surgery. There, a few days later, he died before he could learn of Taylor's report that gave credit for winning the battle to Ringgold's flying artillery.

The next morning, May 9, 1846, dawned clear on the plain of Palo Alto, though smoke from the previous day's battle still smudged the air. The battered Mexican force had retreated quietly to a new position that General Arista considered impregnable. This was the Resaca de la Palma, a shallow ravine that had once been part of the bed of the ever-changing Rio Grande. The resaca formed an arc facing the road from Point Isabel to Matamoros. The road crossed the ravine and was the only way through acres of dense chaparral. If Taylor's army was to relieve the American fort opposite Matamoros, this was the way it must come. But would Taylor, still badly outnumbered, dare to attack such a formidable position? Arista, sure he would not, settled down in his luxurious tent to compose dispatches.

Taylor called a council of war. The terrain, he knew, was formidable, the chaparral so tangled on

42

both sides of the road that infantrymen could only inch their way through. And Arista's cannon, protected by the resaca, commanded the road. While Taylor's senior officers were counseling caution, Captain Duncan of the artillery happened to pass Taylor's tent. What would you do, Taylor asked the young officer. "We've whipped them," Duncan said, "and we can again." Taylor replied, "That is my opinion, Captain Duncan," and, turning to his other officers, said, "Prepare your commands to advance."

Taylor's scouting patrols quickly drew a blast of fire from the resaca. The general immediately ordered Lieutenant Randolph Ridgely, who had taken over for Ringgold, to gallop up the road with his battery and engage the Mexicans while infantry units tried to work their way through the chaparral on both sides of the road. Sam French, riding forward with Ridgely, had never before felt so exposed and lonely, "leaving the entire army behind, moving down the road through the woods without any support whatever." Finally Ridgely, French and their guns were within 100 or so yards of the enemy's batteries. They unlimbered their guns and "at this fearful proximity" laid down a heavy fire.

Meanwhile, just off the road to the left, Kirby Smith was leading his company of the 5th Infantry forward as best he could. His men grimaced and swore as the thorny brush tore at hands, faces and clothes. The terrain "broke us up into small parties," Smith said, and "the enemy's grape and cannister were whipping about our ears and the smallshot falling thickly amongst us."

To the right of the road Sam Grant was trying to move his men of the 4th Infantry forward "wherever a penetrable place could be found." Once he had gotten close to the resaca the "balls commenced to whistle very thick overhead, cutting the limbs of the chaparral right and left. We could not see the enemy, so I ordered my men to lie down, an order that did not have to be enforced."

Ridgely's exposed artillerymen were falling so fast that he sent French to ask Taylor for reinforcements. Describing the enemy position, French reported, "General, those guns are just in front and can be taken." Taylor immediately ordered Captain May, the flamboyant leader of the dragoons, to charge the

Mexican guns. May's horsemen rode furiously for the front, reached the Mexican guns and bowled the gunners away, but the momentum of their charge carried them to the far side of the ravine. By the time they could turn their hard-mouthed mounts, the Mexican artillerymen had regained their pieces.

This outraged Taylor, who thundered, "Take those guns, and by God, keep them!" The assignment fell to the men of Kirby Smith's 5th Infantry, who now jumped over the lip of the resaca, running hard, bent forward, their muskets at the ready, while "from right to left the most desperate hand-to-hand fighting ensued. The enemy here fought like devils." There was not enough time to reload muskets, and both sides fought with bayonets. Gradually, the Mexican troops fell back, and the guns massed in the center of the Mexican line were captured.

Once this center battery fell, Mexican resistance failed and suddenly a rout began, soldiers fleeing toward the Rio Grande. The Americans were right behind them, "keeping up a run, and yelling like mad!" General Arista came out of his tent, made one attempt to rally his cavalrymen and then joined the rout. At the river Mexican soldiers fought for the use of the only two boats they found there, and in the words of a Mexican observer, many "threw themselves into the river with their clothes and arms, and almost all were drowned." Back at the resaca the Americans inspected the baggage that the fleeing Arista had left behind and found his solid silver dinner service. American accounts put the total of Mexicans dead, wounded and missing at 1,200, though Arista officially reported less than half that number. The Americans had 33 dead and 89 wounded.

Taylor spent a few days attending to his wounded and assuring his supplies, and then prepared to cross the river and take Matamoros. Arista proposed an armistice but Taylor countered that it was too late to talk of armistice: if the town resisted, he would destroy it. On May 18, ferried by Mexican boatmen, the Americans crossed to find Arista's army already in flight toward Linares, more than 60 miles away, leaving behind some 400 wounded. Taylor made no attempt to follow. Instead, he consolidated his hold and began using Matamoros as the staging ground for his next move, deeper into northern Mexico.

Outfitted for war in dazzling variety

Americans of the 1840s favored military uniforms as dazzling as the dream of Manifest Destiny they pursued. Plumes, fringe and scarlet silk adorned the garments bought by regular officers and even those issued to enlisted men.

Among the volunteers, each regiment proudly flaunted its own distinctive style—a reflection of the provincials' disdain for the federal government and its standing Army. "Let 'em go to hell with their sky blue," said an Indiana soldier decked out in dark blue and silver lace. "I'll be blowed if they make a Regular out of me." Splendid as some of these uniforms were, they proved to be woefully inappropriate for campaigning in Mexico. Wool caps and jackets were either too hot or too thin to fend off cold. Shoes disintegrated and the chaparral shredded shirts and trousers. With only a few exceptions, the uniforms that survived the war were those saved for dress parade.

THOMPSON'S PATENT SPURS

This handy, nonregulation kit could be carried inside a pocket and came with an auger to fit the spurs to any shoes or boots.

REMAINS OF A KNAPSACK

The patriotic design was hand-painted on this canvas flap, all that remains of the pack that held most of a soldier's gear.

CAPTAIN DUNCAN'S FATIGUES

A jacket and forage cap worn by artillery Captain James Duncan are among the few articles to have survived combat intact.

INFANTRY MAJOR'S EPAULETS

In full dress, the length of the fringe on an officer's shoulders indicated his rank while a brass numeral identified his regiment.

AN ELITE CORPS' FULL DRESS

An ostrich plume and heavy embroidery on sword belt, collar and cuffs marked officers of the elite Topographical Engineers.

A PRIVATE'S FATIGUES

The wool uniform of a regular included leather belts to support a cartridge box. The same trousers were worn for dress.

NEW YORK MILITIA SHAKO

With a gaudy plume, this bell-crowned militia cap resembles a style abandoned by the Regular Army before the war.

AN OFFICER'S DRESS SHOES

These shoes could be worn on either foot. Not until 1851 was military footgear made to the shapes of right and left feet.

NEW YORK COLONEL'S COAT

This elaborately trimmed jacket with tails reflects European styles that had an influence on both U.S. and Mexican uniforms.

OFFICER'S CARTRIDGE BOX

A major commanding a New Orleans artillery unit buckled this leather case onto the crossbelt of his full-dress coat *(right)*.

MISSOURI MILITIA HAT

This officer's dress chapeau, similar to a plumed version worn by generals, could be folded flat to be carried under the arm.

MAJOR POLK'S COAT

The President's brother, Major William H. Polk, wore this coat. The tiny D on each remaining button stands for dragoon.

ARTILLERY MAJOR'S COAT

Flaming grenades on the collar and gilt crossbelt ornaments marked the Washington Artillery Battalion of New Orleans.

COAT OF A MARINE "MUSIC"

Bright jackets like this identified musicians, called Musics, as noncombatants. They often doubled as stretcher-bearers.

MARINE CORPS SHAKO PLATE

A pugnacious eagle appeared in various forms on much U.S. gear; an eagle holding a snake in its beak was Mexico's emblem.

A SEAMAN'S SUMMER TROUSERS

Many sailors passed the time aboard ship doing "fancy work" such as the embroidery on these lightweight bell-bottoms.

MARINE MAJOR'S UNIFORM

In 1840's fashion this museum mannequin wears the hat slightly cocked; four-button cuffs show that he is a field officer.

Mexican uniforms: elegant touches for the elite

The Mexican army dressed for war was a study in spectacular contrast that mirrored the social and political extremes of the young nation. In the tumultuous decade before the war, governments changed an average of every five months and nearly every new regime created elite new military units, each more magnificently turned out than the next.

After 1839, new and detailed regulations prescribed reasonably standard uniforms, such as the officer's coat shown below. Under these rules the common soldiers, primarily peasants and convicts, were to be issued colorful but relatively plain cloth coats and trousers, with leather shakos. Mexico, however, had supply problems even more severe than those of the United States, so the rank and file often fought in sandals and cheap cotton garments as ineffectual against the elements as the uniforms of the American enemy.

A LANCER'S HEADGEAR

A metal helmet, topped by a mortarboard (and now missing its plume), was worn by the Jalisco Lancers, a crack cavalry unit.

A DIVISION GENERAL'S COAT

Heavily embroidered but less colorful than the full-dress version, the jacket at left was worn with a sash of light-blue silk.

CAP PLATE FOR GRENADIERS

The members of Santa Anna's household guard wore this Mexican coat of arms on heavy black bearskin hats 20 inches tall.

OFFICER'S BELT BUCKLE

Infantrymen wore gold or brass accouterments such as this buckle. Cavalrymen wore white metal such as silver or pewter.

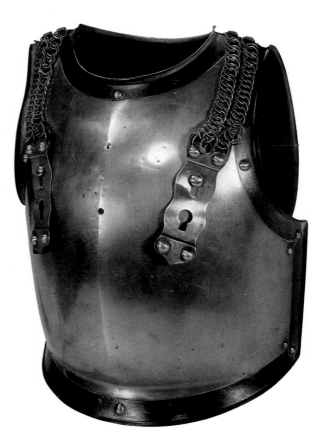

OFFICER'S NECK GORGET

This bit of combat armor was more decorative than protective. It was worn around the neck, suspended by short ribbons.

A CAVALRYMAN'S ARMOR

This helmet and breastplate were the specified uniform of the Tulancingo Cuirassiers. Actually, they rarely wore them.

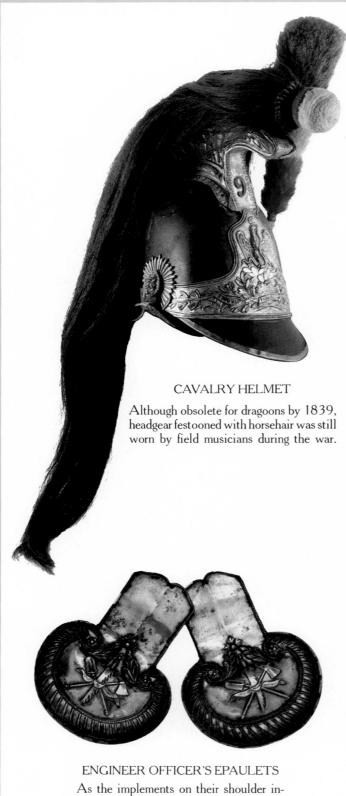

CAVALRY HELMET

Although obsolete for dragoons by 1839, headgear festooned with horsehair was still worn by field musicians during the war.

ENGINEER OFFICER'S EPAULETS

As the implements on their shoulder insignia suggest, the Engineers served as builders and scouts who could also fight.

ARTILLERY LIEUTENANT'S COAT

Exploding bombs embroidered in silk on the collar identify the artillery; the lieutenant's single shoulder epaulet is missing.

CAVALRY SHAKO

Wide horizontal metallic bands indicate that the wearer held a high rank; the lion's-head hooks on each side held a chin strap.

A CHOICE OF SHAKO PLATES

The Mexican national arms in a sunburst *(below)* was a typical emblem on the 20 kinds of shakos Mexicans wore in the 1840s. The fiery bomb *(bottom left)* was worn by the grenadiers and the crossed cannon *(bottom right)* by the artillerymen.

REGIMENTAL OFFICER'S COAT

A biblike plastron buttoned onto the front of this dress jacket replaces the usual broad lapels worn by generals and staff officers.

2 | Mexico finds a leader

After their defeats on the Rio Grande, the Mexicans needed a leader—and the Americans handed them one. Former Mexican President Santa Anna, in political exile in Cuba, persuaded President Polk he would begin peace talks if he were allowed through the U.S. blockade. Back in Mexico and installed as a compromise president, Santa Anna instead began to revitalize the army *(right)* at San Luis Potosí.

A few weeks after Santa Anna's return, Taylor, having won Palo Alto and Resaca de la Palma, took Monterrey, the major stronghold in the north. These American successes stung the Mexicans. Yet few leaped to the rescue of the homeland that the "gringo" invaders—in the words of a Mexican chronicler—had "presumed to pollute with their arrogant feet"; it took months for Santa Anna to assemble an army of 25,000.

If recruiting an army was difficult, paying for it was a nightmare. The Mexican national treasury was nearly empty. Some provincial governments and the Church, though better fixed, opposed Santa Anna's resurgence and donated almost nothing. Of the money Santa Anna did raise, he spent too much on fine uniforms and too little on food for his hungry troops.

Then, hoping to destroy Taylor's depleted army, Santa Anna marched his half-prepared force 300 miles north in February 1847 to engage the Americans at Buena Vista. As it happened, the forced march to battle and a chaotic retreat afterward depleted Santa Anna's army more than the fighting, and stacked the deck against him— and Mexico— for the rest of the war.

Civilians watch Santa Anna drill his brigades at San Luis Potosí. The soldiers practicing with muskets were lucky; many troops, to conserve ammunition, had never fired a shot before facing the Americans.

MAJOR GENERAL ZACHARY TAYLOR

MAJOR GENERAL WINFIELD SCOTT.

GENl WILLIAM J. WORTH.

GENERAL D. E. TWIGGS.

A patriotic romp that became a tour in hell

The electrifying news of General Zachary Taylor's impressive victories against superior numbers on the Rio Grande reached Washington on May 23, ten days after passage of the war bill. Since the people of the United States had believed Taylor and his small force of regulars to be in dire jeopardy, the results of Palo Alto and Resaca de la Palma produced a wave of relief and excitement. Taylor, the unsung, unlettered frontier commander, became a national hero almost overnight; President Polk quickly made Old Zach a major general. Volunteers thronged the recruiting depots, eager to share in what promised to be an exciting, short-term romp south of the border. Patriotic verse appeared that, if slight in poetic value, lacked nothing in fervor: "Arm! arm! your country bids you arm! / Fling out your banners free— / Let drum and trumpet sound alarm, / O'er mountain, plain and sea."

In democratic fashion that reflected the mood of the time, the hastily formed volunteer units elected their officers, most of whom unfortunately had little, if any, military background. The men themselves received virtually no training. This inexperience would tell heavily in the arduous campaign to come when Taylor carried the war into the interior of northern Mexico. When green troops broke and ran the following February during the final battle of the northern campaign, Taylor's army came within an ace of being beaten and destroyed. Despite their inexperience, most of the volunteers, many tempered by a frontier upbringing that stressed self-reliance and an early introduction to firearms, fought hard and well under conditions much harsher than they had expected.

In two of the fiercest battles in early American military history, at Monterrey and Buena Vista, volunteers played a decisive role. As a result Taylor, by the end of February 1847, held tenuous control of not only the border but also the northern tier of Mexico. To the frustration of those who hoped for a quick end to the war, however, his successes were not enough to persuade the Mexicans to sue for peace.

As the months went by, volunteers and regulars alike found themselves plagued by an enemy more deadly than Mexican arms. Of the 116,000 who served, almost 13,000 died—making the war, for its size, the deadliest in American history. Yet as tough as the fighting became, battle casualties were only an incidental cause of death. Rampant disease, bred of filthy camps, contaminated food and water, and constant exposure to the elements, was the principal killer. Amoebic dysentery, diarrhea, yellow fever and other illnesses not then identified infected the American ranks. The men, in their ignorance, blamed the brackish water they drank, and often they were right. They continued eating local fruits, vegetables and other "delicacies" that their systems could not tolerate. By war's end, 1,721 Americans had died in action; 11,155 were dead from disease and exposure. And they kept on dying. An unusually high mortality rate in the Army in the years immediately following the war was blamed on the lingering effects of diseases contracted during service against Mexico.

The volunteers' hot enthusiasm was cooled somewhat when they reached New Orleans, the main staging center for the volunteer force. At the War of 1812 battlefield east of the city where many of the troops camped, the men found life neither healthful

These American generals were shuffled like the playing cards bearing their images. President Polk replaced Taylor with Scott. Taylor's second in command was Worth, then Twiggs, then Worth again.

nor pleasant. In the words of one contemporary historian, "mud and water covered what was below their boot-tops while mosquitoes covered what was above." Conditions were even worse aboard the ships that carried some volunteer regiments from New Orleans to Corpus Christi and Point Isabel on the Texas coast. The men were "packed like sardines in the dirty holds of schooners or brigs." When Gulf storms struck, the men vomited, cursed and prayed while horses, tethered belowdecks, were maddened with fear and tried to kick the planking to matchwood.

The recruits who sailed to war, nevertheless, suffered a shorter term of misery than those forced to walk all the way across south Texas, via San Antonio. This march to Matamoros, where Taylor's army was encamped, was comparable to the trek that had tested Taylor's original force of well-disciplined regulars. One volunteer unit that hiked across Texas during the summer of 1846 was Company H of the 2nd Regiment of Illinois Foot Volunteers, whose elected officers included a lieutenant named Adolph Engelmann. Engelmann was a steady, generous man who conscientiously wrote a series of letters meant for family and friends back home. In one letter, describing the inhospitable deserts of Texas and northern Mexico, he observed, "All plants here have thorns, all animals stings or horns, and all men carry weapons."

The Texas sun blazed down on Engelmann and his Illinoisans, burning them raw while alkaline dust rose in choking clouds. Alternately, torrential rainstorms forced them to march "up to our knees in water." Once beyond the Nueces, their worst problem was a lack of drinking water. On occasion Engelmann's men marched 30 miles before finding another water hole. Dehydrated and exhausted, men collapsed along the way. After waiting out the worst of the heat, those who could got up and staggered on, reaching camp in ones and twos through the night. Sometimes the supply wagons lagged behind too, and then the men went hungry. Finding good water was such a relief that once when Engelmann discovered a small clear creek he "spent the balance of the afternoon lying in the water." He felt "much refreshed."

As they neared the Rio Grande, the green troops were often alarmed by strange noises and assumed that Mexican troops or some other menace was near.

One night a guard Engelmann had posted thought he heard a bear. Another guard thought it was an Indian. Engelmann and a sergeant rooted about and "after much investigation, we found a toad."

Another volunteer unit marching across east Texas to join Taylor was the Tennessee Cavalry; one cavalryman, a young private named George Furber, kept a detailed journal. The Tennesseans, Furber reported, threw away their rubberized and tin canteens because, uninsulated, the water in them heated during the march. Instead, they made their own canteens from gourds, hollowed, dried, corked and carried by a strap. They learned about the suddenness of south Texas storms when they went to sleep by starlight and awakened at midnight to driving rain and wind so strong that they could not raise their tents.

As they neared the Rio Grande, the Tennesseans came upon a series of inviting oases—small ponds filled with clear water. When they drew near, however, they found the water saturated with salt. The ponds looked so clear and tempting because the salt had killed off all life; no grass, fish or even insects could live in or near them. The Tennesseans rode on, talking wistfully among themselves about the wells back home, the creeks that fell from the Tennessee hills, the springs that never failed. Soon they were in more trouble as their horses—fine mounts accustomed to good treatment—began to die. One horse tottered into camp and collapsed on a tent, to the shock of the soldier inside.

Finally the men found a pond that was drinkable, if barely. Someone remembered there was a keg of whiskey in one of the wagons. Broaching the keg, they found that adding whiskey made the water, if not appealing, at least amusing. At last, dusty, dirty, throats aflame and horses staggering, they reached Matamoros. Then, their exhaustion overcome by rowdy exhilaration, they went to town to celebrate.

Matamoros was just the place for it. Taylor had crossed the Rio Grande and taken the town on May 18, after letting General Arista and his Mexican force leave and limp southward toward Linares. The first volunteers had arrived four days later, and thereafter the town swarmed with American soldiers.

By midsummer Taylor had some 14,000 men on the Texas-Mexico border with time on their hands.

The paired images of General Arista
(above) and General Paredes *(below)*
contrast their actual appearance, at left, to
the popular view, at right, of prejudiced
Americans who considered all Mexicans
"savage, barbaric, immoral and corrupt."

Two English-language newspapers were started to chronicle the doings at the boardinghouses, bars and restaurants that sprang into existence. One saloonkeeper opened a bowling alley, and two others quarreled over which of them had invented a drink named in honor of the Army's leader, Old Rough and Ready, a concoction of wine and cordials that was guaranteed to send any soldier reeling into the street. Stores sold American goods, including ice brought in from the North. A theater was improvised and a troupe of actors arrived. The audience—armed, drunk and loud—generally put on a more spirited show than the performers. American preachers arrived and held services, but they and a quickly organized temperance society had a hard job countering the effects of the Rough and Ready and other wines—whiskey having been prohibited by Taylor.

Relations with the resident Mexicans deteriorated and some nasty incidents occurred. The elected officers were almost powerless to keep discipline among their volunteer troops, some of whom robbed, and occasionally killed, Mexican civilians. Taylor, from his headquarters tent pitched in the shade of a small tree about half a mile from town, threatened to courtmartial the culprits.

But his threats had little effect on the lawless troops. Serious fights and even riots broke out among the soldiers. On the last day of August the Georgia Regiment erupted in an all-out melee. By the time the 4th Illinois had quelled the riot, three men were dead and several wounded. Spoiling for action, the men also popped off their muskets or rifles at passing game—or at nothing at all. So much ammunition was flying about that Lieutenant George G. Meade decided that passing a day in his tent was as perilous as being in battle. West Pointer Meade, the future victor of Gettysburg, derided the volunteers as "one costly mass of ignorance, confusion and insubordination."

While his soldiers raised hell, Taylor worried about the logistic and strategic problems he should have considered months earlier. At first he lacked supplies for an army as large as his had become. When the supplies finally began to arrive on the Gulf Coast, he lacked wagons and steamboats needed to get them to Matamoros. Gradually his sweating supply officers—Ulysses S. Grant among them—round-

ed up wagons and pack mules, and by late July a dozen shallow-draft steamboats were working the Rio Grande. One was skippered by a rugged, ambitious young man named Richard King, who a few years later would found the famous King Ranch on land that Taylor had crossed on his march to Matamoros.

President Polk and the War Department, eager to bring the war to a swift and decisive conclusion, began to press Taylor for a comprehensive plan. Taylor, who had given little thought to long-range strategy, equivocated. He knew that he intended to thrust southward and take Monterrey, the important capital of Nuevo León province. From there he might proceed to Saltillo, 50 miles beyond Monterrey, and advance on another of northern Mexico's major cities, San Luis Potosí. Perhaps that would persuade the Mexicans to sue for peace.

But Polk and his advisers, including William Marcy, the blunt-spoken Secretary of War, were becoming convinced that Mexico City itself would have to be taken before the Mexican government would negotiate. How did Taylor feel, Marcy asked, about going overland to Mexico City?

At this point Taylor became cautious, not to say evasive. He was hearing a political siren song as the Whig Party rallied behind Taylor—the hero of Palo Alto—hoping that his newfound popularity would enable him to win the White House for the party in the 1848 election. Old Rough and Ready, so long a modest, retiring man, found the idea of being a Presidential candidate rather intoxicating. He suspected that Marcy and Polk were pressing him to undertake an impossible mission, hoping that he would fail and be disgraced. So Taylor responded that crossing 1,000 miles of semidesert to attack Mexico City would be difficult at the very best. Meanwhile, he would commit himself only to taking Monterrey.

As men continued to swarm into Matamoros, Taylor began moving them upstream to the town of Camargo, which seemed to be the logical staging point for the assault on Monterrey. First to go were the regulars of the 7th Infantry, who filed aboard river steamers on July 6, led by General William Jenkins Worth. It took the steamers nine days to travel up some 250 miles of rain-swollen river. The 5th Infan-

The "perfect purgatory" of a soldier's life in camp

Between battles the Americans had plenty to gripe about in letters home. They were tormented by weather too wet or dry, too hot or cold, and by "myriads of crawling, flying, stinging and biting things!" The water was often "green with slime" and "acted as an instantaneous emetic" on men already suffering from dysentery and fever. Food was often scarce, and beef supplied by Mexican contractors (including Santa Anna) was so putrid and gummy that if thrown "against a smooth plank it would stick." Said a lieutenant: "We are in perfect purgatory here."

Still, most took the hardships right in their stride. Wrote a levelheaded Tennessean, "It is nothing more than we expected. Supper over, we collect in squads, sing songs, tell tales, chew our tobacco, smoke our pipes."

Three army cooks, lucky enough to get fresh meat, prepare a meal for their outfit.

Some grimy soldiers launder their clothing at streamside. Hard campaigning in difficult country often reduced uniforms to tatters.

try soon followed the 7th. The volunteers moved in late July, some by boat but many more overland.

The boat ride was unpleasant—one steamer burst a boiler and most of the men aboard were killed. The march from Matamoros to Camargo was worse. The troops followed a more-or-less straight route south of the Rio Grande, reducing the distance to be covered to some 120 miles. Having left the river, the men again found water scarce and the heat and dust of Mexico's summer appalling. A Maryland volunteer officer recalled that the urge for something to drink became so great that "when we reached a pond, which was nothing but a hog-wallow, men and horses rushed pell-mell frantically into it, all semblance of rank and organization forgotten. I saw men fall down in convulsions on this march," he continued, "frothing at their mouths, clutching the sand with their hands, and left to lie until nature and the shadows of night restored them to consciousness and strength."

Conditions at Camargo were almost as bad. Taylor had chosen to bivouac his army in a hot and pestilen-

tial hole, the worst of all the Mexican towns in the vicinity. The main camp lay in a sun-baked bowl of rocks where every day the temperature reportedly climbed above 100°. Dust infiltrated everything— food, clothes, skin, eyes, mouth. The camp was infested with snakes, tarantulas, scorpions and armies of ants. "Last night the ants tried to carry me off in my sleep," wrote one soldier.

Then disease struck. Its ravages had been bad enough at Matamoros, where it was common for a 900-man regiment to have 150 on sick call; at Camargo sickness spread through the camp like flame. The volunteers understood little of camp sanitation, and dysentery and yellow fever raged unchecked. Some 1,500 American soldiers died of disease— almost as many as would die of battle wounds in the entire war. At times 30 per cent of Taylor's command was bedridden.

"The large hospital tents," wrote an officer of the Ohio volunteers, "were constantly full—the dead being removed at sunrise and sunset, but to make room

An anti-Catholic lithograph sold in American cities alleges that Mexican clerics abandoned Matamoros to save their wine and women.

THE MEXICAN RULERS,
migrating from Matamoras — with their Treasures —
LITH. & PUB. BY F. & S. PALMER, 43, ANN ST. N.Y.

T. B. Peterson Agent 98 Chesnut St. Philadelphia.

for the dying." Eventually, the camp ran out of wood for coffins and burial details began to inter bodies wrapped only in blankets. Tom Tennery, a private with an Illinois regiment, was at Camargo for six weeks and recorded in his diary the death of a friend about every other day. "At four o'clock this morning Theophilus Johnson died," Tennery wrote. "We lamented his death though not so much as we would if we had not despaired of his recovery a week ago, and witnessed his sufferings."

Again, as at Matamoros, lawless troops harassed the local Mexican civilians. Hardest on civilians— and on anyone else who got in their way—were the Texas Rangers, who became notorious for their violent and sportive ways. The Rangers, formed just after the revolt of 1836, were small companies of horsemen organized to travel swiftly with light arms to protect the Texas frontier against Indians, Mexican bandits and, occasionally, Mexican soldiers. At Taylor's request, when the war began several Ranger companies had been banded into a cavalry regiment

headed by Colonel John C. (Jack) Hays, and other Texans flocked to join it. One of Hays's company captains was Sam Walker, who on the eve of Palo Alto had slipped through the Mexican lines to bring Taylor a report that Fort Brown was holding out.

Another company was led by Ben McCulloch, a quiet man with bold features, a broad forehead and deep-blue eyes; like Taylor, McCulloch was said to grow calm in the face of danger. McCulloch quickly made himself one of Taylor's most valuable scouts, but in the meantime his company and others built a fiery reputation.

The Rangers attracted the roughest men on a rough frontier, and they looked the part. Someone described their uniform as "a dirty shirt and a five-shooter." The artist-soldier Samuel Chamberlain thought that "with their uncouth costumes, bearded faces, lean and brawny forms, fierce wild eyes and swaggering manners, they were fit representatives of the outlaws which make up the population of the Lone Star State." Lieutenant Colonel Ethan Allen

Colonel Jack Hays, the tough commander of Taylor's Texas Rangers, put Samuel Colt's bankrupt firearms business back on its feet in 1846 with an order for 1,000 six-guns—two for each of his 500 men.

Hitchcock, a member of Taylor's staff, was more generous in his appraisal: "Not any sort of uniforms, but well mounted and doubly well armed: each man has one or two Colt's revolvers besides ordinary pistols, a sword, and every man a rifle."

The Mexican civilians were terrified of the Rangers, and for good reason. Texas and Mexico had been abrading each other for 10 years, ever since Texas had proclaimed its independence, and deep hatreds had sprung up on both sides of the Rio Grande. Despite the fact that they were now part of the invading U.S. Army, the Rangers spent much of their time rooting out and dispatching old enemies.

"Our orders were most strict," one Ranger wrote, "not to molest any unarmed Mexican, and if some of the most notorious of these villains were found shot, or hung up, in the chaparral, the government was charitably bound to suppose that during a fit of remorse and desperation, tortured by conscience for the many evil deeds they had committed, they had recklessly laid violent hands upon their own lives."

A major villain, to Texans' eyes, was General Antonio Canales, known as the Chaparral Fox, whose irregular cavalry for years had plundered the Texas frontier, robbing and killing under cover of the flag of Mexico. McCulloch led a probe deep into the Mexican interior in search of Canales, during which the Rangers covered 250 miles in 10 days and never took off their boots.

They missed Canales but reported to Taylor that the route he planned to take to Monterrey lacked the water to support an army. Instead, they recommended advancing by way of Mier, a town on the Rio Grande whose name had become a bitter rallying cry for Texans second only to the Alamo; some 250 Texans, captured there in 1842 after a sharp engagement in Texas' sporadic border war with Mexico, had been cruelly maltreated and eventually put to death. From Mier the route turned upward, away from the river, to Cerralvo at the edge of the Sierra Madre.

Taylor had learned to trust the Rangers as scouts and as cavalrymen, however little he cared for their violent ways. "On the day of battle," he said, "I am glad to have Texas soldiers with me, for they are brave and gallant; but I never want to see them before or afterward." He sent some Rangers to seize Cerralvo and hold it until his army could get there.

In mid-August the army stirred itself to move. Taylor thought the whole force too unwieldy and decided to take only about 6,000 men to Monterrey, half of them his trusted regulars. Before he left he assembled the entire army at Camargo and it bolstered the men to see how many they were in total.

Grant, still assigned to quartermaster duty—which he considered "shirkers' work" and hated—recounted the agonies of dealing with the pack mules. "Sheet-iron kettles, tent-poles and mess chests were inconvenient articles to transport" on mules, Grant later wrote. "It took several hours to get ready to start each morning, and by the time we were ready some of the mules first loaded would be tired of standing so long with their loads on their backs. Sometimes one would start to run, bowing his back and kicking up until he scattered his load; others would lie down and try to disarrange their loads by attempting to get on top of them by rolling on them." Grant added dryly, "I am not aware of ever having used a profane expletive in my life; but I would have the charity to excuse those who may have done so, if they were in charge of a train of Mexican pack mules at the time."

General Worth and the 1st Brigade of the 2nd Division moved out first and made their way from the festering pit of Camargo to Cerralvo in seven days over an awful road where every stone seemed sharp. Next came General Persifor Smith with the 2nd Brigade, then General David Twiggs with the 1st Division, a group of regulars and volunteers. Taylor himself, looking, said one of his officers, as "glum as a bear," reached Cerralvo on September 9. He remained suspicious that Polk, Marcy and others in Washington were conniving to embarrass him. But he was cheered to find that Cerralvo had enough potable water "to supply New York City," as well as pleasant groves, pastures and a fine view of the Sierra Madre foothills. Major General William O. Butler with a division of volunteers brought up the rear. Taylor's force totaled 6,640 men and officers.

The march to Cerralvo was not without alarms. A thousand Mexican dragoons drifted down the road just ahead of the Americans, keeping a close watch. They were led by the same General Torrejón who had taken Thornton's force before the battle of Palo Alto. The Americans were used to mingling with the Mexican civilians. When they saw a civilian on the road, it was their custom to ask if there would be a fandango, or dance, in the next town that night. Now the Mexicans were responding with undisguised relish: *"Sí. Mucho fandango a Monterrey!"*

The Mexicans had in fact prepared quite a reception at Monterrey, where they had massed some 7,300 troops. Their army had mostly recovered from its demoralizing defeat at Resaca de la Palma. The temporarily disgraced General Arista had marched the survivors to Monterrey, and in the summer of 1846 this nucleus had been reinforced by large contingents marching north from Mexico City.

The Mexican commander in Monterrey was General Pedro de Ampudia, a 41-year-old Cuban who had come to Mexico to join its revolution and had

prospered in the years since. Governor of the state of Nuevo León as well as chief of the Army of the North, Ampudia had a formidable—and deserved—reputation for cruelty and ghoulishness. Two years earlier he had captured a political agitator and a small group of his followers. As Ampudia described it later, "I granted him the necessary time to make his will and to receive the spiritual aids of religion and then had him shot." Ampudia ordered the corpse buried for a few moments in consecrated ground, then directed it to be dug up and "exposed as a public spectacle." After 12 hours of this, he had the head severed, boiled in oil and displayed in a glass jar. Thirty-eight of the agitator's followers were executed without trial.

Monterrey was a 250-year-old city with a population of 15,000. Ampudia, for good reason, considered it an impregnable stronghold against which the American Army would destroy itself. On the south, the city was protected by mountains and the Santa Catarina River. To the west, guarding the road to Saltillo and the interior of Mexico, were two steep-sided hills, Independencia and Federación, both fortified and garrisoned with troops and guns.

To the north—the direction from which the Americans would approach—was a formidable bastion, an unfinished cathedral containing eight cannon and 400 men, surrounded by a wall and moat. The Mexicans called it the Citadel, and the Americans soon dubbed it the Black Fort because of its dark stone walls. To the east was a four-gun redoubt named La Tenería because of a nearby tannery. Near La Tenería was another fort called El Rincón del Diablo, or The Devil's Corner, and still a third bastion that defended the bridge over a canal flowing through the city. Even the interior of the city was fortified. Loopholes for sharpshooters had been cut in the stone walls of the houses and their flat roofs were equipped with sandbag parapets from which Mexican infantry could enfilade the streets. The American Army would have to pierce all of these obstacles manned by a well-armed force twice its size.

The American advance guard, Taylor among them, came within sight of this formidable fortress-city at 9 o'clock in the morning on September 19, 1846. There, across fields of corn and pastures where cattle grazed, lay Monterrey's white houses partly hidden

ARMY OF THE NORTH.

GENERAL IN CHIEF. HEAD QUARTERS, MONTEREY SEPTEMBER 15 TH 1846.

It is well known that the war carried on to the Republic of Mexico by the Government of the United States of America is unjust, illegal and anti-Christian, for which reason no one ought to contribute to it.

The Federal Government havingbeen happily re-established, à largenumber of Batallions of the National Guard in the States of Coahuila, St. Louis Potosi, Guanajuato, Zacatecas, Queretaro and others, are ready to be on the field and fight for our independence.

Acting according with the dictates of honour and in compliance with what my country requires from me, in the name of my Government Ioffer to all individuals that will laydown their arms and separate themselves from the American Army, seeking protection, they will be well received and treated in all the Plantations Farms or Towns, where they will first arrive and asisted for their march to the Interior of the Republic by all the Authorities on the road, as hasbeen done with all those that have passed over to us.

To all those that wish to serve in the Mexican Army, their offices will be conserved and guarranteed.

PEDRO DE AMPUDIA.

A leaflet issued by General Pedro de Ampudia, sprinkled with misspellings and faulty grammar, urges Americans to defect before the battle of Monterrey. His appeal attracted fewer deserters than earlier ones.

by green trees. A little to the right crouched the menacing Citadel. While Taylor examined the tranquil scene, a puff of smoke rose from the Citadel; a 12-pound ball flew straight at Taylor, tore up the ground and rolled to rest nearly at his feet. Another ball dropped nearby and a party of Mexican cavalrymen advanced. Colonel Jack Hays's Texas Rangers were ordered to charge. At this the Mexicans turned away in an apparent attempt to lure the Texans toward the Citadel's guns. But Taylor recalled Hays and ordered the Army to make camp out of range in a beautiful grove of pecans and live oaks.

The Army was in high spirits. The victories at Palo Alto and Resaca de la Palma had given the regulars confidence that they could defeat any Mexican force. The volunteers, who had missed the earlier battles, were curious to "see that as yet unseen biped, a Mexican soldier." They swarmed out of camp to gawk at the Citadel's dark walls, and the Texas Rangers showed off their courage and horsemanship by riding in front of the walls "like boys at play on the first frail ice." Taylor finally ordered the men to cut out the theatrics; there would be real action soon

enough. No one acquainted with Taylor doubted it.

Taylor sent out scouts and that evening held a council of war. He had never before attacked forts built by military engineers and so, with a mistaken optimism that would cost many lives, he planned to assault the northeastern edge of town, knifing between the Citadel and the smaller fort, La Tenería. Then the attacking troops would take the next redoubt, El Diablo, and fight their way house by house toward the grand plaza at the city's heart. Old Rough and Ready had no idea what a difficult task this would prove to be; he gave no orders for a systematic preliminary artillery bombardment. He had not brought enough heavy artillery with him in any case, and the flying artillery's shells would be ineffective against the strong walls of the forts. As always, Taylor put his faith in the bayonet, and in the courage of his men.

It was evident, however, that any assault on Monterrey could succeed only if the Americans also took the two fortified hills to the west, Federación and Independencia, whose heights commanded the city as well as the Saltillo road, down which Mexican reinforcements might come. Scouts reported that the road could be reached despite the Mexican artillery on the two hills. So Taylor, ignoring the military maxim that a commander must never divide his force in the face of superior numbers, determined to send 2,000 men, including the Texans, to take the hills. The commander would be the ruddy-faced, 52-year-old Kentuckian, General Worth. His force would make a wide sweep and attack from the west. Taylor would feint to the east to preoccupy the Mexicans there. Then the two forces would drive into the city from the west and the northeast, crushing the Mexicans (it was hoped) in a nutcracker.

Worth's column set out at 2 p.m. on September 20, looking, a soldier watching them wrote, as polished as though they were standing "Sunday inspection at Fort McHenry." They were guided by a Mexican prisoner who was encouraged to tell the truth by the presence of "a hempen cravat about his neck." Worth's men went about seven miles across difficult terrain, skirmished with a Mexican patrol and spent an uncomfortable night without food or shelter as rain streamed down on them. The next day they moved toward the two threatening hills.

Just after dawn Hays's Texans, in the lead, bumped into a mass of waiting Mexican lancers. The story is told that Hays, brandishing a saber and calling out in clear Spanish, challenged the lancers' commander to a duel. Hays's men were startled: he was murderous with a pistol but weak with a saber. The Mexican agreed, dropped his lance and charged, his men thundering behind him. Hays abandoned his saber, drew a pistol, shot down the Mexican officer and galloped back to his men. "Dismount," he is said to have shouted, "and get behind your horses! Here they come, boys! Give 'em hell!"

The Rangers dropped off their horses, some scurrying under a nearby fence, and opened a devastating fire on the lancers. The Texans were soon reinforced by infantry and two flying-artillery batteries. Three times the Mexicans charged; "I have never called a Mexican a coward since," one of the Rangers later wrote. When it was over the Mexicans had lost 100 men and were reeling back. Worth's column drove on until it cut the Saltillo road.

Now the two hills lay between the Americans and Monterrey. The problem was to take them.

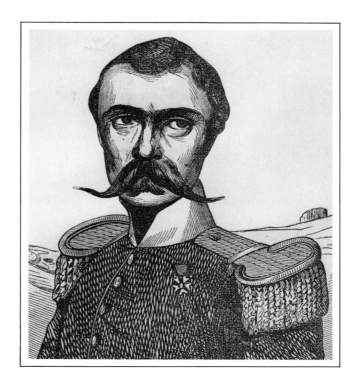

Guerrilla General Antonio Canales was at least as shifty as he looks in this caricature. Instead of harassing the advancing Americans, he tried for a deal setting himself up as local ruler under U.S. protection.

The hills were actually long ridges pointing toward the city. Federación stood to the south, across the Saltillo road and across the shallow Santa Catarina River. The guns from its two emplacements could, in American hands, help to subdue Independencia hill. The Americans waded through the waist-deep river that afternoon and started up Federación hill. Dismounted Rangers and artillerymen, soon reinforced by the 7th Infantry, thrust toward the smaller, higher emplacement while the 5th Infantry went after the larger emplacement, a fort called El Soldado. The men attacking the small emplacement were first to succeed, taking the earthwork after a brief exchange of gunfire and a sharp hand-to-hand struggle. They then turned its gun on El Soldado until the 5th Infantry swarmed up and took that fort in a rush.

Success. But on the other side of the city what had started as a feint by Taylor had turned into a full-scale battle—and a costly disaster.

Taylor started the day in a jocular mood. "Get up, Kirby," he told his paymaster, "and come with me and I will give you a chance to be shot." The first

Formidable Monterrey, "a city of stone" fortified inside and out, confronted Taylor's army in September 1846. Only after three days of savage fighting was the U.S. flag run up in the Citadel (center rear).

charge was to go in and simply test the Mexican guns, but it was badly led and soon got out of hand.

The old professional, General David Twiggs, who should have been in command, was in the habit of taking a laxative the night before action. "A bullet striking the belly when the bowels are loose," he explained to one of the junior officers, "might pass through the intestines without cutting them." But he had apparently taken an overdose, and that particular morning he was indisposed. As a result, a brevet colonel named John Garland led the charge; he struck almost down the center, between the Citadel on the right and La Tenería on the left. There his 800 men, the 1st and 3rd Regiments and the Washington-

Baltimore Battalion of volunteers, were caught on the front and on both sides by a shower of canister that whipped and tore the long lines. The men ran forward, hunched over, shoulders drawn in, clutching their muskets, the wounded falling with screams, the survivors jumping over bodies, stumbling, falling, seeing iron cut the dirt around them.

They passed the range of Black Fort and La Tenería's fire increased. Without thinking they stumbled back to the right and succeeded only in bringing their whole line under the Citadel's guns. They turned farther to the right, which brought them closer to the loopholed houses of the city. The Mexican soldiers inside and on the roofs poured volley after volley of

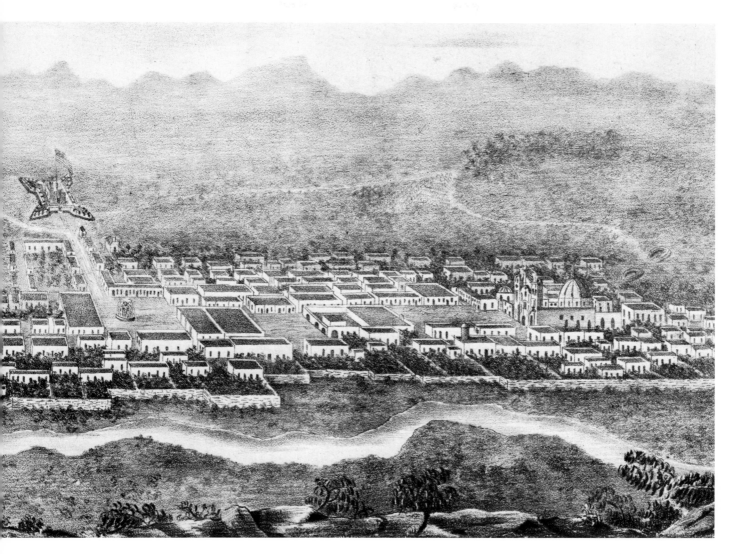

musket fire into the stumbling, cursing Americans. "Showers of balls were hurled upon us," wrote Captain Henry. "There was no resisting the deadly, concealed fire, which appeared to come from every direction. On every side we were cut down." Henry saw some of Colonel William Watson's men urging him to retire. "Never shall I forget the animated expression of his countenance when, in taking a drink from the canteen of one of his men, he exclaimed, 'Never boys, never will I yield an inch! I have too much Irish blood in me to give up!' A short time after the exclamation he was a corpse." A few minutes later, savaged beyond endurance, the Americans began falling back, again under fire from the Citadel.

Taylor, knowing from the sound of the gunfire that a serious fight was in progress, ordered more troops forward. Among them were three more companies of the 4th Infantry, which charged La Tenería and were cut to pieces. Ulysses S. Grant was in that charge, in direct disobedience of orders to remain in camp as a quartermaster in charge of supplies. "My curiosity got the better of my judgment," Grant wrote in his memoirs, "and I mounted a horse and rode to the front to see what was going on. I had been there but a short time when an order to charge was given, and lacking the moral courage to return to camp—where I had been ordered to stay—I charged with the regiment." Grant thought that "about one-third of the men en-

General Worth's division swings westward around Monterrey to cut off its Mexican garrison as Taylor attacks the city from the northeast. Worth later stormed and captured Mexican artillery positions on two of the surrounding hills, Independencia *(left)* and Federación *(right, foreground).*

gaged in the charge were killed or wounded in the space of a few minutes. We retreated to get out of the fire." As the 4th Infantry reeled back, Grant gave his horse to the exhausted regimental adjutant; minutes later the adjutant was killed.

The order came to withdraw, but not everyone heard it. One who did not was Captain Electus Backus who, according to his memoirs, rallied the fragments of several companies of the 1st Infantry—perhaps 100 men in all—and threw them forward. They came to the tannery for which La Tenería was named. It was "filled with the enemy, who opened fire on us," Backus recalled, but they "were soon destroyed or dispersed." He mounted the tannery's roof and saw that he was *behind* both the fort and other Mexican positions. One of these was a distillery 120 yards away where Mexicans posted on the roof were firing to the north from behind sandbags. But there were no sandbags on the western side, and Backus' men, themselves protected by the tannery roof's two-foot stone parapet, cleared the distillery's roof with musket fire. Backus now heard the command "Retire in good order," but "not knowing from what authority it proceeded, I retained my position." Thus Backus was in place when the next charge began.

Now came a brigade of volunteers commanded by John Quitman, a brigadier general from Mississippi, driving straight into the flailing guns of La Tenería. Leading the charge was the 1st Tennessee Infantry, which had a quarter of all American casualties on this first day of battle—most of them in the few minutes under those guns. Backus saw them coming and saw that the gorge, or entrance, at the rear of La Tenería was open. Crouched behind their parapet on the tannery's roof, his men began pouring heavy musket fire right into the fort. "The effect was electrical," Backus recalled. As his men paused to reload, he noted, "the enemy was in full retreat toward Fort Diablo." Backus and his men jumped off the tannery building and followed the Mexicans, trying to cut off their retreat. Right behind Backus' men came the Tennesseans. La Tenería was at last in American hands and an American flag went up. Now, barely, the Americans had a hold in Monterrey.

The tenacious Taylor, once involved in a fight, was rarely willing to quit. Down the center he sent the Ohio Regiment, driving into the city past Bragg's flying artillery battery, which had been beaten bloody, its men and horses down, "making the ground about the guns slippery with their gasped foam and blood."

The Ohioans ran into fire from the fortified bridge; they paused, circled and advanced past the Tennessee regiment, now regrouping. With General Butler, Taylor's second in command, in the lead, they drove on El Diablo. The waist-deep canal that flowed into Monterrey from the east blocked them, but they plunged across; some stopped to drink and were killed on the bank. Beyond lay a low wall and they came to rest behind it, sheltered for a moment from El Diablo's musket fire. Mexican sharpshooters leaped on the fort's wall to fire, and American marksmen cut them down. Soon, however, a hidden battery opened pointblank on the Americans, forcing them to seek what shelter they could. Butler was wounded, the regimental commander went down and the Ohioans, "being more than decimated," began to fall back toward the walls of La Tenería.

Darkness finally ended the fighting and a chill rain began. Wagons creaked through the night, picking up the wounded, and the surgeons went to work. Much later, in the dark, Major Luther Giddings and his exhausted men of the Ohio Regiment were slumped at a table, eating. Someone brought a lantern and they saw that "the table was covered between the plates and cups with thin strips of human flesh and clots of gore." The surgeon, rather enjoying the Ohioans' distress, said he had used the table in a hospital tent and had "only cut off some legs and arms upon it."

The terrible day was done, 394 of Taylor's men had been killed or wounded and the defenses of Monterrey had only been scratched. The next day, however, General Worth and his men on the western side of Monterrey achieved one of the memorable triumphs of the war. Reveille was at three in the morning, and the cold, hungry troops, having spent another rainy night in the open, launched their attack in the predawn darkness on heavily armed Independencia hill.

Like Federación, it was essentially a ridge protected by two forts. The higher one was little more than a gun emplacement, but halfway along the ridge and considerably lower stood the ruin of Bishop's Palace, its heavy walls bristling with cannon. It was the key

A soldier-artist's record of Monterrey's fall

Texas Rangers raise up Old Glory during the battle for a palace west of Monterrey.

A fair number of eyewitnesses illustrated the fierce three-day battle at Monterrey, but the most vigorous pictures were painted by a soldier who saw none of the action. He was Samuel Chamberlain, a husky 16-year-old dragoon private from Boston who was still en route to Mexico when the battle ended. In the following weeks, after visiting the battered town and pumping its captors for details, he painted these watercolors of key clashes and incorporated them in *My Confession,* a lusty narrative of his wartime exploits.

Chamberlain soon saw plenty of action, and his experience later stood him in good stead. During the Civil War he rose to the rank of brigadier general.

Preceded by a howitzer *(right),* Yankee soldiers burst through the back gate of the palace. Soon the Mexicans fled east, into the city.

Trading shots with defenders, Americans fight their way down a Monterrey street.

Jubilant Texans, perched on a roof that overlooks Grand Plaza, watch as Mexican soldiers and civilians prepare to evacuate the city.

to Monterrey's western defense. Rain continued to fall as the men started up the steep slopes toward the smaller fort; the downpour muffled the noise of their advance. They climbed steadily, half blind, slipping on mossy rocks, sliding in mud, cursing, equipment knocking against rock, and they were still far from the top when dawn broke. A Mexican picket rose up suddenly, shouted *"Quién viva?"* and fired. His ball struck Captain Richard Gillespie in the stomach and killed him. A storm of musket fire flailed down on the Americans, who now fired as they climbed, hand over hand, to within 20 yards of their goal.

To the north of the city, as the rain subsided, Taylor's men could see the drama unfolding on Independencia. Among them was Sam French, by now attached to Braxton Bragg's battery, which had been so battered the day before. "Our men could be seen climbing up from rock to rock and the smoke from every musket indicated whether it was fired *up* or *down* the hill. Gradually the circles of smoke moved higher and nearer as our men ascended and when, near the top, they commingled into one, the excitement was intense. Troops on both sides looked on in silence." Soon "the top smoked like a volcano and we could see our men leaping over the parapets and the Mexicans retreating down the slope."

A 12-pound howitzer had been painfully dragged up the slope, piece by piece, and reassembled; with it, Worth's men began to bombard the Bishop's Palace. At the same time, American infantry began to probe along the ridge, off the crest on each side. A Mexican sortie came out, keeping to the crest, and when the Mexicans were between them, the two American groups opened fire, shooting upward. It was an impossible position for the Mexicans; each move they made exposed them on one side of the ridge or the other. In a moment they broke toward the palace. The Americans charged so close behind that the Mexican gunners in the palace could not fire without hitting their own men. The Mexican infantry, panic-stricken, swept over the walls and the Americans went with them, firing, bare bayonets reaching for the defending gunners. The Mexicans broke again and burst out of the front doors of the palace and down the hill toward Monterrey. Below, Sam French and his men cheered and hurled their caps into the air.

The Bishop's Palace dominated the battlefield; its loss changed everything, and though there had been little action on the east side of Monterrey that day, General Ampudia began withdrawing into the center of the city. His men, who had fought well, were bitter, but gradually they moved back and Taylor's attacking force was given what the day before they had been unable to take.

At dawn on the third day, September 23, the Americans realized that the Mexicans had withdrawn from the outskirts, and they began to press toward Monterrey's grand plaza. But inside the city the Mexicans waited in great force, sharpshooters poised at their loopholes and heavy cannon mounted to hurl charge after charge down each street approaching the plaza. The Americans, thrusting inward, were safe enough on the side streets, but the through streets, faced with houses flush to the street, were like bowling alleys from which there was no escape. Captain Henry wrote that Mexican bullets swept the streets, "as if bushels of hickory nuts were hurled at us."

This fighting was hardest on the American artillerymen, who were forced to man their pieces unprotected in the streets. French, with Bragg's battery, said that a Mexican volley "rattled like hail on the stones." Dismounting, French turned toward his gun and found the two men at the muzzle had been hit. "One poor fellow put his hands to his side and quietly said, 'Lieutenant, I am shot,' and tried to stop the flow of blood." French had two ropes tied to the tail of his howitzer. After the gun had been pulled out into the street and fired, several members of the gun crew would pull the gun to shelter behind the wall of a house, load it and light the fuse. Others would then frantically pull it back into the street, where it fired again. After two hours, even firing this way, four of French's five gunners had been hit.

Infantrymen worked their way slowly into the city. The routes to the plaza, Grant recalled, "were commanded from all directions" by Mexican artillery.

Around the plaza the flat roofs of the houses "were manned with infantry, the troops being protected from our fire by parapets made of sand-bags. All advances into the city were thus attended with much danger. While moving along streets which did not lead to the plaza, our men were protected from the fire, and from the view of the enemy except at the crossings; but at these a volley of musketry and a discharge of grape-shot were invariably encountered. The 3rd and 4th regiments of infantry made an advance nearly to the plaza in this way and with heavy loss."

Within one block of the plaza, the unit Grant was with found they were short of ammunition. The commanding officer, Colonel Garland, asked for a volunteer to take a message back to General Taylor requesting either more ammunition or reinforcements. Grant offered to go. "Before starting I adjusted myself on the side of my horse furthest from the enemy and, with only one foot holding to the cantle of the saddle, and an arm over the neck of the horse exposed, I started at full run." At each intersection Grant took a burst of fire, but he flashed through with such speed that neither he nor his horse was hit.

As Taylor's men worked toward the plaza from the north and east, Worth's men came from the west. They had an easier time, for they had the wit to come through the buildings instead of around them. The stone was soft and a man with a pick could quickly open a hole in the house's side, put in a shell with a three-second fuse and blow out a wide opening. The troops would then rush in, clear out any snipers on the roof and blow out the next house's wall. By late afternoon the Americans were closing on the plaza from both sides and a Mexican appeared with a white flag. Instantly a Texas Ranger shot and killed him. This slowed Mexican efforts to surrender only a few minutes, when another white flag appeared.

General Ampudia, although he still had a huge volume of ammunition on hand, knew all that remained was a final bloody spasm on the grand plaza. He had been "out-generaled, outwitted and out-maneuvered from first to last," as one rather biased American observer put it, and now there was nothing left but to seek a truce. Taylor's troops were bloodied and exhausted, and he was glad not to be forced to endure that final spasm. Ammunition was low, and there were hundreds of sick and wounded to be cared for. The rest were so tired, sweaty and bedraggled, said one observer, that "they were as dirty as could be without becoming real estate." So Taylor accepted an armistice proposal that allowed the Mexican troops to march out with their arms two days later.

Understandably, there was consternation in Washington when it became known that Taylor for the second time had failed to destroy a beaten Mexican army. He had allowed Arista to leave Matamoros; now he had done the same thing again in his agreement with Ampudia. Taylor defended himself by pointing out that he had once more broken the Mexican Army of the North and held that part of the country without dispute. His excellent, optimistic reports, written by William Bliss (by then a brevet major), thrilled the nation. Across the United States the idea of Taylor for President gained strength, although many of those who fought with him at Monterrey had lost confidence in his leadership.

Old Zach Taylor still had one more Mexican general to face and one more battle to fight. That wily fox, Santa Anna, the one man who could rally the Mexicans to effective resistance, was in Mexico City, raising an army that he hoped would be strong enough to punch Taylor back across the Rio Grande and to meet any other threat from American arms as well.

In one of the Mexican War's classic ironies, it was the United States government that had helped to manage Santa Anna's return to power from political exile in Cuba. This bizarre twist evolved from President Polk's persistent, and mistaken, belief that the Mexicans would eventually listen to reason, sell their claims to Texas, New Mexico and California and end the bloody conflict. Santa Anna himself had fed that idea when, as early as February 1846, he sent an emissary from Cuba to Washington who suggested that the refugee general was the only Mexican politician strong enough to conclude a negotiated peace — and that he would agree to trade the territory Polk wanted, for $30 million.

Polk had ruminated over the idea and, during the summer of 1846, dispatched an emissary of his own to Cuba. Santa Anna agreed to try to end the war and in return the U.S. Navy permitted Santa Anna to slip

through its blockade of the Mexican coast. But Santa Anna had no intention of making peace.

The Napoleon of the West had little trouble capturing control of the Mexican government. President Mariano Paredes was detested by the people and had the failures at Palo Alto and Resaca de la Palma on his head. By midsummer his power was gone, and on July 31 the garrison at Veracruz mutinied and pronounced itself loyal to Santa Anna. Paredes tried to rally troops in Mexico City — and they took him prisoner. At this juncture Santa Anna, still in Cuba, left his favorite pastimes — drinking and wagering on cockfights — and landed at Veracruz on August 16, a month before the fighting at Monterrey. Then, in his shrewd way, he retired to his estate and let public support build. It was on September 15 — four days before Taylor reached Monterrey — that Santa Anna entered Mexico City. He did not immediately take the presidency, however; instead, he began to rally the army to repel the invaders, a very popular idea. The fall of Monterrey simply added impetus to his task.

In Washington, as the year wore on, Polk grew ever more disenchanted with Taylor and the lenient armistice terms. Realizing that his scheme to restore Santa Anna had backfired, Polk became even more convinced that an American army would have to bring pressure on Mexico City itself to get the peace treaty he sought. Polk turned to Winfield Scott, the senior general whom he personally detested, and ordered him to prepare a coastal invasion and an assault on the heart of Mexico.

Scott set out almost immediately for the theater of war, having informed Taylor by letter of the change in plans. This letter, though couched in cautious and even gentle terms, brought the bitter news that Scott needed the cream of Taylor's experienced troops for the new expedition. Taylor's duty would be simply to hold Monterrey, which he should have been able to do with a reduced army. The letter struck Taylor like a thunderbolt. An officer with Taylor when the letter came recalled that the general sat down to dinner, spread mustard unseeingly over meat, potatoes, bread and dessert and ate it all without a word.

A second letter that Scott wrote to Taylor had a more severe effect than ruining Taylor's dinner. A copy of the letter, which repeated the request for

Mr. Polk. OH!—WHAT A FIX THESE THINGS ARE IN! WILL NOBODY HELP ME?

Taylor's best troops and outlined the coming campaign, was captured by the Mexicans and fell into Santa Anna's hands.

Santa Anna had been recruiting troops with difficulty. Considering the problems of supplying an army with an exhausted treasury, it was a tribute to his leadership that he managed to raise some 25,000 men. It is not clear to what extent the capture of Scott's letter decided Santa Anna's course, but it did convince him that there would be time to take his army north, whip Taylor's now depleted force and still get back in time to meet Scott's attack. If he could defeat Taylor, and then march southward and repulse Scott, the war could still turn around. So he moved his ponderous army north in a grueling march to San Luis Potosí, reorganized the 20,000 or so

who had not died or deserted on the way and in late January, 1847, set out to confront Taylor.

Taylor by now was morbidly convinced that every order from Polk, Marcy or others in Washington was designed expressly to torpedo his chance for the Presidency. In this mood he decided to disregard his orders to stay at Monterrey and advanced deeper into the Sierra Madre to Saltillo, which guarded the strategically important Rinconada Pass. There he prepared his army as best he could to meet Santa Anna, who Taylor soon realized was headed in his direction. Except for Bragg's artillery and a few other regular units, his best troops had all been ordered to the Gulf Coast to join Scott's expedition. A 2,400-man force, mostly volunteers, under the highly efficient General John E. Wool, was diverted from targets in another

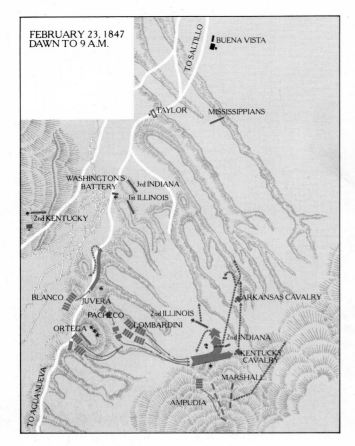

FEBRUARY 23, 1847
DAWN TO 9 A.M.

TO SALTILLO

BUENA VISTA

TAYLOR

MISSISSIPPIANS

WASHINGTON'S
BATTERY

3rd INDIANA

1st ILLINOIS

2nd KENTUCKY

BLANCO

JUVERA

PACHECO

ORTEGA

LOMBARDINI

2nd ILLINOIS

ARKANSAS CAVALRY

2nd INDIANA

KENTUCKY
CAVALRY

MARSHALL

TO AGUA NUEVA

AMPUDIA

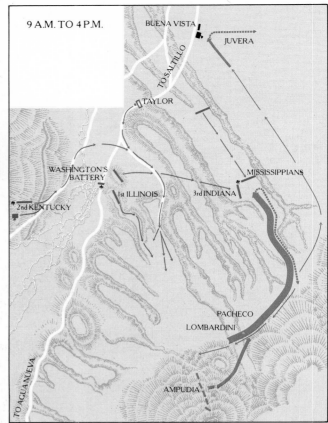

9 A.M. TO 4 P.M.

BUENA VISTA

JUVERA

TO SALTILLO

TAYLOR

MISSISSIPPIANS

WASHINGTON'S
BATTERY

1st ILLINOIS

3rd INDIANA

2nd KENTUCKY

PACHECO

LOMBARDINI

TO AGUA NUEVA

AMPUDIA

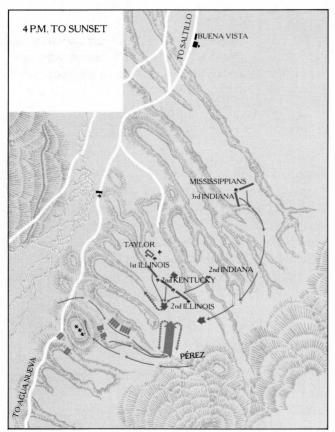

4 P.M. TO SUNSET

TO SALTILLO

BUENA VISTA

MISSISSIPPIANS

3rd INDIANA

TAYLOR

1st ILLINOIS

2nd INDIANA

2nd KENTUCKY

2nd ILLINOIS

PÉREZ

TO AGUA NUEVA

THE BLOODY DAY AT BUENA VISTA

The battle began *(above, left)* when General Ampudia drove a U.S. force under Marshall from a key mountain position and Blanco, attacking a U.S. strong point at La Angostura, was stopped by U.S. artillery. Then Lombardini and Pacheco routed the 2nd Indiana, forcing back the 2nd Illinois and the Kentucky and Arkansas cavalries as well. Taylor moved toward the fighting about 9 a.m. *(above)* and sent Jefferson Davis' Mississippi Rifles and the 3rd Indiana to halt the Mexican advance. Formed in a V, the volunteers repulsed the Mexicans, while Juvera made a fruitless end run against Buena Vista. Taylor then sent the 1st Illinois and 2nd Kentucky to intercept the thwarted Mexicans. At about 4 p.m. *(left)*, he ordered an attack that foundered before a force regrouped under Pérez. As the bluecoats were about to give way, the Mississippians and the 3rd Indiana, led by artillery, disrupted Pérez' columns for good.

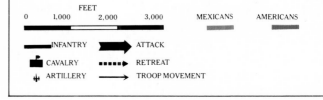

FEET

0   1,000   2,000   3,000   MEXICANS   AMERICANS

INFANTRY   ATTACK

CAVALRY   RETREAT

ARTILLERY   TROOP MOVEMENT

At Buena Vista, Taylor, on Old Whitey *(center)*, directs the advance of Bragg's artillery *(right)* and Davis' Mississippi Rifles *(left)*.

part of northern Mexico to reinforce Taylor. Wool's arrival gave Taylor a total of about 6,000 men.

The stage was set for the battle of Buena Vista, the last of Taylor's career. It was a unique battle. It was the only one that the U.S. Army fought almost totally with volunteers—some of whom panicked and endangered the entire force. It was also the only battle in which the Americans were entirely on the defensive, receiving the Mexican attack. And it was the only battle that the Americans almost lost—in which, in fact, their force was almost destroyed.

Having pushed beyond Saltillo to a large ranch, or hacienda, called Agua Nueva, Taylor sent the reliable and daring Ben McCulloch of the Texas Rangers to locate Santa Anna. McCulloch found the advancing Mexicans 60 miles to the south at Encarnación. Slipping into the huge enemy camp at night, he climbed a hill from where, the next morning, he calmly surveyed the Mexican army. The Ranger got back through

enemy lines the next night and delivered his report to Taylor on the morning of February 21. "Very well, Major," Taylor said, "that's all I wanted to know. I am glad they did not catch you."

The Americans immediately withdrew to a narrow defile located three miles south of a ranch called Hacienda Buena Vista. It was a tight little valley known as La Angostura, or The Narrows, through which ran the main road from the south. This was the road, Taylor figured, that the advancing Mexican army would take. To the right, facing southward, was a network of eroded gullies and ditches that made an attack there impossible. Near the road itself General Wool, who was charged with laying out the defense, placed some artillery and infantry. On the left, several long spurs from the nearby mountains stretched practically to the road. Here, where much of the battle would be fought, Wool stationed most of his volunteer infantrymen and the balance of his field artillery.

81

Santa Anna, having driven his 20,000 troops across the desert for some 200 miles from San Luis Potosí to Encarnación, prodded them another 35 miles to Agua Nueva, seven miles south of the American position. On the way he lost 5,000 men to exhaustion or desertion. At Agua Nueva he found that U.S. troops had burned stores in an advance supply dump there and had withdrawn hastily northward. Santa Anna assumed, wrongly, that the whole U.S. Army was in retreat; he spurred his men forward without letting them fill their canteens. On the morning of February 22, the Mexican army fetched up against the Americans, deployed in their defensive position in the narrow valley along the Saltillo road. Santa Anna still had about 15,000 usable troops; Taylor had some 4,500 on the line of battle while others guarded the supplies in the rear.

Santa Anna sent forward an emissary under a white flag with a demand that Taylor surrender or risk annihilation. Taylor's reply, laundered of expletives by Major William "Perfect" Bliss, read: "I beg leave to say that I decline acceding to your request." Mexican infantry opened fire and a column moved toward the American left, which was ranged on the rocky spurs of the nearby mountains. An American column advanced and inconclusive skirmishing ensued.

Night fell and at 6,000 feet the winds were icy. The troops huddled by their weapons and shivered in a cold rain. Mexican cavalry was reported roaming to the north, and Taylor went back to Saltillo that night to shore up his defenses there; Jefferson Davis' Mississippi Rifles went along. At one time Davis and Taylor had been at bitter odds for very personal reasons. Davis had been a young regular officer when he began courting Taylor's daughter, Knox. For two years Taylor, unwilling to see his daughter become a soldier's wife, forbade the marriage. Finally, Davis resigned from the Army and Taylor relented. Knox and Davis were married, but seven weeks later she died of malaria. Now Davis was back in uniform, at Taylor's side, as a commander of volunteers.

The Mexican attack came early on the 23rd, aimed at the American left, which held a plateau east of the road. The Mexicans advanced, two divisions strong, aided by cannon fire. The 2nd Indiana Regiment was positioned to take the brunt of the attack and in front of the Hoosiers was Lieutenant John Paul Jones O'Brien with three small field guns.

O'Brien kept up a battering fire until, with the 7,000 charging Mexicans nearly at his guns' muzzles, he realized no other shots were hitting them. Looking around, he saw that he and his gunners were alone—the 2nd Indiana volunteers had broken and were running back pell-mell, taking four companies of Arkansas mounted riflemen with them. All were in a state of confusion and panic; there had been a mistaken order to withdraw, instantly countermanded, but it was enough. Released, they went flying back. Some ran miles before stopping and did not see action again that day. Some of O'Brien's horses were down and some of his gunners were dead; instantly he rallied those who were left, abandoned one four-pounder and rode out of the jaws of the onrushing Mexicans.

Driving the tattered, fleeing 2nd Indiana Regiment before them, the Mexican troops next crashed against the 2nd Illinois; it too gave way before the men, muskets and shattering cannon fire. But the Illinois troops gave way slowly, in order. Then the Mexicans came within range of the strong point in the American line, a battery of artillery commanded by Major John Washington, a distant cousin of the first President. The major's gunners, working their deadly pieces in rhythm, stopped the advance—for the moment.

But the lines had been breached and turned; the Americans no longer controlled the plateau but were stretched in a long line paralleling the valley. Swinging around them, Mexican cavalry bypassed the combat in an attempt to strike Taylor's supply train at Hacienda Buena Vista and thus bottle up the Americans for the killing stroke. It was the most perilous situation Taylor's army had ever faced.

At this moment Taylor and his escort "appeared most fortunately" on the field, having returned from Saltillo with Davis' Mississippi Rifles. The general, on Old Whitey, took up his position, calmly, where he could see and be seen, and Davis' men ran forward in long lines. They reached a point where two ravines met as the Mexicans came hurtling down, supported by cavalrymen in overwhelming numbers. The 2nd Indiana was broken and gone, but the 3rd Indiana was coming up to support the Mississippi men. There was no time, however, to wait for the Hoosiers; Davis led

A LITTLE MORE GRAPE CAP. BRAGG!!

Entered according to the act of congress in the U.S. District court Clerk's office in the year 1847.

ROUGH AND READY AS HE IS.

Fac simile of G^l ZACH. TAYLOR from a Daguerotype full lenght likness taken at Buena Vista, by A. H. Wm Smith.

Political cartoons published in the journal *Yankee Doodle* boost war hero Zachary Taylor as the Whig Presidential candidate in the 1848 election. The cartoon at right lists Taylor's successes and names him the king of trumps. Below, the popular general scores a strike in a bowling alley named after his famous victory; the tenpins he is knocking down represent Whig politicians mentioned as his rivals for the nomination.

THE KING OF TRUMPS.

BUENA VISTA ALLEY.

OLD ROUGH AND READY—"ANOTHER TEN STRIKE, CAPTAIN BRAGG."

his men into the onrushing Mexicans. The Mississippians held their fire at first, and "then their little line blazed forth a sheet of fire," wrote an American officer who had been there. "Men went down before it as ripe grain falls before the reaper." Davis gave a shout; the Mississippians flowed down into the ravine and up the other side, fighting with bayonets, and the battered Mexican column wavered.

There was a momentary lull. Then Mexican cavalry swept down the left side of the American line and struck Archibald Yell's Arkansas cavalry in a melee of flashing sabers and pennanted lances. Yell was killed and many of his men fell with him, but the Mexican charge was broken and the lancers rejoined the main battle, where the Mexican infantry was gathering to try once more to shatter the American left.

By that time the 3rd Indiana had arrived and with the Mississippi Rifles they formed a wide angle—the V of Buena Vista, they called it later. Mexican infantrymen and lancers charged into the open end of the V. They came expecting the Americans to fire, and when they were only 80 yards away and no fire had come, they slowed and finally stopped, perhaps puzzled by the silence of the American guns. Then the Americans let go, sheets of flame spurting from two directions on the stationary targets at only 80 yards. The Mexicans tumbled and rolled under this blast of metal, bodies shattered, blood pouring, weapons lost, men crawling away over heaps of bodies, drawing back out of the fire. The V of Buena Vista marked the turning point of the battle.

But the fighting was far from over. No sooner was the attack on the left broken than fresh Mexican soldiers punched straight ahead onto the plateau. Again O'Brien's batteries, what was left of them, were there, taking the brunt of the attack until all of his remaining gunners were gone and his horses dead. He got out—barely—with his life; he left his two remaining six-pounders in Mexican hands.

Once again the Mexicans were driving, and again the flying artillery broke them. Bragg and Captain Thomas W. Sherman, flogging their exhausted horses, brought their little guns squarely into the Mexicans' path and opened fire at musket range.

It was here that Taylor uttered the lines that helped carry him into the White House. Turning to Bragg, he asked, "What are you using, Captain, grape or canister?" "Canister, General," replied Bragg. "Single or double?" asked Taylor. "Single," said Bragg. "Well, double-shot your guns and give 'em hell, Bragg." So Bragg put double charges of the bullet-filled cartridges in his guns and let fly. The first salvo staggered the Mexicans, and by the third salvo they were in retreat; the last major Mexican thrust of the day had been turned back. Taylor's calm injunction, usually misquoted as "A little more grape, Captain Bragg," entered American folklore.

All night the exhausted Americans lay on their arms in the cold, without fires, without unharnessing the exhausted artillery horses, awaiting the onslaught of the morning. When morning came the Mexicans were gone, taking O'Brien's cannon and claiming a victory. For the Americans the sight of the Mexicans' dust clouds was a relief "beyond description." Even Taylor, who seldom showed his emotions, embraced General Wool in a bear hug.

There was no more major fighting in the north. Santa Anna reeled southward, his army riddled by desertion, disease and battle casualties, to begin assembling a new force to meet Scott. In time Taylor went home to his beckoning political career.

Sam French lay on a cot in Saltillo for 40 days with a ball in his leg. Hit during the fighting around Bragg's artillery by a one-ounce musket ball, French felt as though he had been struck by a club. He could not stand, so while the battle continued, he had his men place him in his saddle, where he stayed all day fighting pain and nausea, fearful that if he took to a wagon, he would be abandoned in an American retreat. Now the surgeons could not locate the ball and so refused to cut for it. French knew he would die if it did not come out and he was sure he knew where it was. He summoned the surgeon. "I placed my finger over where I was sure the ball was then located and told him to perform his duty." The doctor, operating without anesthetic, did locate the musket ball. "I was watching his face intently and the moment he touched the ball I saw an expression of delight come over his countenance." After three days French was able to sit up on the edge of his cot, "and some days after that, with crutches, I went to the door and looked into the street." And then Sam French went home too.

The flyer above announces the showing of a picture of General Taylor and his staff *(right)*, painted by William Garl Brown Jr. after the battle of Buena Vista. Americans eagerly paid a 25-cent fee to see one of the few good likenesses of the commander. In the painting Taylor, standing in the center, shows his preference for simple quarters and casual attire. Taylor's aide, Major William Bliss, sits at his right while at left his horse Old Whitey is held ready.

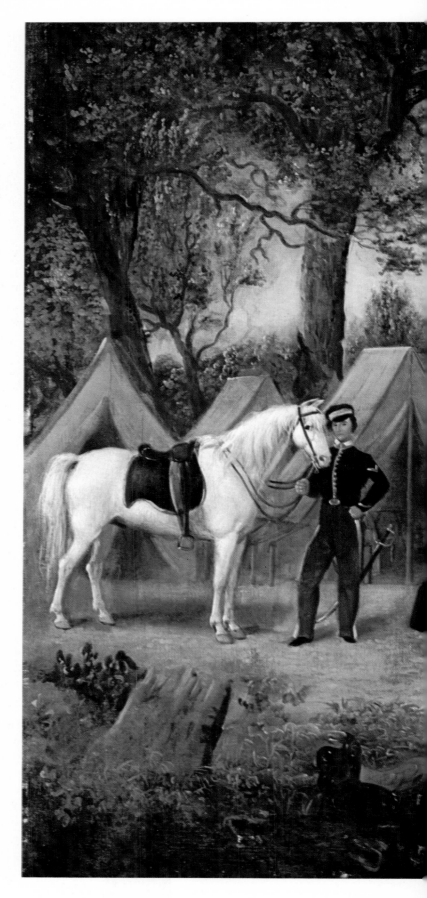

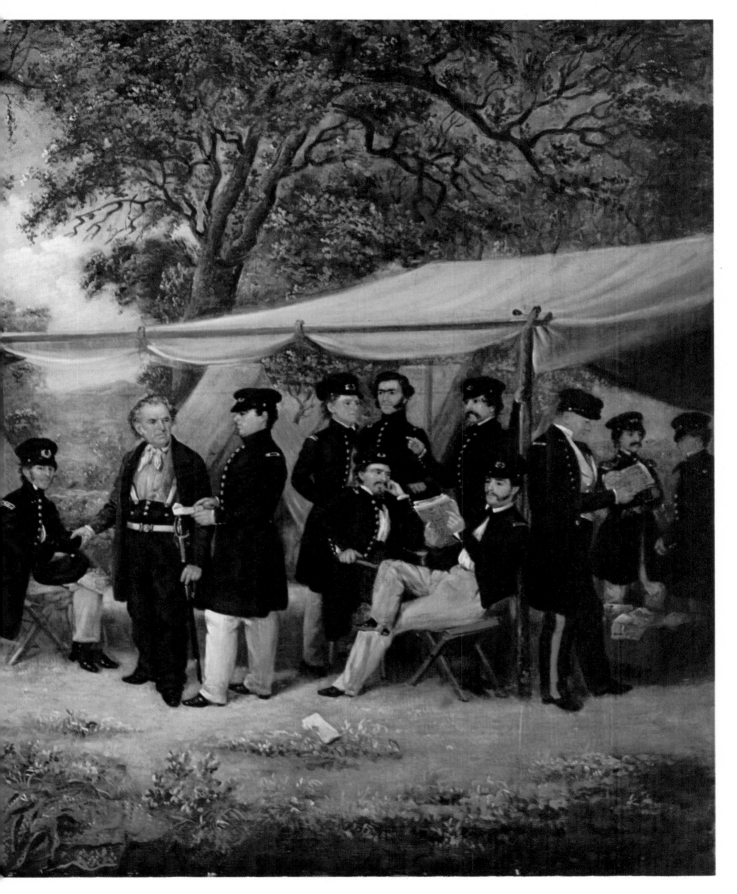

American guardians of a subdued city

Major Lucien Webster's artillery *(below)* helped disperse Mexican dragoons who had lurked near Saltillo to ambush Taylor's retreat, had he lost at Buena Vista.

In 1847 an itinerant American daguerreotyper, his name long forgotten, began the illustrious history of war photography by recording these images of U.S. occupation troops in and around Saltillo, Mexico.

Daguerreotypy, the forerunner of modern photography, was an awkward process that required an exposure of at least several seconds to record an image. Consequently, stationary subjects were needed, and action pictures of combat were impossible.

The relative calm of Saltillo provided good working conditions, and the daguerreotyper stayed on, perhaps as late as January of 1848, when General John Wool, the commander of the occupation army, ejected all of the Americans "who cannot satisfactorily account for themselves, as well as gamblers." Since the record ends here, the eviction order might well have included the world's first war photographer.

The Virginia Regiment of volunteers, on parade in Saltillo, harbored malcontents who abetted a brief mutiny of the North Carolina Regiment against its commander.

General Wool (the horseman left of center) attempted to curb guerrillas by fining their Mexican sympathizers. In only a few months he reported collecting $8,000.

An American horseman is silhouetted against a church in Saltillo. The balmy climate and striking architecture helped relieve the boredom of occupation troops.

The Santiago Cathedral in Saltillo, begun
by the Spaniards early in the 18th Century, served General Taylor as a hospital
for his soldiers wounded at Buena Vista.

Youthful Mexicans pose amiably with a U.S. Army officer. Since no battle had been fought in Saltillo, its citizens did not act openly hostile toward the Americans.

3 | Westward to capture a great prize

In June of 1846, Brigadier General Stephen Kearny rode out of Fort Leavenworth, Kansas, with an army of only 1,458 men. His orders were to invade Mexican California, the prize that would open the Far West, and to secure New Mexico on the way. Unknown to Kearny, other American forces were already invading California, but their blunders would give him time to join the hectic little campaign.

Kearny's dragoons took Santa Fe unopposed, but their race west slowed to a two-month trudge over mountains and deserts. The journey was even harder for the unit shown here, a battalion of Mormons who had fled persecution in Illinois and joined up to seek a haven in California. The recruits spent 15 harrowing weeks blazing a route to the Pacific for Kearny's wagons, which could not cross the mountains. They finally staggered into San Diego shoeless and half starved. Their trek very nearly justified their commander's boast: "History may be searched in vain for an equal march of infantry."

California bound, the ragged and thirsty Mormon Battalion reaches a riverbank and sets to work grading a ford for the wagons to cross.

97

California: the hectic, controversial conquest

The Spanish-speaking inhabitants of Sonoma, California, a "most dull and ruinous" outpost some 35 miles north of San Francisco Bay, were jolted from sleep at dawn on June 14, 1846, by an armed party of American settlers. The Americans, wearing greasy buckskins and "about as rough a looking set of men as one could imagine," strode belligerently into the home of General Mariano Vallejo, Sonoma's most prominent citizen. The astonished Vallejo asked the intruders what they wanted; oddly, none had any clear notion. Vallejo asked if his estate had been taken. That much, at least, the Americans could affirm, and they added that he was their prisoner.

Vallejo then went to his room and, as one bemused American recounted, "soon reappeared with his sword girded on, which he offered to surrender to them; but as none of the party manifested any disposition to receive it, he returned to his room again and replaced the sword." Instead, Vallejo offered hospitality — brandy from his cellar. The Americans and their host then sat down to a more relaxed discussion of what to do next.

Thus began an early episode in the taking of California, one that epitomizes the confusing and often comic uncertainties of this phase of the war with Mexico. Acquisition of the large and potentially priceless Mexican province of upper California and the even larger province called New Mexico was the United States' major aim in the war, yet their conquest was not accomplished by the traditional clash of armies. Only relatively small groups of men were involved and the initial victories, like the taking of Sonoma, were nearly bloodless. Later battles took their toll of lives; but even

these losses were minimal compared with the numbers killed in Mexico itself.

In California Commodore Robert F. Stockton led a motley army of tender-footed U.S. sailors on long overland marches against a mounted, lance-wielding enemy, while in New Mexico Brigadier General Stephen Watts Kearny encountered a foe more adept at posturing and talking than at fighting. Nonetheless, it was a time of testing and of nerves stretched taut. The American settlers in California, most of whom had retained their U.S. citizenship, felt they had to protect their homesteads and their future, with or without the help of their distant government. The military men, for their part, were operating alone, with broad and sometimes conflicting orders; there were months in communication time from Washington and news of developments in Mexico proper. Indeed, the Americans in California had started their own war before they knew that war had officially been declared.

The leaders of the California campaign were men of decisive and independent natures — egotistic, ambitious and jealous of their prerogatives — but they also were given, after each flamboyant action, to cautious glances over their shoulders as they wondered if they were moving toward great success or career-crushing failure. Their uncertainty resulted at least in part from the campaign's unusually murky beginnings.

"I held a confidential conversation with Lieut. Gillespie of the Marine Corps, about eight o'clock p.m., on the subject of the secret mission on which he was about to go to California. His secret instructions and the letter to Mr. Larkin, United States consul at Monterey, in the Department of State, will explain the object of his mission."

So wrote President Polk in his diary on Thursday, October 30, 1845, half a year before the beginning of the war with Mexico. Four days later, 33-year-old

John Charles Frémont's early expeditions raised U.S. hopes for westward expansion. By December 1845 he was back in California with a party of armed "explorers."

Hardened veterans of Frémont's California Battalion gather for a reunion a year after the war ended. The battalion, founded at Sonoma (*opposite*) in July of 1846, helped capture Los Angeles in August.

Archibald Gillespie left Washington, posing as a civilian commercial agent with business in California. In a note to Secretary of the Navy George Bancroft, the excited Gillespie wrote, "I cannot say what I would wish at a moment like this, setting forth on an adventurous enterprize, but I can assure you, you will not regret having named me for this service."

Gillespie was loaded with papers. He carried a copy of the orders for Consul Thomas Larkin (which he memorized and then destroyed), as well as orders for Commodore John Drake Sloat, Commander in Chief of the U.S. Pacific Squadron then lying at Mazatlán on the western coast of Mexico. He brought a letter of introduction to Brevet Captain John Charles Frémont of the U.S. Topographical Engineers, who had left earlier for the West on a "surveying" expedition, and he had a packet of private letters to Frémont from his wife, Jessie, and her father, the influential Senator Thomas Hart Benton of Missouri.

Though he made as much haste as possible, the undercover Marine officer did not reach California for almost six months; by then the impetuous Frémont had already had one run-in with California authorities—to diplomat Larkin's dismay—and some anxious American settlers in the area were on the verge of their own revolt. Gillespie's active participation later in the fighting for California, the secret orders he carried and the contents of Frémont's letter from Senator Benton—

who was an ardent expansionist—all stimulated a controversy over the motives of both Frémont and the Polk administration that has never been fully resolved.

In December 1845, as Gillespie made his way across Mexico, the 32-year-old Frémont came down the western slope of the Sierras into California at the head of a small party of heavily armed men, guided by his good friend Kit Carson. Frémont had already made a name as an explorer of the West, and this expedition, his third, led him to seek a shorter southern route to California and an easier road between Oregon and the interior of northern California.

Early in his career, Frémont had been strongly influenced by his father-in-law and Benton's like-minded colleagues. Discussions with these proexpansion politicians, Frémont said, "gave shape and solidity to my own crude ideas." On the eve of his first expedition, in 1842, the young explorer had been aroused by the visions of the older men. "I felt I was being drawn into the current of important political events; the object of this expedition was not merely a survey; beyond that was its bearing on the holding of our territory on the Pacific; and the contingencies it involved were large." This sense of destiny was part of the baggage Frémont brought with him on his third trip west.

An accomplished man, Frémont was physically strong and a demonstrated leader who, despite his youth, inspired something like reverence in the hardened men who followed him. Many were old comrades from earlier expeditions, among them experienced mountain men like Carson, Joseph Walker and Alexis Godey, and a dozen Delaware Indians who later formed Frémont's personal bodyguard. But the young explorer was also marked by an almost too-powerful urge to prove his worth and by a quickness to perceive slights and take offense, characteristics that would rise to the surface under the pressures of this expedition.

Frémont's party had split up for the winter crossing of the mountains, and most of the men and baggage were entering the province farther south. Once reunited, the group numbered 62 in all, a larger force than was needed for simple exploration. Indeed, it constituted a small army in that sparsely populated country. For years afterward there was a suspicion that Polk had sent Frémont to California to foment revolution. Yet

such an order to Frémont would have been in direct conflict with Polk's instructions to Commodore Sloat of the Pacific Squadron. Polk still hoped to buy California, and Sloat was ordered to be "assiduously careful to avoid any act which could be construed as an act of aggression." Should Sloat learn "beyond a doubt" that war with Mexico had been declared, he was to sail north, seize San Francisco Bay and "blockade or occupy such other ports as your force may permit." But even in that instance he was urged "to preserve, if possible, the most friendly relations with the inhabitants" and to encourage them to remain neutral.

Of all the attitudes the Californios might adopt, neutrality was probably least likely. True, they were a hospitable and pleasure-loving people, in the Spanish tradition. "You might as well attempt to extinguish a love of air in a life preserver as the dancing propensity in this people," marveled Walter Colton, a U.S. Navy chaplain who became the first U.S. *alcalde,* or mayor, of Monterey. Colton was also impressed by the Californios' passion for horsemanship. "They think nothing of riding a hundred and forty miles in a day, and breaking down three or four horses in doing it," he wrote. Certainly the country they inhabited was bountiful.

"Nature rolls almost every thing spontaneously into their lap," Colton said. "Were it possible for a man to live without the trouble of drawing his breath, I should look for this pleasing phenomenon in California."

However, in the 12 years prior to 1846, four revolutions against Mexico had erupted in the province, and on the eve of war with the United States, California was, in effect, an independent republic. The government in Mexico City had accepted that state of affairs, recognizing a civil chief named Pío Pico, who served as governor from Los Angeles, and a self-appointed military chief named José María Castro, who ruled from Monterey in the north. Pico and Castro themselves were at swords' point over control of the treasury and customhouse at Monterey, then the principal port, and civil war between forces led by the two rivals appeared inevitable. To the world at large California "seemed a derelict on the Pacific."

While some Californios were adamantly opposed to foreign intervention of any kind, others thought that annexation—whether by Great Britain, France or the United States—would be a welcome relief from the present turmoil. Americans made up the largest foreign element, numbering some 700 out of a non-Indian

Commodore John Sloat's Pacific Squadron rides in the harbor of captured Monterey. On July 7, 1846, Sloat took the tiny capital unopposed, proclaimed himself the Californios' "best friend" and promised to respect their civil and property rights.

population of only about 8,000. But the chances that the United States might acquire California peacefully were reduced by what one historian called the "Anglo-Saxon's instinctive feeling of superiority to other races." Reflecting this condescending, often contemptuous, attitude, one Yankee described a single-room Californio dwelling—in which a poor family of 10 or 15 members slept on the dirt floor—as a "promiscuous dormitory." He added that "the thicker they lie, of course the less covering they need."

Mixed with this condescension, however, was a healthy sense of awe at the grand scale on which some of the Californios lived. "Two thousand horses, fifteen thousand head of cattle, and twenty thousand sheep," Colton wrote, "are only what a thrifty farmer should have before he thinks of killing or selling." Eager to share in this wealth, American settlers had been entering California quietly for a decade. By 1845 they were disturbed by the turbulence that threatened to engulf, or even evict, them. The Sacramento Valley, where most of them had staked their claims—often without benefit of legal sanction—was astir with the rumor that any foreign settler who did not become a Mexican

citizen would be expelled and his land confiscated.

These developments were being watched carefully by the U.S. government, in the person of Thomas Larkin. A wealthy Massachusetts-born merchant in Monterey, Larkin had been appointed consul in 1844. In that year, the U.S. whaling fleet in the Pacific numbered 650 vessels and 17,000 men. San Francisco Bay was immensely valuable as a refuge for whalers, and it would be even more important if the nation became embroiled in a war with Britain over possession of Oregon. Polk aimed to win California through infiltration and subversion, and Larkin, who was liked and trusted by the Californios, made an ideal consul. On Polk's order, Secretary of State Buchanan wrote to Larkin that the President would not try to induce California to join the United States, "yet if the people should desire to unite their destiny with ours, they would be received as brethren."

Such were the secret instructions Gillespie carried, but by the time they were delivered, Frémont had stirred up a hornet's nest and severely damaged chances for a peaceful American acquisition of California.

Upon arriving in California, Frémont went first to Sutter's Fort, the fortified trading post at the junction of the American and Sacramento rivers owned by the genial Swiss immigrant John Augustus Sutter. In less than three years, gold would be discovered nearby, and Sutter's huge estate, New Helvetia, would be overrun by hordes of fortune hunters. But in December 1845, the fort was the center of a small, self-sufficient empire. Indians who worked the fields for miles around were paid with special coinage redeemable at Sutter's stores. The fort itself, approximately 170 by 425 feet with adobe walls 15 feet high and three feet thick at the base, was guarded at all times and protected by 12 cannon. Sutter was cautiously maintaining a neutral position between Californio authorities—from whom he had received the title to his nearly 50,000 acres of land—and the foreign settlers, who looked on New Helvetia as a protective base.

Frémont paused long enough to replace his mounts and restock his supplies, then set out for Monterey, which was described by an American of the day as "a mean, irregular collection of mud huts, and long, low, adobe dwellings, strewn promiscuously over an easy slope, down to the water's edge." There he explained to José María Castro, the Californio military commander, that he simply needed a place to winter before continuing his explorations in Oregon. Castro agreed; it was understood that the American expedition would stay out of the populous coastal areas.

By mid-February Frémont's 62 men were camped at a ranch 13 miles southeast of San Jose. They were lean and sun baked, and each carried a hunting knife and a long 26-pound rifle. Only a fool would have failed to recognize them as fighting men, probably the most efficient military force then in California.

One day in February Frémont, despite his agreement with Castro, saddled up and moved his men south to within 25 miles of Monterey. Frémont's motive was not clear, but Castro accused the Americans of aiming to incite revolt and ordered them to leave California. Instead, the touchy Frémont moved his men to nearby Hawk's Peak in the Gavilan Mountains, threw up battlements and hoisted the United States flag. Suddenly, to everyone's surprise, Frémont was at war— which was more than could be said for the nation he represented. The first hostilities on the Rio Grande

were still weeks away. In a note to Larkin, Frémont said grandly that "if we are unjustly attacked we will fight to extremity and refuse quarter, trusting our country to avenge our deaths."

Frémont held the peak for three days, while Castro gathered a small army and several pieces of artillery. When Castro appeared, with a force that outnumbered the Americans 3 to 1, Frémont surveyed the situation and decided to go to Oregon after all. He slipped away on the night of March 9.

The immediate threat of hostilities was over, but Larkin was still concerned: the captain's rash actions might result in bloodshed and reprisals against settlers. Larkin wrote to Commodore Sloat at Mazatlán asking that a warship be sent to Monterey to protect American lives and property. Sloat received the request on April 1 and promptly dispatched the sloop of war *Portsmouth,* under Commander John B. Montgomery.

Meanwhile, Frémont drifted slowly north, careful to avoid the impression of flight. In early May he reached the Klamath Lake area of Oregon. There, to his surprise, he was visited by Marine Lieutenant Gillespie.

Gillespie had been a long time coming. He had reached Monterey on April 17, 1846, and had delivered orally to Larkin the instructions he had memorized about five months earlier; then he headed north to look for Frémont. En route, Gillespie heard the latest news of the deteriorating relations between the United States and Mexico. He also had Larkin's appraisal of the Californios' probable response should the American Navy attempt to capture the coastal ports. Larkin had informed Castro that "our flag may fly here in thirty days," whereupon the commandant reportedly declared that "war is preferable to peace."

Thus, in addition to the private letters from Jessie Frémont and Senator Benton, Gillespie brought Frémont the news that war was almost a certainty and that Castro had vowed to fight. Frémont and Gillespie met on May 9, 1846, on the shores of Klamath Lake. Though they could not have known it, this was the day American troops were winning the battle of Resaca de la Palma; the Mexican War had begun.

That night Frémont decided to retrace his steps. "What we are to return to California for no one knew," Edward Kern, an artist member of Frémont's expedition, wrote to his brother. "But to return was sure of

creating a row with the yellow bellies." Frémont reached the Sacramento Valley in late May and found the settlers there ripe for action and the overall situation in California degenerating into chaos. Castro was arming to take the field at Los Angeles against Governor Pico, who was equally convinced that one or the other of them had to go. Castro was also threatening to expel the American settlers by force.

Most of the men who had settled along the Sacramento were frontier-hardened, well-armed and excellent marksmen. When Frémont reappeared they turned to him for leadership, alarmed by rumors of a possible Indian attack instigated by the Californios. Frémont, believing it his duty to pre-empt such a move, led a party of about 50 men in a surprise raid on the Indian villages. They galloped down the valley one morning, striking village after village and scattering the Indians with gunfire. By dusk they had broken any chance of an Indian uprising—if that possibility had ever existed.

Hardly had the dust settled from this exercise when new trouble rose in the hot June air. A man named Knight, who operated a ferry landing on the Sacramento, rushed to Frémont with word that a party of soldiers sent by Castro was rounding up horses for a campaign against the settlers. The settlers boiled over at the

news, but in fact, it appears that Castro's target was still Governor Pico in the south.

Whether or not Frémont directly ordered it, a tall, rawboned frontiersman named Ezekiel "Stuttering" Merritt—whom Frémont later referred to as his "field lieutenant"—gathered a dozen or more settlers and set out after the detachment of Californios. At dawn on June 10, Merritt's party surprised the soldiers in their camp on the Cosumnes River south of Sutter's Fort. The Americans took the nearly 200 horses and freed the men, giving them each a mount and sending them back to Castro with the message that if he wanted his horses, "he must come and get them."

High on this success, the Americans soon mounted another dawn assault—on Sonoma, the northernmost California settlement and the only military garrison for miles. This raid definitely was planned by Frémont, though he again refrained from personally taking part.

Sonoma was not much of a prize. It had been set up in 1835 by Mariano Vallejo, who was then commandant of northern California, to counter a Russian advance out of Fort Ross to the north. By 1846, however, many of its adobe houses were collapsing into mud and its plaza was strewn with the bones of slaughtered cattle. Sonoma had nine brass cannon but none were usable, and no soldiers were there when 33 American settlers, led by "Stuttering" Merritt and William B. Ide, a shrewd jack-of-all-trades from Vermont, routed Vallejo and his compatriots from their beds.

Frémont later defended the action at Sonoma as a "prompt precautionary measure," but the treatment of Vallejo was needlessly harsh. The man was a leading advocate of peaceful annexation with America. Now, after his brandy was consumed, more hostile spirits took over, and Vallejo, with 17 other Sonoma citizens, was taken under guard to Sutter's Fort, where Frémont held him prisoner for nearly two months.

The Americans next took over Sutter's Fort itself. When Sutter protested, Frémont said that "if he did not like what he was doing, he would set him across the San Joaquin River, and he could go and join the Mexicans." Sutter had been sharing meals, brandy and evening walks with his "prisoners" until Frémont relieved him of control. Edward Kern was given charge—and marveled at his quick rise from artist to military commander of a fort. After that time, Frémont referred to the place as "a fortified post under my command."

In Sonoma, meanwhile, the settlers under Ide tried to clothe their insurrection in legality by declaring the establishment of the "Republic of California," a scheme they saw as a natural preliminary to joining the United States. They raised a new flag designed by William L. Todd, whose aunt in Illinois not long before had married a country lawyer named Abraham Lincoln. Todd's ensign contained a large star, a grizzly bear and the words "California Republic." Some Californios sniffed that the bear looked more like a pig, but thereafter the short-lived nation was known as the Bear Flag Republic and its followers as Bear Flaggers.

The Bear Flaggers next issued a proclamation produced by William Ide. One settler, William Baldridge, remembered the genesis of the document this way: "Ide was a strong, active, energetic man, and, in our judgment, was possessed of many visionary if not utopian ideas. Consequently, within a short time he was the most unpopular man among us. Finally he was seized with a fit of writing, which continued almost incessantly for several days, all the time keeping his own counsel." Ide's proclamation was based roughly on sentiments expressed previously by Thomas Jefferson. It guaranteed peace and security to all law-abiding citizens and vowed to overthrow the California government for being incompetent, selfish and oppressive.

Castro could not let this challenge go unanswered. He had no troops north of San Francisco Bay, but he soon collected 160 men farther south and sent a third of them, under Captain Joaquín de la Torre, to the relief of Sonoma. In a skirmish on June 24, the Bear Flaggers killed at least one of de la Torre's men and wounded several more; the rest went galloping southward. The Bear Flaggers suffered no casualties.

All of this served to draw Frémont out of his thin guise of neutrality: with American settlers under attack, he felt justified in acting openly. The Bear Flaggers in Sonoma held a fine Fourth of July celebration. They organized a 250-man California Battalion, comprised of settlers and members of Frémont's original expedition; Frémont was elected its commander, with Gillespie as his adjutant. In his acceptance speech Frémont outlined his intentions, which were nothing less than to march south to seize the whole of California. No longer was this a simple uprising of men in the Sacramento Valley interested only in their own protection. Now they were a conquering force, committed to making California their own.

Without knowing that his country was at war and without authority, Frémont had precipitated a revolution and then had assumed its command. He may have excused his actions on the ground that desperate times call for desperate deeds, but evidently he realized that he was in a risky spot. He quietly wrote out his resignation from the U.S. Army, dated it and sealed it in an envelope with a letter to be sent to Senator Benton should his great gamble fail. But luck was with Frémont. Forty-eight hours after the California Battalion was formed, Commodore Sloat, who had at last arrived aboard the frigate *Savannah,* raised Old Glory over the customhouse in Monterey.

Commodore John Sloat of the five-ship Pacific Squadron was elderly, ill and poorly suited for command. Many years of peacetime duty had made him cautious and he tended to vacillate when faced with important decisions. Sloat heard of the first clash of Zachary Taylor's troops on the Rio Grande as early as May 17. But three weeks went by before the commodore received what he considered authentic confirmation of the fighting at Palo Alto and Resaca de la Palma. The next day he finally started up the coast to carry out his orders to seize California's ports.

Sloat reached Monterey Bay on July 2 to find that Larkin still hoped California might be brought peacefully to the American side. Three days later this hope was shattered by a letter from Commander Montgomery of the *Portsmouth,* at San Francisco Bay, describing Frémont's activities in the interior. Surely, Sloat thought, Frémont must have official approval to be operating in such an openly warlike fashion.

Thus encouraged, Sloat ordered Montgomery to seize the tiny community of Yerba Buena and sent Captain William Mervine and a small party ashore to demand the surrender of Monterey. Mervine returned with a reply signed by artillery Captain Mariano Silva. Silva was "withdrawing and leaving the town peaceful and without a soldier." Two days later at Sonoma, as guns roared in salute, the insurrectionist Bear Flag came down and the Stars and Stripes went up. Francisca Vallejo wrote to her husband, still a captive at

Sutter's Fort, "The danger is past. I and sister Rosa are not afraid any more for your life." The timorous Commodore Sloat had taken control of northern California.

Frémont was equally relieved. Now that the U.S. Navy had arrived to give the color of legality to his operations, he left Sutter's Fort for Monterey, where he and his men could be enrolled in the service of the United States. Tales of their ferocity had preceded them, and on July 19 the inhabitants of Monterey watched from behind their barred windows as a long line of shaggy trail-roughened men, led by Frémont and his bodyguard of Delawares, entered the town. They rode two by two, their heavy rifles held ominously with one hand across the pommels of their saddles.

Frémont and Gillespie boarded Sloat's ship and repaired to the commodore's cabin. Already fearful that he himself had gone too far, Sloat quailed on learning that Frémont had been acting on his own initiative. The Navy commander declared that he had no intention of beginning land operations nor would he support Frémont in doing so. Then, beside himself with agitation, he hurried out of his cabin.

Rescue from this impasse was at hand, however, in the person of Commodore Robert Stockton, who had arrived at Monterey a few days earlier in the frigate *Congress* with authority to take over for Sloat.

If Frémont was the first major figure in the California conquest, Stockton was certainly the second. Commodore Stockton was a smallish man of 51, vain, bombastic, excitable, with excellent political connections. He was a competent seaman with a good naval career behind him, but he thirsted for bigger things and California seemed just the place to achieve them. In character and self-esteem he was not unlike Frémont. The two of them got along famously.

Sloat wanted only to be rid of the whole problem. On July 23 he turned command of shore operations over to Stockton and a week later sailed for home. Stockton eagerly mustered the Bear Flaggers into service as the California Battalion of the United States Troops, with Frémont in command as major and Gillespie as a captain and the second in command. Ezekiel Merritt was given the rank of major, recommended for the post of quartermaster and awarded 2,000 Mexican silver dollars—which he and some of his friends imme-

Patrolling occupied New Mexico, horsemen of General Kearny's

Kearny's sure-footed mules follow a precarious trail along a spur

Army of the West pass a Pueblo village outside Santa Fe. Kearny himself, leading a small force, later headed west to invade California.

close to Arizona.   The flag flies over the tiny port of San Diego, which Kearny's men described as merely "a few adobe houses."

diately spent on a royal bout of food and drink. How Merritt qualified for the job "was to everyone a mystery," one settler reflected, unless "somebody entertained the idea that quartermaster meant the ability and duty to quarter a beef!"

Stockton, now in total command, issued a proclamation annexing California to the United States and vowed to drive Castro and all other resisting Californios out. He said he would march at once "against these boasting and abusive chiefs" who had "violated every principle of national hospitality and good faith toward Captain Frémont and his surveying party."

Castro had removed himself to Los Angeles, where he mended his fences with Governor Pico and began putting together an army to resist the Americans. Stockton set out to crush him with one stroke. Frémont's men would go by ship to San Diego and march north, while Stockton would land a force of sailors and Marines at San Pedro, some 35 miles below Los Angeles. On July 26 the California Battalion set sail. These frontiersmen may have been tough soldiers but they were poor sailors; soon almost all, including the redoubtable Kit Carson, were seasick. "We were all very low in our minds," Frémont later reported.

But as the Americans approached from two directions, the defense of Los Angeles began to melt away. On August 9, Castro warned Governor Pico that he could muster no more than "one hundred men, badly armed and worse supplied" and was thinking of quitting the country. The following night Castro, the governor and a few supporters fled south, while most of the rest of their force dispersed to their homes.

On August 13, Stockton's sailors, followed by Frémont and his men, marched into Los Angeles unopposed. Andrés Pico, the governor's brother, and José María Flores—who would both figure prominently in later developments in California—were captured but were freed when they promised not to bear arms against the United States. The war—if what had happened so far in California could be called that—seemed to be over. But the ease of this early conquest was deceptive; the Californios would not stay subdued for long.

Stockton issued a new proclamation. It announced that California was now part of the United States, that its people were American citizens and that civil government would be established and elections would be held. Proudly he wrote to Washington that "the flag of the United States is flying at every commanding position, and California is in undisputed military possession." Stockton's proclamation also imposed a curfew from 10 p.m. to sunrise and declared that any person found armed outside his home without permission would be subject to deportation as an enemy. These harsh regulations undoubtedly contributed to the turmoil that soon developed.

The third great figure in the taking of California was at this time sitting comfortably in Santa Fe, New Mexico, which had fallen as easily as California. Stephen Watts Kearny was an ironhanded old frontier cavalry officer with a rigid sense of propriety. If Frémont and Stockton were much alike, Kearny was like neither—and before the final California conflict ended, he would clash with both. Indeed, Kearny's quarrel with Frémont ultimately would destroy Frémont's military career.

Kearny, then in his fifties, had fought in the War of 1812 and had spent almost 30 years on the Western plains. He had, said a man who rode with him, "the look and carriage of the soldier." He was efficient, effective, courteous, quiet and very tough. For the past 10 years he had been the commanding colonel of the 1st Dragoons at Fort Leavenworth in Indian Territory, perhaps the finest single unit in the United States Army. Kearny was a tough disciplinarian and his men watched their step. A popular barracks story had him interrupting a subordinate who addressed his men as "gentlemen." Kearny snapped, "There are colonels, captains, lieutenants and soldiers in this command, but no such persons as 'gentlemen.'"

At the same time, though, Kearny had the wisdom to be more flexible with the high-spirited, unmilitary volunteers—mostly Missouri farmers—who were sent to his command as the Mexican War began. Out of pure curiosity, they tended to follow him aimlessly around Fort Leavenworth. Once he boarded a steamboat and told the sentry to keep his volunteer escort ashore. They immediately rushed the sentry, thrust him aside and boarded. According to a St. Louis *Reveille* correspondent, the volunteers slapped Kearny on the back and cried gaily, "You don't git off from us, old hoss! for by Ingin corn we'll go plum through fire and thunder with you. What'll you drink, General?" Kearny gave up trying to look offended and offered to share a glass of wine. Huh! Wine was women's drink. "Why in thunder don't you go for the corn juice, General? It's the only stuff for a military feller to travel on."

On May 13, 1846, just after he signed the declaration of war, President Polk ordered Kearny to ready the 1st Dragoons for travel and to prepare to receive 1,000 mounted volunteers who would be raised immediately. His mission: to protect the valuable trade along the Santa Fe Trail, move into Santa Fe and take New Mexico for the United States. Kearny at once set about organizing what came to be called the Army of the West. A month later came further orders: when he had settled affairs in Santa Fe, he was to move on to "conquer and take possession of" California—where U.S. Navy forces, it was presumed, would already hold the ports—and to establish a civil government there. Kearny was also promoted to brigadier general, as befitted his enlarged command.

In early June the 1st Regiment of Missouri Mounted Volunteers began arriving at Fort Leavenworth. They held an election and the easy winner as colonel and commanding officer was Alexander Doniphan, a huge frontier lawyer. Doniphan (who years later would stand back to back with Abraham Lincoln in the White House and prove himself half an inch taller) was a born leader who made men want to follow him.

As quickly as they could be made ready, Doniphan's men were started on the road to Santa Fe; they moved in small detachments, a procedure that helped conserve the grass and water along the route. Soon Kearny's full army was on the move—1,458 men, 459 horses, 3,658 draft mules, and 14,904 cattle and oxen. For artillery he had a dozen six-pounders and four 12-pound howitzers.

Most of the men were unaccustomed to long marches, especially in the heat and dust of the arid plains. But Kearny pushed them up to 32 miles a day. Regulars and recruits alike cursed and moaned, but they made it, "the long-legged infantry" as a cavalryman put it, outpacing the horses. In 29 days they covered nearly 550 miles.

Near the end of July they came to Bent's Fort, the only permanent post between the Missouri River and Santa Fe. Like Sutter's Fort, it was a center of trade, news and rumor. Every passerby consistently stopped,

Indians camped outside its thick walls to swap skins for manufactured goods, and the great wagons of the Santa Fe trade paused regularly. "The Fort is crowded to overflowing," Susan Magoffin, the wife of an American trader, recorded in her diary. "Col. Kearny has arrived and it seems the world is coming with him."

Kearny anticipated relatively little trouble in Santa Fe and had agreed to send any surplus troops south to reinforce General John Wool in Chihuahua. Like California, New Mexico was so far from the Mexican capital that for years not much effective Mexican control had been felt there. Its people had little commerce with Mexico but had long engaged in a highly profitable trade with merchants in St. Louis.

From Bent's Fort, Kearny issued a proclamation announcing that he was entering New Mexico with a powerful force "for the purpose of seeking union with and ameliorating the conditions of its inhabitants." He also sent a letter—part conciliatory and part threatening—to New Mexico's governor, Manuel Armijo. The letter urged Armijo, who was also commandant general of the province's modest soldiery, to accept the inevitable. A dozen dragoons under Captain Philip St. George Cooke carried the message; with them went Susan Magoffin's brother-in-law, James Magoffin, a famed trader with strong connections in Santa Fe.

Long before Magoffin reached Santa Fe, Kearny's men were on the march. On August 2 they started southward across the stretch of near-desert that led from Bent's Fort toward the climb to Raton Pass, the entryway to Santa Fe. For four days they marched almost without water, the temperature climbing to 120°, the wagons falling back, the horses collapsing, the men burying their fellows who could not survive. Wolves followed the column. When a water hole was encountered, the lead men usually rushed to use it, spoiling it for those behind. Private Marcellus Edwards described the water in one hole as "so bad that one who drank it would have to shut both eyes and hold his breath until the nauseating dose was swallowed."

As Kearny's army advanced, scouts brought in Mexican prisoners daily—soldiers, alcaldes, shepherds, priests—anyone who might have information about the enemy force. Kearny found the military men among these prisoners so pathetic that he remarked to his aide, Lieutenant William H. Emory, "If I have to

Kearny's men carried water, when they could find it, in the three kinds of canteens below. The wood tended to dry out and leak, India rubber made the water taste terrible and tin often caused it to overheat.

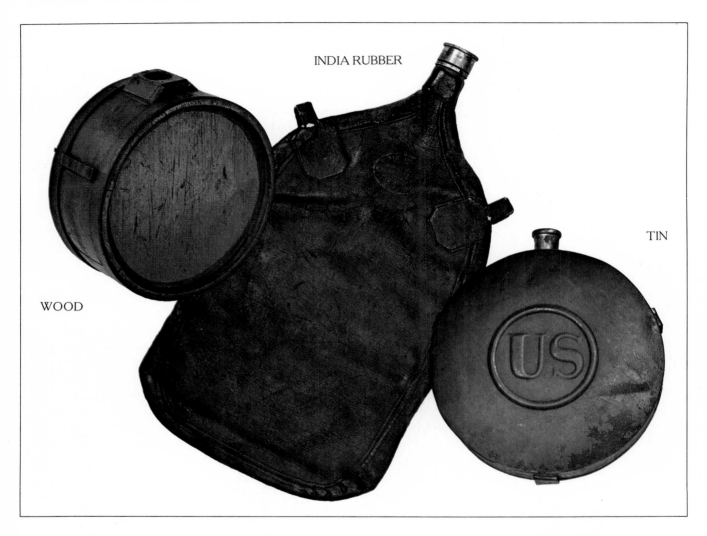

INDIA RUBBER

WOOD

TIN

fire a round of grape into such men I shall think of it with remorse all my life."

The nights grew cold as they approached Raton Pass, climbing to an altitude of 7,754 feet. On August 7 they were through and gazed over the magnificent Sangre de Cristo Mountains toward Santa Fe.

The next day Governor Armijo, who had been appealing in vain to the Mexican commander at Chihuahua for men, called on New Mexicans to rally against the invaders. About 4,000 Mexicans and Indians under Colonel Manuel Pino met at Canoncito in Apache Canyon and prepared to make a stand. On August 12 Magoffin's party reached Santa Fe and he delivered Kearny's letter. Magoffin fluently argued for American occupation, saying that New Mexicans

would be much better off dealing with their trading partners than adhering to their nominal government in Mexico City. But Armijo declared that since the people seemed ready to fight, he must lead them.

Apache Canyon was a chasm through a wall of stone, in places only 40 feet wide. Here, for the first time, a battle appeared imminent. A Missouri volunteer wrote later that the "men were in as fine spirits as I have ever seen them—every fellow at his post—determined that Franklin County should not be unknown to *fame*. We each of us stripped off our coats, shouldered our Rifles, and marched off at double quick time to enter upon our career as soldiers."

But Armijo canvassed his officers and found them all opposed to fighting. His troops already were slipping away, and soon he and his 90-man personal body-guard were riding hard—away from the Americans. Kearny learned of all this from New Mexico Secretary of State Nicholas Quintaro, who, like many in Santa Fe, was an American sympathizer. Quintaro arrived in Kearny's camp riding a mule and roaring with laughter. "Armijo and his troops have gone to Hell," he cried, "and the canyon is all clear."

Thus Kearny's Army of the West took Santa Fe without spilling a drop of blood. The Americans passed through the canyon and got their first sight of the "irregular cluster of low, flat roofed, mud built, dirty houses," which looked to them more like "a prairie-dog village than a capital." They entered a city that was silent except for the wails of frightened women. The women recovered, however, and were in attendance a few days later when Kearny threw a massive ball at which 500 people danced until dawn.

Kearny took several measures to ensure the occupation of New Mexico would go smoothly. In order to make the American presence known, he visited the settlements downriver as far as Tomé, below Albuquerque, accompanied by a force of 700 dragoons and volunteers. Kearny also had Doniphan and another soldier-lawyer prepare a law code for the territory. He appointed Charles Bent, an American from Taos, as territorial governor and signed peace treaties with several hostile Indian tribes.

With the first part of his mission thus accomplished, Kearny dispatched Doniphan's Missourians on a long trek *(pages 112-113)* to join General Wool at Chihuahua and he set out for California at the head of 300 dragoons. In early October, near Socorro on the upper Rio Grande, the column met a party of men headed east. Kearny's assistant staff surgeon, John S. Griffin, described the encounter: "About ten o'clock while marching along, some 8 or 9 men came charging up to us with an Indian yell. These turned out to be Kit Carson, the celebrated mountain man and his party on his way to Washington with an express from Capt. Stockton of the Navy and Col. Frémont announcing that they had taken California." Learning this, Kearny decided to send 200 of his now evidently unneeded dragoons back to Santa Fe. He prevailed upon Carson to return to California as his guide and marched on to take control of the province on the Pacific.

Kearny's troops were disappointed. "Most of us hoped," wrote Dr. Griffin, "that we might have a little kick up with the good people of California but this totally blasted all our hopes." Exactly two months later, however, the much-diminished Army of the West would have a "little kick up" that would nearly eliminate it altogether.

Back in California, unknown to Carson or Kearny, sweet success had long since turned sour. The Californios felt no real loyalty to Mexico and had little interaction with government in their daily lives anyway. They seemed generally willing to accept U.S. rule, provided nobody trampled their dignity and sensibilities. Unfortunately, however, the Americans did just that.

Stockton, who wanted to invade western Mexico next, had no interest in ruling California. Frémont, he decided, would be governor. Stockton planned to sail south, land at Acapulco and lead an attack on Mexico City. He would need his whole naval force, so he ordered Frémont to return to the Sacramento Valley and expand the California Battalion to 300 men to replace the sailors garrisoned along the coast.

Stockton turned Los Angeles over to Gillespie as military commandant of the south, leaving him a garrison of 48 men from the California Battalion. It turned out that Gillespie was the wrong man to run Los Angeles, which was the center of anti-American feeling in California. The tall, redheaded Gillespie spoke fluent Spanish but held the Californios in contempt and treated them rudely. He not only strictly enforced Stockton's curfew and the ban on Angelenos bearing arms but also outlawed reunions in homes and even forbade any two persons to walk in the street together. His soldiers were discontent with duty in the south and so undisciplined that even Gillespie felt the Californios "could have no respect" for them.

At about 3 a.m. on September 23, 1846, a turbulent fellow named Sérbulo Varela led some 20 street toughs in an attack on Gillespie's garrison. The Americans beat them off readily enough, but news of the incident electrified the Californios, who began to dig up arms they had buried for safekeeping. By night a full revolt was under way and the next afternoon some 300 Californios rallied at one of Castro's old military camps about a mile from the American barracks.

The epic march of Doniphan's splendid Missourians

For nearly six months, Americans at home were kept on tenterhooks by reports of the rousing exploits of Colonel Alexander Doniphan and his Missouri Mounted Volunteers.

In December 1846, Doniphan's 856 troopers were sent from New Mexico into northern Mexico to reinforce Wool's division, and before they emerged on the Gulf Coast they had trekked more than 2,000 arduous miles and won two sensational battles. It mattered little that they did not find Wool in time to be useful.

They had written a splendid chapter into the annals of high adventure.

Everything about the expedition tickled the American fancy. The men, including lawyer Doniphan, knew little about the military arts. They traveled with no commissary, no uniforms, no pay and—because the colonel preferred it—no discipline. They seemed unfazed by waterless days in the desert and weeks with no food but flour baked in ashes.

Though he was an amateur, Doniphan showed a flair for battle tactics.

Surprised by a Mexican force at Brazito, he beat off the enemy in half an hour. Outside Chihuahua, in a battle named after the nearby Sacramento River, he used his wagons as a moving fort to maneuver into a good defensive position (below). Outnumbered 3 to 1, they killed some 300 Mexicans but lost only three.

By the end of the march, the Missourians' one-year hitch was nearly over, and none re-enlisted. Perhaps that was Doniphan's fault; he had spoiled the men for the real Army.

Late in the battle of Sacramento, Doniphan's men meet a charge by enemy lancers. Breaking the attack, they captured a Mexican fort

Colonel Doniphan *(left)* pooh-poohed his battle successes, claiming that he merely moved his men up and turned them loose. It was inevitable, he said, that "the enemy first recoiled, then gave way, then fled."

Fancifully depicted in snappy uniforms, Doniphan and his Missourians prance across the cover on a popular song glorifying their march. Actually, they started out in buckskins and ended up in tatters.

and then marched gaily into Chihuahua.

Col. DONIPHAN'S GRAND MARCH.

RESP'LY DEDICATED TO THE OFFICERS & MEMBERS OF THE
MISSOURI VOLUNTEERS,
Composed by A. WALDQUER, by the Publishers.
LEADER OF THE ORCHESTRA OF THE ST. LOUIS THEATRE.

Leadership was assumed by Captain José María Flores, an intelligent and able military man who, along with Andrés Pico, had been captured and released on parole when Los Angeles was first occupied. Flores, like Castro, had long taken a stand of uncompromising hostility toward the United States. Breaking his parole, he issued a proclamation declaring California's independence of all foreign rule and laid siege to Gillespie's position. The war so recently finished was on again.

On the night of September 24, Gillespie sent John Brown (who because of his build was known as "Juan Flaco"—roughly "John Skinny") to get help from Stockton at Monterey. Messages on cigarette paper were hidden in Brown's hair. Five days later, however, with no relief in sight, the badly outnumbered Gillespie surrendered to Flores. Under rather generous terms granted by the Californios, the Americans were allowed to march out with their arms to San Pedro, where they boarded the U.S. merchant ship *Vandalia*. But contrary to the surrender agreement, rather than sailing immediately for Monterey, Gillespie stayed in the harbor and awaited rescue by Stockton.

Revolt flared in other towns along the southern coast. The little American detachment at Santa Barbara—nine men under Lieutenant Theodore Talbot—escaped into a chaparral, which the pursuing Californios set ablaze. The Americans stole across the countryside on foot. "I suffered more from downright starvation, cold, nakedness and every sort of privation," Talbot wrote to his mother, "than in any trip I have yet had to make, and I have had some rough ones." A month later the detachment limped safely into Monterey. In San Diego the American garrison fled to the *Stonington,* a whaler in the harbor, and although the Yankees retook their barracks after a few days, they were under siege for a month.

Thus Stockton was right back where he had been before he drove Castro out of California. The debacle was largely his own fault since, like Gillespie, he treated the Californios contemptuously and seemed uninterested in any sort of negotiated settlement.

Stockton had learned of the uprising in Los Angeles from "Juan Flaco" Brown, the Paul Revere of California, who had galloped most of the length of the province in record time to deliver the news to the commodore aboard his flagship in San Francisco harbor.

Captain Mervine in the *Savannah* was immediately ordered to Gillespie's rescue. Gillespie was still aboard the *Vandalia* when Mervine arrived, and 24 hours later 225 men from the *Savannah,* plus Gillespie's detachment, went ashore to try to recapture Los Angeles. The move was ill considered. Mervine's men had no ambulances, no supply train and no artillery. Their captain knew nothing about conducting a land campaign, particularly against the masterful horsemanship of the fast-striking Californio lancers. Mervine, said Gillespie, "was without reason."

Flores, meanwhile, was planning a campaign of guerrilla warfare. The mounted Californios had more mobility on land than their opponents and Flores hoped to keep the Americans confined to the coast. All food supplies, cattle and horses were to be driven to the interior, out of reach.

The opposing forces met on October 8 on the plains between San Pedro and Los Angeles, north of Rancho Dominguez. The Californios, led by Flores and José Antonio Carrillo, placed their single piece of artillery, a four-pounder, athwart the road. The gun had been hidden in the garden of an elderly lady named Ignacia Reyes, and thus the encounter came to be known as the battle of the Old Woman's Gun.

Mervine marched his men out in close column, with Gillespie's riflemen acting as skirmishers on the right and left flanks. Carrillo found the tightly bunched column an ideal target. When the Americans were within 400 yards of his line, he ordered the fieldpiece fired. Mervine formed his men into a square and ordered a charge. The Californios looped *reatas* about the cannon, pegged them to their saddle horns and galloped out of range. Mervine ordered another charge on the gun. But the Californios had reset the piece and found their target. Shot slashed into the American square. Then the gun was hauled out of reach again.

Three times Mervine charged, only to have the gun evade him. Under the devastating fire, he decided further pursuit was hopeless and called for a retreat. Ten Americans had been wounded and four of them died. That afternoon, after two more skirmishes on the road back to San Pedro, Mervine and Gillespie's weary men reboarded their ships.

To the north, Stockton and Frémont were preparing another two-pronged attack on Los Angeles. Frémont, after a false start in a chartered merchant ship, made ready to march overland from Monterey, while Stockton, in the *Congress*, sailed down the coast to San Diego, which he retook after some minor skirmishing.

Now Stockton had to prepare for real war. He was faced with the prospect of conducting an extensive campaign on land with a force made up almost entirely of sailors. Only perhaps a third of his men carried muskets. The rest were armed with carbines and boarding pikes—hardly the best weapons with which to fight Californio cavalry lancers. Though anxious to attack quickly, Stockton realized his seamen needed more instruction in land fighting. So the commodore drilled them in rudimentary military commands—"march," "halt," "form in line" and so on.

The Californios, meanwhile, had convened an assembly, set up civil government and named Flores as governor and military commander. Despite his recent successes, Flores was hampered by inadequate supplies. He had hardly any money or ammunition, and only 400 men. He divided his force into three parts: Castro would take 100 men north close to San Luis Obispo to watch Frémont; about the same number, led by Captain Andrés Pico, would watch San Diego; and Flores would keep the largest force near Los Angeles to counter either Frémont or Stockton.

Northern California, meanwhile, remained more or less in American hands except for one uprising around San Francisco. Like the revolt in the south, this one was caused by the harsh treatment meted out by the Americans stationed there. The Californios captured Lieutenant Washington A. Bartlett, acting alcalde of San Francisco, and tried to trade him for another American, Captain Charles Weber, whose behavior the Californios found especially objectionable.

In late December an American expedition of some 100 Marines and volunteers, led by Marine Captain Ward Marston, set out for Santa Clara to punish the rebels. On January 2, 1847, Marston encountered about 120 Californios under Francisco Sanchez, former military commandant of San Francisco. The ensuing battle was brief but deadly, at least by California standards: four Californios were killed and five wounded. The Americans suffered two men wounded.

The next morning Marston and Sanchez agreed to an armistice while the Marine consulted his superiors about terms for a permanent cease-fire. On January 6, on the assurance that no further abuses would be committed against the Californios, Sanchez agreed to the unconditional surrender demanded by Marston's superiors, and the war in northern California was ended.

As Stockton and Frémont prepared for the coming action, Kearny and his 100 dragoons appeared from the east. They had reached the headwaters of the Gila River on October 20 and had followed it down, dragging their cannon over violent terrain. The mountains often sloped directly into the river, forcing them into one arduous crossing after another. The views were wonderfully picturesque, Dr. Griffin wrote, "but the fact is we have had so much of the grand & sublime scenery that I am tired of it." Their horses and mules were short of fodder and steadily weakening.

At the point where the Gila pours into the Colorado they paused, seeing fires in the distance. Lieutenant Emory led a party of 20 men forward and found a group of Californios herding horses to Sonora. They seized the men and horses and discovered letters exulting that the "detestable Anglo-Yankee yoke" had been thrown off in California.

This was shocking news for Kearny, who had sent two thirds of his command back as unneeded. Mounting his men on the captured horses, Kearny drove them on to the last, and worst, leg of their march: across the Colorado Desert. Men and animals collapsed in growing numbers. Finally, on December 2, the exhausted soldiers reached the summit of the coastal range and saw below them the gorgeous, waving yellow grass of the valley of the Agua Caliente. Soon they rode into the ranch of Long John Warner, which served southern California as a center of commerce and social life much as Sutter's Fort did the north. There the men sank gratefully into the hot springs to wash away the weeks' accumulation of burning alkaline dust.

From Warner's, Kearny sent a message 60 miles to Commodore Stockton at San Diego. Stockton dispatched Gillespie, with 39 men and a fieldpiece, and the reinforcements joined Kearny's advancing force on December 5. Gillespie brought word that a detachment of Californios under Andrés Pico was camped nine miles ahead at the Indian village of San Pascual and relayed the suggestion from Stockton that Kearny

"beat up the Camp." That night a dragoon patrol led by Lieutenant Thomas C. Hammond crept close to the enemy encampment and a deserter from Pico's force actually entered the camp to spy for the Americans. But the heavy sabers of the patrol rattled so loudly that the Californios were alerted.

Though the element of surprise was gone, Kearny decided to attack at dawn. He outnumbered the Californios 2 to 1; nevertheless, it was a strange decision, given the shape of his men and their mounts after the grueling march. Gillespie described Kearny's army as "way-worn soldiers, whose strength and spirits seemed to be entirely gone." Most of the horses and mules they rode were "jaded and famished." Kearny was soldier enough to know that his chances would be better if he assumed a defensive position and dared the enemy to come to him. But he and his men had trekked all the way from Fort Leavenworth without firing a shot. Besides, both Carson and Gillespie spoke disparagingly of the Californios' readiness and ability to fight. Kearny was unwilling to wait. At 2 a.m. on December 6, he gave the order to saddle up and move out despite a cold rain dampening the powder in the carbines that the dragoons carried.

It was near dawn when they sighted the Californios. "The weather had cleared," Gillespie wrote afterward,

"the moon shone bright as day almost, but the wind coming from the snow covered mountains made it so cold we could scarcely hold our bridle reins." Captain Abraham Johnston, Kit Carson and a dozen dragoons, on the best horses, were in the lead followed by Kearny and his personal bodyguard of six or seven men. Close behind came the main body of dragoons and Gillespie's detachment, a combination of Bear Flaggers and sailors. Kearny ordered an advance at a trot, but Johnston apparently misunderstood and threw his men forward at a charge. Thus separated from the main column, Johnston's men pounded into the Californios' camp, scattering men and horses. Before the rest of Kearny's force could provide support, the Californios rallied and opened fire. A bullet in the head killed Johnston on the spot. Carson was unhorsed and, as he recalled later, "I barely escaped being trodden to death, since I was in advance and the whole command had to pass over me."

The Americans were forced to retreat. Seeing Kearny's main force approach, Pico's men fell back about half a mile to a level plain. Again the Americans charged, but every man at his own pace, those on mules and worn horses straggling in disarray behind the handful of fresh horses in the lead. The Californios spun about, couched their lances and slashed into the strung-out Americans, whose weapons either had been discharged or had misfired in the rain. In the 30-minute melee that followed, American gun butts and sabers were no match for the long, sharp Californio lances backed by the power of galloping horses.

"Our advance was perfectly at their mercy," wrote Dr. Griffin later, and little mercy was shown. Gillespie was thrown from his horse, his saber pinned beneath him. A lance thrust from behind struck above his heart, making, as he wrote later, "a severe gash open to the lungs. I turned my face in the direction of my assailant, when one of the Enemy riding at full speed, charged upon me, dashed his lance at my face, struck and cutting my upper lip, broke a front tooth, and threw me upon my back, as his horse jumped over me." Eighteen Americans were killed on the spot and 18 more were wounded. Gillespie fainted on the field from loss of blood, and Kearny, who received two ugly lance wounds, temporarily had to relinquish command.

Griffin worked frantically on the casualties afterward. Some men had up to eight wounds. "Generally,"

A New York volunteer's departure for war is shown as a flight from penury. Actually men of his unit were chosen for skills and intended to help colonize California.

ONE OF THE CALIFORNIAN BO-HOYS TAKING LEAVE OF HIS GAL.

Griffin wrote, "they seem to aim with their lances so as to strike a man near the kidneys." The number of Americans who finally died was 22. It was the bloodiest battle of the California campaign. "This was an action," Griffin said caustically, "where decidedly more courage than conduct was showed." Of the 80 Californios engaged, no more than a dozen were wounded and none were killed.

The Americans held the field and made their camp. "When night closed in," said William Emory, who was brevetted a captain for his actions during the battle, "the bodies of the dead were buried under a willow to the east of our camp, with no other accompaniment than the howling of the myriads of wolves attracted by the smell."

Kearny's second in command, Captain Henry Turner, sent mountain man Alexis Godey for more help from San Diego. The Army of the West, in the meantime, tried to move on. There were no wagons to transport the wounded, who jolted painfully on travois—stretchers supported by horses at one end and dragged along the ground at the other—and the Californios continually harassed the tattered column. On December 7, Kearny camped on a small hill near Rancho San Bernardo after dislodging the Californios from the height. In the process Kearny lost the few cattle he had left. "We are reduced to mule meat," Griffin wrote, and thereafter the place became known as Mule Hill. They were surrounded by patrols of mounted Californios, they were short of water and they had no fodder for the animals.

The next day Carson and two others volunteered to try to reach San Diego. The Californios knew the elusive Carson was in the camp and had thrown three cordons of lancers around the hill's base to keep *El Lobo*—The Wolf—from getting through. At dusk the three messengers removed their shoes, discarded their canteens and wormed their way down the hill on their bellies. They slipped through the first cordon, then the second and the third. Finally they were among trees where they could stand up. But they were barefoot and had 30 miles to go over rocks and cactus. They made it, only to find a rescue force already being readied.

Before daybreak on the 11th, when the beleaguered Americans had given up hope of relief and were preparing to march out fighting, Lieutenant Andrew V. F. Gray arrived with 215 sailors and Marines. In the face of these reinforcements the Californios melted away. The next day Kearny's battered command entered San Diego and his men at last saw the Pacific Ocean.

Kearny and Stockton immediately began to plan the next stage of the campaign—the retaking of Los Angeles. Frémont had started south from Monterey with the

California Battalion, which now numbered 428 men. They drove a herd of cattle ahead of them and slaughtered 13 each day. One incredulous observer estimated that they consumed 10 pounds of beef per person per day, adding that they seemed to prosper on the diet.

Fearing ambush along the coast, Frémont turned up into the Santa Ynez Mountains; on Christmas Day, 1846, he crested the mountains above Santa Barbara and started down in a howling storm. Water fell in sheets, and the shrieking sea wind blinded both men and animals. The path was obliterated, and more than 100 pack horses stumbled and slid into the raging streams and were drowned. "All traces of the trail," Frémont later wrote, "were washed away by the deluge of water. At night we halted in the timber at the foot of the mountain, the artillery and baggage strewed along our track, as on the trail of a defeated army."

Frémont reached Santa Barbara and took it without a fight, but by the time his troops were ready to move again, the column commanded by Stockton and led by Kearny had set out from San Diego toward Los Angeles without him. Kearny traveled as always, sleeping on the ground in a single tent, but Stockton, said Dr. Griffin, carried a complete bedroom suite with a great bedstead and night tables. The column moved slowly because the sailors, reduced to wearing homemade canvas footgear after their shoes had worn out, suffered from sore feet. "If they only had shoes," Griffin wrote, "there is certainly no reason why they should not make first rate soldiers."

On January 8, 1847, the Stockton-Kearny army reached the San Gabriel River, not far from Los Angeles. Flores' force numbered nearly 500 men, but they were inadequately armed and lacked enough powder for prolonged fighting. Flores mounted four pieces of artillery overlooking the river. Kearny ordered artillery broken out to cover the crossing, but Stockton, an inept tactician, countermanded the order. They would cross unguarded. They did—and only the inferior quality of Flores' powder and the poor aim of his gunners spared American lives.

"As the line was about the middle of the river," wrote Captain Emory, "the enemy opened his battery, and made the water fly with grape and round shot. Our artillery was now ordered to cross—it was unlimbered, pulled over by the men, and placed in counter battery on the enemy's side of the river." Here Stockton, whose personal courage was unquestioned and who had laid many a gun at sea, personally zeroed in his artillery and silenced two of Flores' guns.

Then, shouting "New Orleans" in memory of Andrew Jackson's great victory on that day 32 years before, the Americans charged toward the hill held by the Californios. Halfway there, Emory said, "the enemy made a furious charge on our left flank. At the same moment, our right was threatened." The Americans formed hollow squares, as Stockton had taught them to do in the hasty weeks of training before the battle, "and after firing one or two rounds, drove off the enemy." The Californios fell back in confusion toward Los Angeles. Since Stockton had no cavalry, he did not pursue them. The battle had taken 90 minutes; on each side two men were dead and several wounded.

The next day the two forces met again on the plain of La Mesa, about six miles from the river. Many of Castro's men had deserted, but he deployed about 300 of the remainder in a line across Stockton's route. After two and a half hours of fighting, during which Flores' artillery used up nearly all its powder but accomplished little, the Californios retired from the field for good. In this exchange, remarkably, only one Californio and not a single American soldier had been killed.

On January 10, Los Angeles was reoccupied, and Gillespie himself raised the American flag he had been forced to haul down almost four months earlier. Four days later, in a driving rainstorm, Frémont led his 400 men into the town, carrying with him, much to the surprise of Kearny and Stockton, a treaty of surrender signed by the Californios. Frémont had encountered what was left of Flores' army just north of Los Angeles and, without bothering to check with either of his superior officers, had drawn up articles of capitulation that were signed on January 13 at the Rancho Cahuenga. The terms of the Treaty of Cahuenga were most generous; in effect, they demanded only that the Californios agree to stop fighting. Griffin wrote later, "We took the wind out of Frémont's sails by capturing the Puebla—and whipping the enemy on the 8th & 9th, but he has shown himself the better politician by negotiating first with the enemy."

Peace now reigned between Californios and Americans, but almost at once the American commanders entered into open contention with each other.

Kearny had arrived in California with orders from the President to subdue the country and establish a civil government with himself as its leader. But when he got there a government already had been formed by Stockton, and the commodore refused to turn over command. Frémont unwisely allowed himself to be caught in this imbroglio.

Stockton, as promised, appointed Frémont the governor of California. Although Kearny was Frémont's superior officer, Frémont told him that he would follow only Stockton's orders.

Frémont had guessed wrong. Stockton's replacement, arriving in late January, took one look at Kearny's orders and accepted them. In mid-February Colonel Richard Mason arrived from Washington with new orders that clearly gave Kearny command of all land operations in California. Without telling Frémont of the clarifying orders, Kearny sent Mason to relieve him. The two had such hot words that Frémont challenged Mason to a duel, which Kearny managed to head off at the last moment. Thus the California campaign ended, as it had begun, in confusion.

When Kearny started east in June 1847, he ordered Frémont to accompany him and, on reaching Fort Leavenworth, had Frémont arrested for mutiny and disobedience. That winter in Washington, after a highly publicized court-martial, Frémont was found guilty and ordered dismissed from the Army. President Polk accepted the court's verdict but remanded its sentence. Frémont, outraged, resigned anyway.

Stockton never launched his hoped-for invasion of Mexico's west coast. He traveled overland to Washington, and after the war, resigned from the Navy to serve as a Senator from New Jersey. Although his harsh policies had made the conquest of California far more costly than it might have been, a large part of the final American success was due to the mobility that Stockton's ships provided and to the well-disciplined seamen and Marines of his "gallant sailor army."

Kearny went on to further service in the occupation of Mexico. In 1848, like so many other Americans there, he contracted dysentery; he was dead within the year. Frémont was soon back in the West, embarked on a civilian career marked by dramatic ups and downs. In 1850 he was elected one of the new state of California's first two United States Senators, and in 1856 he was nominated the first Presidential candidate of the infant Republican Party. But ill luck and rash judgments dogged him and eventually he died in poverty in New York City, a continent removed from the golden prize that he had been among the first to reach for.

A military triumph of landbound sailors

An unlikely group of 600 sailors, Marines and dismounted dragoons made up the U.S. force that marched on Los Angeles in the last battle of the California campaign. Led by Commodore Robert Stockton and Brigadier General Stephen Kearny, the Americans left San Diego in December 1846. They hoped to draw General José Flores' lancers—"the most expert horsemen in the world"—into a decisive battle.

Except for six field guns, the Americans were lightly armed: a third had muskets, the rest made do with carbines or boarding pikes. But they were better troops than might have been expected. Sailors, noted Kearny's aide, "properly handled, made very good infantry. Their habits of discipline aboard ship made the transition easy."

The first test of discipline came on January 8 at the San Gabriel River, 10 miles from Los Angeles. Flores' lancers drove a herd of half-wild horses at the Americans. But Stockton formed his men in a hollow square—the classic defense against cavalry—and their fire diverted the stampede.

Whenever possible the Americans fought and even marched in their bristling square, safely enclosing their wagons and cattle. They forded the San Gabriel *(right)*, drove off the lancers and that night—still in a square—camped where they had fought.

The following day they marched in their awkward but secure formation to the plain of La Mesa where the lancers again charged the square, gamely but in vain. Even in retreat the lancers' horsemanship was impressive. Without dismounting, they continued to strip the dead horses in the field, carrying off bridles, saddles, and their dead and wounded to the hills. But they had had enough. "We all considered this as the beginning of the fight," wrote Kearny's aide, "but it was the end of it."

Stockton's men, looking like two-dimensional cutouts in these battle sketches by a

American skirmishers in close order fall back to protect their field guns as the

Navy gunner, cross the San Gabriel with their artillery. The river here was "100 yards wide, knee-deep, and flowing over quick-sand."

Californios attack. Sailors on the left flank and Marines on the right flank repulsed the lancers, who then retreated to the adjacent hills.

Protected by a double line of pickets, the Americans camp in a square on the San Gabriel battlefield, their muskets stacked close at hand.

"The enemy pitched his camp on the hills in view," wrote Lieutenant William Emory later, "but when morning came he was gone."

Their artillery driven out of range by Stockton's gunners, Californio lancers charge the American square from every side on January 9,

1847, at La Mesa. The Americans' musket fire, augmented by grapeshot from the cannon at the corners, made the square impregnable.

4 | Building up to strike the heartland

By November 1846, the United States Army, reinforced with thousands of volunteers and aided by the Navy, had overrun Monterrey under Taylor, occupied Mexico proper as far south as Saltillo and conquered most of California and New Mexico. The Mexican Army of the North had been routed. Yet Santa Anna refused to negotiate a peace settlement.

President Polk therefore set in motion a plan that echoed the daring thrust of the Spanish conquistador Cortés, 300 years earlier: breach Mexico at Veracruz, its principal port, then strike inland to seize the capital city. Major General Winfield Scott, General in Chief of the Army, drew up the master plan for the operation.

To be sure of success, Scott's concept demanded an amphibious assault force—assembled at an island (*below*) off the Mexican coast—of a scale unmatched in U.S. history for a century.

126

Ferried to Lobos Island in the Gulf of Mexico by more than 200 ships, soldiers camp on the coral beaches and prepare for the invasion.

The race against a foe deadlier than guns

All day the transports have been arriving, coming down before the gale like race horses," wrote Captain Kirby Smith in February of 1847 as he watched the Army's fleet of chartered merchantmen deliver thousands of troops and tons of supplies to Lobos Island in the Gulf of Mexico. Major General Winfield Scott had chosen Lobos as the launching point for an invasion of Mexico and an assault on the capital city that President Polk had authorized when he realized that nothing less would force the Mexicans to negotiate a peace.

The next three months would involve Scott's army in two perilous actions. Before the end of April, Scott would stage America's largest amphibious landing up to that time and successfully besiege Mexico's principal port, Veracruz. Then he would march inland to clash with a revived Mexican army under Santa Anna near the mountain village of Cerro Gordo.

Lobos was ideal for Scott's purposes. Though 180 miles by sea from Veracruz, its commodious anchorage was fairly well protected from savage Gulf storms that could wreak havoc on ships at anchor. For the gathering troops, Lobos seemed pleasant enough, although it was the hottest February most of them had known. A Philadelphia newspaper correspondent observed: "Today, by Fahrenheit, in the shade, I scored 92°. If this is *winter,* what will summer be?"

Scott did not intend to stay long enough to find out. The build-up of Lobos Island continued in fits and starts for four weeks, an interminable delay by Scott's timetable. He and his expedition were pitted against an

implacable deadline: the approach of the spring onslaught of yellow fever—the *vomito*—in Veracruz and the low country around it. If Scott could not take the city, then fight his way by late April into the highlands beyond the reach of this scourge, it would destroy his army more efficiently than Mexican grapeshot. Yellow fever, though no one knew it, was carried by mosquitoes. American soldiers bitten by them would fall ill within a few days. After another week, four of every 10 men stricken would die.

Little wonder that Scott was impatient with the logistic foul-ups that kept him at Lobos day after precious day. Transports he had ordered were canceled by mistake. Bad weather delayed other sailings for as long as a month. Troops were sent to the wrong ports. In letters to Commodore David Conner, commander of the U.S. Home Squadron in the Gulf of Mexico, and to Secretary of War Marcy, Scott warned that the date of the invasion was edging ever closer to the beginning of the yellow-fever season.

In the capital, President Polk and Secretary Marcy were no less displeased with the snail's-pace progress of the war, though their concern was as much political as military. To avoid a rout of the Democratic Party in the approaching midterm elections, Polk had hoped for a quick, negotiated victory when he sent Taylor to the Rio Grande in 1846. That summer, Senator John C. Calhoun of South Carolina wrote to an acquaintance, "The administration and the country are already tired of the Mexican war, and are in as great haste to get out of it as they were to get into it."

Since Santa Anna's reinstatement as president, however, there had been little hope for a negotiated peace. Because of the turbulent political atmosphere in Mexico, Santa Anna's hold on the government was shaky; he was more the creature than the maker of public opinion. Mexicans were suspicious of the ease

General Scott, though a stern commander, unabashedly relished his victories. Hearing that the guns of Veracruz had been silenced, he nearly dragged the messenger from his horse with a jubilant embrace.

with which the resilient general had passed through the American blockade in August and they were incensed that in October he had evacuated Tampico—allowing the U.S. Navy, without firing a shot, to capture the port as a marshaling point for part of Scott's army. The Mexican Congress delivered the *coup de grâce* to negotiations when it passed a resolution that seemed to be aimed directly at Santa Anna: just to speak with U.S. officials was ruled treasonous and punishable by death. Even if he had wanted to, maneuvering for an early peace would have been risky for Santa Anna.

The only option remaining for Polk was to conquer Mexico, and that course could also backfire politically. Democrat Polk feared that General Scott, a potential Whig Party candidate for the Presidency in 1848, might ride into the White House on the crest of a brilliant military victory.

Scott gradually collected 9,000 troops, less than half the number his campaign plan called for. He had only one third of the munitions he needed and fewer than half of the special surfboats he had ordered built to ferry his men ashore. Nevertheless, the American commander was pleased with the forces he had. "This army is *in heart,*" he wrote to Secretary Marcy. "And, crippled as I am in the means required and promised, I shall go forward, and expect to take Veracruz." Scott's troops shared his high spirits. "All things look auspicious of success," Major John R. Vinton wrote to his mother. "I am only afraid the Mexicans will not meet us & give us battle."

February slipped by and Scott could delay his attack no longer. On March 2, he and his army sailed from Lobos for Veracruz. As his command ship *Massachusetts* steamed past the fleet of sailing transports crowded with cheering soldiers and blaring bands, the men of Scott's old artillery regiment in the War of 1812 sent up a barrage of huzzahs. A lieutenant standing beside Scott remarked that the artillerymen had not forgotten him. "No," Scott allowed, "the rascals want to fight; they are no better than they were thirty-three years ago, when I commanded them; they were always for getting into the hottest part of it then."

A few months earlier, Scott's prospects for commanding the invasion had seemed almost nonexistent. Impatient with civilian meddling in military affairs, he had

written Marcy a letter that all but accused President Polk of political sabotage. "My explicit meaning," he wrote scathingly, "is that I do not desire to place myself in the most perilous of all positions:—*a fire upon my rear, from Washington, and the fire, in front, from the Mexicans.*" The letter was all the excuse Polk needed to fire Scott as the leader of the Mexican expedition—and he seized it.

Scott remained General in Chief of the Army, however, and he forged ahead with the planning of operations. Aware that Veracruz was for all practical purposes impregnable from the sea, Scott proposed to establish a beachhead and besiege the city from there. To accomplish this against a Mexican force he expected to number more than 20,000, Scott was willing to attack with only half that many, with the guarantee that his army would quickly be doubled by 10 new volunteer regiments. To prevent a rout on the beach, Scott planned to land a massive first wave of 2,500 troops and eight artillery pieces.

The complexity and daring of the plan made it imperative that a truce be reached between Polk and Scott. It was clear to Marcy that no other man besides Scott—in or out of the Army—could pull off this invasion. Consequently, the Secretary of War turned his energies toward persuading the President to achieve a reconciliation with his foremost general. Marcy received unexpected support from Senator Thomas Hart Benton, the powerful Missourian who earlier in the year had proposed himself to Polk as commander of the expedition. Polk had tried to push through Congress a measure creating a lieutenant-generalcy for Benton—a rank higher than Scott's. When the move failed, Benton grudgingly endorsed Scott. Polk's Cabinet, fearing that all other proposed commanders lacked military experience, also supported Scott.

The President reluctantly embraced his nemesis. "I have strong objections to Gen'l Scott," read his diary entry for November 17, "and nothing but stern necessity and a sense of public duty could induce me to place him at the head of so important an expedition."

Two days later Winfield Scott walked out of the White House, reinstated as commander of the invasion. Scott was by no means the natural leader of men that Zach Taylor was, but he was a better strategist. He was then 60 years old and he had been a general for

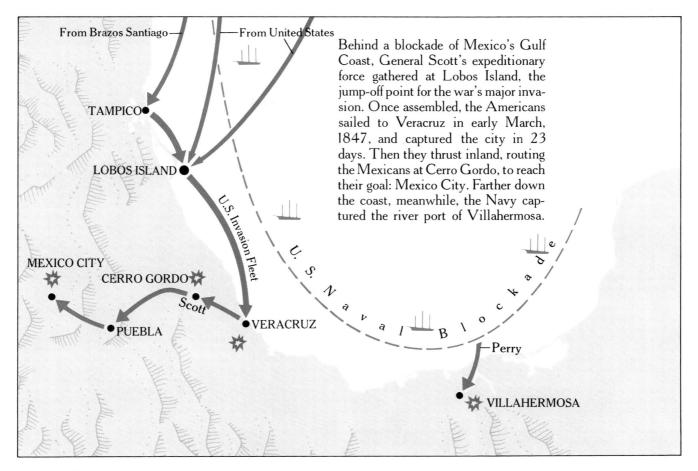

From Brazos Santiago— —From United States

Behind a blockade of Mexico's Gulf Coast, General Scott's expeditionary force gathered at Lobos Island, the jump-off point for the war's major invasion. Once assembled, the Americans sailed to Veracruz in early March, 1847, and captured the city in 23 days. Then they thrust inland, routing the Mexicans at Cerro Gordo, to reach their goal: Mexico City. Farther down the coast, meanwhile, the Navy captured the river port of Villahermosa.

TAMPICO

LOBOS ISLAND

U.S. Invasion Fleet

MEXICO CITY

CERRO GORDO

Scott

PUEBLA

VERACRUZ

U. S. Naval Blockade

Perry

VILLAHERMOSA

more than half of those years—earning his first star as a brilliant artillery officer in the War of 1812. His insistence on military spit-and-polish had earned him the nickname Old Fuss and Feathers.

Scott promptly submitted a list of the men and matériel he would require and ordered work begun on the flat-bottomed, double-ended surfboats he wanted to put his army ashore. The boats, designed by Navy Lieutenant George M. Totten and built in Philadelphia, came in three graduated sizes so they could be stacked inside one another for shipment. Each one could carry at least 40 soldiers.

On November 23, Scott got his marching orders. Before embarking in New York, he wrote to Taylor a tactful but—to ensure military security—cryptic letter requisitioning the experienced core of Taylor's army. Scott intended to meet with Taylor at Camargo, brief him on the plan and issue the orders that would start Taylor's troops moving toward staging points at the mouth of the Rio Grande and at Tampico.

Headwinds extended the passage time from New York to New Orleans from the customary 12 days to 19, a precursor of the delays that would plague Scott throughout his campaign. He then steamed across the

Gulf of Mexico for the Brazos Santiago—the Rio Grande delta—and headed upriver to Camargo for his meeting with Taylor. Old Zach never showed up. He had avoided the face-to-face meeting by accompanying a column of troops sent to occupy Victoria, an insignificant Mexican town. Unable to deal directly with Taylor, Scott abandoned military etiquette and, through Taylor's second-in-command, ordered the troops he needed to the coast.

When the orders to move reached Captain Kirby Smith, he was comfortably billeted with a Mexican family in Saltillo. Smith wrote home: "After dinner I had lain down upon my counter to take a *siesta* and had hardly composed myself, when to my surprise my friend, Lt. A—of the Dragoons, roused me with the cry: 'Up! you will be on the march in an hour.' He had just arrived from Camargo with dispatches from General Scott. Major Staniford came to my quarters immediately after, briefly ordering before he put spurs to his horse: 'Have your company ready to march in thirty minutes.'" Half an hour stretched into the next day before the column moved out toward Camargo and proceeded thence by steamboat to the mouth of the Rio Grande. By January 25, Captain Smith and his

Ann Chase, the fast-talking heroine of Tampico

U.S. Consul Franklin Chase left his wife in Tampico.

British subject Ann Chase became an adroit U.S. spy.

The Mexican port of Tampico, a staging point for the invasion of Veracruz, was presented to the United States as a gift by an extraordinary amateur spy. She was Ann McClarmonde Chase, the Irish-born wife of Franklin Chase, an American importer who was the U.S. consul in Tampico. When the war began, Ann persuaded Franklin to leave Mexico for his own safety; she, protected by her British citizenship, would stay behind to run their business.

Franklin departed on June 7, 1846. It was, Ann wrote in her journal, "A sad moment as I have parted with everything my heart holds dear." Then she began her espionage activities. She studied Tampico's harbor defenses and pumped her friends for information on Mexican troop movements. British sailors smuggled her reports to Commodore David Conner of the U.S. fleet blockading the Gulf Coast.

Mexican officials suspected that Ann was spying, and to get rid of her they tried to close her business and confiscate her property. But she stopped them cold by proclaiming her rights as a British citizen "in the most decisive manner."

Ann was often visited by counterspies who professed friendship, and she carefully misinformed them of American war plans. For her master stroke she remarked that "25,000 to 30,000 troops are coming against this place." Then, correctly guessing that the misinformation she supplied would prompt Santa Anna to order the Tampico garrison evacuated, she notified Conner that the time was ripe to seize the port.

A few days later, on November 14, Ann saw a U.S. warship nearing the harbor. She climbed out to her rooftop flagpole and raised the Stars and Stripes. The port fell without firing a shot, and Ann Chase was hailed as "the Heroine of Tampico."

comrades were camped near the Brazos Santiago, awaiting transport to Lobos Island.

For some of the men, the long march was a welcome relief from the boredom of bivouac. Lieutenant George B. McClellan, a young officer with the engineers, wrote in a letter to his mother: "You have no idea of the charm and excitement of a march—I could live such a life for years and years without becoming tired of it. There is a great deal of hardship—but we have our own fun. If we have to get up, and start long before daybreak—we make up for it, when we gather around the campfires at night—you never saw such a merry set as we are—we criticize the Generals—laugh and swear at the mustangs and volunteers, smoke our cigars and drink our brandy, when we have any."

Private George C. Furber, whose company of Tennessee cavalry had seen its horses collapse from exhaustion on the march across Texas three months earlier, was in Victoria when Scott ordered the volunteer division to Tampico. The columns formed up the next morning and began the 10-day march to the coast. In the middle of the division rolled the baggage wagons, including three that were devoted exclusively to the personal baggage of Major General Robert Patterson. It seemed extraordinary to Furber that even a general could require a full wagon, let alone three. Each night, wrote the bemused private, out would come "kitchen furniture (enough for a good sized hotel), bags of vegetables, champaigne baskets and cases of bottles; carpet bags, mattresses, bedding, trunks &c. You would think of prairie wagons loaded for Oregon."

Compared with the regulars, many of the volunteers were a disorderly lot. They ravaged the country as they passed, stealing chickens and cattle, killing local people who objected and sometimes raping the women. As an excuse for their depredations, the volunteers pointed out that American soldiers had been killed and mutilated by Mexican guerrillas. Volunteers were punished if they were caught, but for the most part their crimes went undetected. Scott wrote in disgust to Marcy: "Truly it would seem unchristian & cruel to let loose upon any people—even savages—such unbridled persons—freebooters, &c., &c." Eventually, Scott placed Tampico under martial law.

In the ranks, regulars and volunteers regarded each other with mutual disdain. Kirby Smith assured his wife that local Mexican civilians were almost fond of the regulars but hated the volunteers. West Pointer George McClellan watched an Illinois volunteer company at drill and saw the lead man file off in the wrong direction. " 'Hulloa, there,' says the colonel, 'you man there, you don't know how to file.' 'The hell I don't,' yells the man, 'damn you, I've been marching all day and I guess I'm tired.' "

Conversely, a volunteer captain noted that officers of the Regular Army "seem to think themselves above us Volunteer officers, being cold and distant. Consequently, we act the same way toward them." Private Furber from Tennessee, mocking the stiff discipline of the regulars, observed that "a regular soldier in peace and war had need for only so much brains as will enable him to stand erect, keep his clothing and tent clean and neat and his arms bright, and just language enough to ask for his allowance of eatables. More brains or language are of no value to him for he will never be permitted to use them."

Soon Scott had an invasion army at his command but no way to transport it. Of the 41 ships he had requisitioned to ferry his troops and munitions to Veracruz, 17 were delayed for nearly a month by terrible weather. Ten ships that were to sail empty to Gulf ports and embark troops for the expedition were canceled by mistake. Other ships, which the Army quartermaster at New Orleans was supposed to charter, never appeared. Scott ordered that replacements be engaged at the Brazos Santiago until, ship by ship, he resolved his staggering transport difficulties.

By the 1st of March, eight weeks later than he had hoped, Scott concluded that his army and his supplies were as complete as they would ever be. Now he had to get them to Veracruz.

Of Scott's 11,000 troops, most had already faced Mexican fire. There were two regular divisions, one headed by General Worth, who had led the attack on the fortified hills at Monterrey, and the other by General Twiggs, the robust old cavalry commander whose laxative had kept him from leading the first charge at Monterrey. A division of volunteers was commanded by General Patterson, a veteran of the War of 1812. In Patterson's division were three brigades led by Generals Gideon J. Pillow of Tennessee, John A. Quitman of Mississippi and James Shields of Illinois. Both Quit-

The big guns' victory at Veracruz

Foresight and good fortune combined to give the Americans an easy victory at Veracruz *(right)*. To Scott's surprise—and for reasons still unfathomed—the Mexicans allowed his army to land unopposed *(far right)*. Scott wisely brought ashore cannon borrowed from the Navy to supplement his own artillery and proceeded to bombard the Mexican garrison into submission *(below)*. Thus Scott was spared a costly infantry assault. Altogether, he lost only 13 of his men.

Fort San Juan de Ulúa dominates the foreground in this view of Veracruz under siege.

A Navy battery exchanges fire with the guns of Veracruz. To borrow the cannon from Commodore Perry, the Navy commander,

Soldiers push field guns through soft sand as Scott's army wades onto Collado Beach.

DAILY MAIL EXTRA.

BY MAGNETIC TELEGRAPH
For the Daily Mail
EXCLUSIVELY!

Important News from
VERA CRUZ.

Successful Storming of the Enemy's Outposts.

A SUCCESSFUL LANDING OF OUR FORCES--WATER AND SUPPLIES CUT OFF FROM THE ENEMY---RECONNOIS-ANCE--REDOUBT CARRIED --LOSS OF CAPT. ALBERTIS AND SEVEN MEN--INVEST-MENT OF VERA CRUZ--RES-CUE OF MIDSHIPMAN ROG-ERS, &C.

New York, Friday, }
April 2—2 P. M. }

The New Orleans Picayune of the 25th, just received, contains intelligence of the highest importance.

Memorandum furnished by Capt. Powers, of the schooner Portia.

Capt. Powers, 8 days from Tampico, having been detained at the south and east of Vera Cruz by a heavy 'norther' until the 17th, has arrived at New Orleans.

The U. S. squadron and all the transports left Point Lerardo for Sacrificios 9th March, the transports having on board 12,000 troops. On the morning of the 10th, the troops and marines effected a landing within three miles of Vera Cruz without meeting any opposition from the enemy, as the landing was well covered by constant discharges of bomb shells and round shot from the U. S. steamers and gun boats anchored near the beach, and in front of the landing.

Immediately after, an organization of American forces on the Beach, took up line of march over the Sand hills to the attack of the enemy's outposts and fortifications, situated from 1 to 2 miles from castle and forts of the city, carried every one by storm—not however, without losing 17 men.

[At the above point our communication broke off. It may be inferred from the heading, however, that Vera Cruz was completely invested, and that Midshipman Rogers had been in some way rescued.]

Battle reports were flashed part of the way from Mexico by telegraph. Nevertheless, readers of this Boston newspaper did not learn of the landing at Veracruz until four days after the Mexicans had surrendered.

Scott had to agree—in an early case of interservice rivalry—to let sailors man them.

In this fanciful portrayal of the naval bombardment of Veracruz, U.S. warships glide with furled sails directly under the defending cannon. Actually, the ships lobbed their shells from anchor a mile offshore.

man and Shields had considerable military skill, but Pillow's only qualification for command was that he had been a law partner of President Polk's.

Sprinkled through this army were some familiar faces. Kirby Smith was part of Worth's powerful and professional 1st Division. So was Ulysses Grant, the reluctant quartermaster. A newcomer worth watching was a middle-aged junior officer named Robert E. Lee, who had joined Scott's staff. Lee, a 40-year-old captain of engineers, had never faced enemy fire but had spent most of his 20-year Army career on routine assignments along the Atlantic Seaboard. When war broke out, he had urgently requested combat duty. As Scott's trusted right hand, Lee would make a remarkable record for himself in the campaign to come.

Anchored offshore near Veracruz, Commodore Conner of the U.S. Home Squadron, whose assignment was to support the American amphibious landing, anx-

iously paced the deck of his flagship. It was March 4 and still there was no sign of Scott's transports or of the brig *Porpoise,* which Conner had dispatched to Lobos Island for news. At last, during the early evening dogwatch, a lookout sighted the *Porpoise* escorting the vanguard of Scott's armada.

For the next day and a half the fleet ran down the coast before a northern gale, "more vessels than we could count," an early arrival said, "ship after ship, crowded with enthusiastic soldiers." Another trooper, watching the spectacle from the deck of his transport, recalled that "the whole eastern horizon looked like a wall of canvas." Navy pilots boarded the inbound ships to guide them through the reefs to the anchorage at Antón Lizardo, 12 miles below Veracruz. By March 6, Scott's army, except for some 2,000 troops still en route directly from Gulf ports, lay poised before Veracruz. Aboard the flagship *Massachusetts* the Commander in Chief raised a toast: "Success to the First

Brigade." Worth's men had been selected to lead the dangerous landing.

Scott believed that thorough reconnaissance was the key to victory. He set out in the steamer *Petrita* to inspect Collado Beach, Commodore Conner's choice of a landing site south of Veracruz. Scott also wanted a look at the city and Fort San Juan de Ulúa, which was planted on a coral reef 1,000 yards offshore to protect the port from a seaward attack. Scott took along his entire command staff: Generals Worth, Twiggs, Patterson and Persifor Smith, and Colonel Joseph Totten, the chief of engineers, as well as his two aides, Captain Lee and Lieutenant P. G. T. Beauregard.

What Scott saw of Veracruz and Fort Ulúa confirmed that the city's defenses were impregnable from the sea and that Ulúa might hold out for months even if the city fell. Veracruz was enclosed by walls 15 feet high. On the land side they "extended from the water's edge south of the town to the water again on the

north." A massive granite seawall protected the waterfront; within the city were "more than 100 pieces of heavy artillery." (Some of the best of these weapons had been cast in an American foundry across the Hudson River from West Point and were purchased by the Mexican government before the start of the war.) Fort Ulúa, built by the Spanish two centuries earlier, could train 135 guns, including heavy 10-inchers, on an approaching fleet. As the *Petrita* steamed along the shore, it was obvious that a landing on Collado Beach was the Americans' only choice.

As the steamer headed toward Fort Ulúa, Colonel Totten, who was examining the fort through a glass, announced: "They are manning their batteries." Persifor Smith took the glass and concurred: "They are using their sponges. We shall have a shot presently." A flower of smoke puffed from a cannon. A junior Army officer aboard *Petrita* later described the experience: "Commodore Conner ordered the steam to be stopped,

to the end, as it were, to let them have a fair trial of their skill in gunnery. We lay thus before the castle until they had fired about eight or nine shells, some of them passing some thirty feet above our heads and exploding afterwards; others exploding before they reached us until they began to calculate the charge and the length of the fuse with considerable accuracy and to scatter the fragments of the shell around the boat."

Bracketed by shellfire, the *Petrita* finally withdrew. Colonel Ethan Allen Hitchcock, Scott's chief of staff, was incensed. "We were in a ridiculous position," he told his diary, "in danger with no adequate object, with *no* means of defence, with all of our officers of rank on board." Lieutenant George Meade considered the whole maneuver "very foolish. One shot might have been the means of breaking up the expedition." The

Petrita headed back to Antón Lizardo, none the worse, and Scott gave the word that the landings would take place at Collado Beach.

The invasion began early on March 9, with the transfer of troops from Army transports to Navy warships for the nine-mile ride to the beach. It was an impressive procession, with "the tall ships of war sailing leizurely along under their topsails, their decks thronged in every part with dense masses of troops whose bright muskets and bayonets were flashing in the sunbeams; the bands of music playing; the long line of surfboats towing astern of the ships." When the ships arrived opposite the beach, they found a line of small American gunboats already in position 90 yards offshore. The gunboats' assignment was to lay a covering fire for the surfboats if this became necessary.

The sand appeared deserted, the surf calm. Beyond cannon range rose the walls of Veracruz, lined with spectators. The rigging of visiting merchant ships and men-of-war offshore was thick with sailors. "It put me in mind," a soldier wrote, "of seeing so many crows on trees, watching the dead carcass lying beneath." There was a reason for such foreboding. Mexican cavalry were reported to be milling about in the sand dunes behind the beach. Two or three well-coordinated cavalry sweeps as the Americans waded ashore could turn the landing into a massacre.

At 3:30 in the afternoon Worth's regulars, each carrying four days' rations of boiled beef and sea biscuit, clambered into the surfboats. Just then, George McClellan noted, "a shot whistled over our heads. 'Here it comes,' thought everybody, 'now we will catch it.' " But the shot had come from the other direction: an American ship was having a go at scattering the rumored dragoons. At 5:30 p.m. a cannon signal from the *Massachusetts* sent the surfboats surging toward the shore, their colors flying.

"Not a word was said—everyone expected to hear and feel their batteries open every instant," McClellan reported. "Still we pulled on and on." The boats slipped through the protective screen of gunboats and a small naval gig with General Worth aboard sprinted ahead. Worth jumped into water up to his armpits to be the first on the beach.

"The entire division reached the shore in good order," Kirby Smith said, "everyone leaping from the boats as their keels grated on the sand, wading the short distance that remained. We were at once formed in order of battle and advanced over the sand hills." The Americans found only empty dunes, windswept and untracked. By 10 o'clock that night, all 11,000 men had reached shore without casualty or injury. Whether the easy landing was due to luck or to Mexican miscalculation is a matter open to speculation. Military historians still puzzle over the Mexican commander's failure to defend the beaches.

Brigades led by Pillow, Quitman and Shields began the encirclement of Veracruz, to bottle up the city's 3,360-man garrison and prevent reinforcements from entering. Their progress was hampered by dense chaparral that had to be cut away and by a lack of supplies and land transportation. A fierce storm had blown up

almost immediately after the landing, and during the two days after the initial assault, only 15 wagons and 100 horses made it ashore. Men still on the beach endured a perpetual sandstorm. The beach was alive with voracious fleas. To avoid them, some men laced themselves tightly into canvas bags; Lieutenant McClellan greased his body with pork fat. Despite these discomforts, in only three days the Americans had formed a seven-mile siege line in an arc around Veracruz and had cut off the city's water supply.

Scott met with his "little cabinet" of staff officers to decide his next moves. The advancing yellow-fever season allowed no time to starve the city into submission. General Patterson had advocated taking it by storm. But Scott saw in that approach a barbaric waste of lives; if one man beyond 100 were to be killed, he declared, "I shall regard myself as his murderer." The battle for Veracruz would be a duel of artillery.

The norther finally blew itself out after seven days, allowing Scott to land his field guns. He divided them into four batteries, three of mortars and one of 24-pounders. It was the task of the engineers to place the batteries where they could inflict the most damage while exposing the artillerymen as little as possible to return fire from the city. Colonel Totten, the chief engineer, chose some sites personally, then delegated their preparation to his subordinates. He sent Lieutenant Beauregard to supervise construction of the emplacements for the 24-pounders. Beauregard studied Totten's choice of ground and decided that it was too exposed. He hurried back to try to persuade his superior to shift the guns and mortars to new sites that he had found. Beauregard noted in his memoirs that Totten looked at him oddly but agreed to re-examine the terrain. As the brash young officer recalled, Totten accepted most of his suggestions—but never did give him adequate credit.

By the afternoon of March 22—a day later than Scott had hoped—the American mortar batteries, set up under harassing fire from Veracruz, were ready to reply. General Juan Morales, garrison commander at Veracruz, rejected a surrender demand from Scott as well as an offer of safe conduct for noncombatants within the walls.

A little after 4 p.m., the seven American mortars opened up. As the first American shots lofted toward the city, Mexican gunners in the redoubts along the walls cut loose with an intense return fire. The guns of both sides, said Kirby Smith, "were soon completely hidden by smoke." McClellan wrote that "a perfect storm of iron burst upon us—every gun and mortar hurled its contents around us. The recruits looked rather blue in the gills when the splinters of shells fell around them, but the veterans cracked their jokes and talked about Palo Alto and Monterrey."

The Mexican fire eased after dark, "but ours kept steadily on, never ceasing—never tiring." The shells from the 10-inch mortars took about nine seconds to fly from muzzle to impact, sailing in giant arcs, their fuses sputtering trails of fire "like bright red stars." Their explosions lighted the rooftops of the city.

The Mexicans had to divide their fire among the four American batteries. Consequently, although the enemy was accurate, American casualties were few. A round shot took off most of Captain William Alburtis' head as he sat beneath a tree, and Major John Vinton died of a concussion—without visible injury—when a shell exploded above him. Vinton's letter home, in which he wondered whether the Mexicans would fight, was still in the mail sack.

Two shells struck near Kirby Smith. "One exploded a few yards to our left and one struck about fifteen feet to my right and rolled very near Rossell and myself. We lay very close to the ground some minutes waiting for it to burst. Then I went and examined it and found very fortunately for us that the fuse had been broken off by its striking the ground."

On the second day of bombardment, Colonel Francis Belton, commanding the mortar batteries, wrote to his wife and son that he had been up all night. "From the time of the opening of the batteries to my leaving this morning, some 600 10-inch shells have been thrown into the city—nine out of ten bursting." Belton thought the enemy fire had been slack, but according to Private Furber, the Tennessean, the Mexican shells were powerful, "digging holes in the sand hills of size sufficient to bury a horse."

For all the smoke and fury, Scott's bombardment had not been decisive by the evening of March 23. True, the 10-inch mortar shells lobbed over the walls had a demoralizing effect on the citizens of Veracruz. But the city's walls were undamaged. It seemed clear that even solid balls from the 24-pounders, which had yet to fire a shot, would scarcely dent them.

Anticipating this problem, Scott had arranged with Commodore Conner to bring ashore three of the Navy's most powerful cannon—each capable of firing 32 pounds of solid shot against the walls. He also landed three Navy eight-inch shell guns, which were more accurate than the Army's mortars. Each of the three-ton cannon was dragged from the beach to the battery site three miles away by 200 seamen and soldiers. Along most of the way, according to a Navy officer, they trudged "through loose sand, knee deep, and fording in their passage a lagoon two feet deep and seventy yards wide." Robert E. Lee, who drew the honor of siting the Navy guns, selected a hill a mere 700 yards from the city walls. The battery was so thoroughly camouflaged that the Mexicans at first remained unaware of its presence.

Then on March 24 its screen of brush was pulled away. As Mexican guns swung to concentrate on the new threat, the sailors manning the Navy artillery leaped for cover. A midshipman who watched a sputtering shell follow a powder boy into a trench wrote that "no jack-in-the-box ever sprang up with more sprightliness." The Navy soon answered the Mexicans better than shot for shot, charging and firing their pieces so rapidly that the barrels finally became overheated and had to be left for an hour to cool.

Lee, whose brother Sidney, a Navy lieutenant, commanded one of the guns, stayed with the Navy battery to repair any damage. "The battery's fire was terrific," he wrote in a letter home. "The shells were constant and regular discharges, so beautiful in their flight and so destructive in their fall. It was awful! My heart bled for the inhabitants."

The inhabitants were indeed having their problems. One American shell crashed into a hospital and killed 19 people; when the patients were hurried to another hospital, it too was hit. Houses collapsed and buried their occupants or drove them into the streets, where flying metal cut them down. Food ran short when most of the city's bakeries were put out of commission. Churches filled with frightened children, crying for parents who lay crumpled on the streets.

The Veracruz garrison was hard pressed as well. The Navy guns pounded the Santa Barbara redoubt—

one of the forts built at intervals along the walls—driving the Mexican gunners from their pieces. A shell detonated the magazine of the Santiago redoubt, and the explosion killed every soldier there but one. Shot after solid shot from the Navy's 32-pounders shattered the stone-and-mortar walls. Finally the barrage opened a breach 50 feet wide. "All the batteries are in awful activity," General Scott wrote in his report to Secretary of War Marcy on March 25. "I think the city cannot hold out beyond to-day."

Scott's appraisal was accurate; morale inside Veracruz was collapsing. Late in the afternoon of March 25, the Mexicans asked for a cease-fire, which Scott granted. But he refused a plea to let women and children leave the city, reasoning that the delay caused by such an evacuation would increase the danger of yellow fever and might enable Mexican rescue forces to break through his line. There had already been several sharp clashes with Mexican reinforcements probing for a way to reach the city.

Scott ordered the bombardment resumed and it continued undiminished through the night, accented by the ripping winds and drenching rains of another vicious norther. In the morning Brigadier General José Juan Landero, who had stepped in during the night to save General Morales the dishonor of surrender, called a truce. Three days later, after negotiating a face-saving surrender with Scott, the Mexicans formally gave up the city. Fort San Juan de Ulúa capitulated too; its garrison, dependent on the fallen city for food, was now in an untenable position.

Scott's victory had been swift and unblemished. His losses—13 killed and 55 wounded—were minuscule; his army was in fine condition. At once he began preparing for the march into Mexico. Still, it was almost two weeks before the first of his troops set off. The time was spent in assembling wagons that had been shipped to Mexico in pieces to save space, and in scouring the countryside for horses to pull them. Whatever horses Scott could find he bought at a fair price. But Mexican ranchers often hid their animals, and American foraging parties came up with only a fraction of the number required. More might be found later; Scott's army would march in sections.

Scattered cases of yellow fever already were breaking out in Veracruz. Yet Scott knew he had to leave a small garrison in the city to secure it as a supply depot. He decided to billet the troops on "the waterfront, open to the sea breezes," presumably hoping that the winds would dispel the miasmatic airs commonly believed to cause the dread fever. It was a fortuitous decision: the breezes would blow away the mosquitoes, which were the real villains.

Scott's immediate goal was Jalapa, 74 miles up the National Road to Mexico City, 4,000 feet above sea level—much more healthful than Veracruz for that reason—and the first town of any consequence in the wall of mountains behind the coast. General Twiggs led the first troops out of the city on April 8. His division of regulars had been heavily reinforced with newly arrived volunteers. Patterson's division of volunteers left the next day. Worth's regulars, augmented by new recruits, would follow as soon as transport could be arranged. Scott remained in Veracruz to settle administrative details, promising to join his army immediately if it should encounter serious resistance.

Santa Anna, meanwhile, was still pulling his army together after the ruinous retreat from Buena Vista. He may have deemed Veracruz expendable, but now he knew it was crucial to stop Scott in the lowlands and let disease do the work of musket and cannon. But Santa Anna was a beleaguered man. He had proclaimed the costly encounter at Buena Vista a victory, thus affording himself the aura of success he needed to quell yet another revolt in Mexico City. He had managed to borrow two million pesos from the Church and had used it to lure new recruits. Then he had headed toward Jalapa to join the remnants of his army. It was in bad shape. According to one Mexican report, the ranks "seemed made up of dead men. Their miserable condition caused the skin of many to stick to the bones and its shrinking exposed the teeth, giving the countenance the expression of a forced laugh."

The mountain passes separating Santa Anna from General Scott offered the Mexican commander a broad choice of easily defended terrain where he might block the American advance. He chose a spot 12 miles coastward from Jalapa where the National Road passed between commanding hills as it began the climb into the highlands. Santa Anna established his headquarters near the sleepy town of Cerro Gordo, or "Big

Hill." It was named for the mountain that dominated it, which the Mexicans called El Telégrafo because it had once been a link in a visual communications system between Veracruz and Mexico City.

By April 12, Santa Anna's 12,000 troops were entrenching themselves and laying their cannon at the summits of Telégrafo and neighboring hills. Lieutenant Colonel D. Manuel Robles, an expert engineer on Santa Anna's staff, objected to the sites. As reported by a Mexican writer after the war, Robles feared "that the road might be cut by the enemy, to the rear of the position." Moreover, Robles considered the Mexican left flank vulnerable to a concerted American attack. Santa Anna squelched this contrary opinion with an insult: "Cowards never felt safe anyway."

For three days Twiggs marched his lead division toward Jalapa—and Cerro Gordo—without incident. The impetuous commander was eager for action. He set a pace that was too fast in the hot sun for his siege-weary infantry; soon many of his troops were collapsing in the heat and crawling into the scanty roadside shade. Nonetheless, on April 11 the Americans reached the bridge across the Río del Plan, about three miles downstream from Cerro Gordo. Next morning, a party of dragoons crossed the bridge to reconnoiter. At the cost of several wounded, they learned that a strong force of Mexicans—4,000, they thought—was dug into the hills. Twiggs dispatched a messenger to alert Scott in Veracruz. Then, with no more information about his enemy than he could gather from that one sharp exchange of fire, General Twiggs ordered an attack at dawn, and damn the odds.

Before the assault could begin, Patterson's division arrived and Twiggs was persuaded to postpone the attack for 24 hours to let the road-weary newcomers gain strength for the battle. Patterson himself was ill, but the next day he pulled himself out of a sickbed and, as the senior officer present, suspended the operation. They would wait for Scott, who had ridden out of Veracruz with an escort of dragoons as soon as he heard about the Mexican opposition.

Scott pitched camp on April 14 near the bridge across Río del Plan. Instead of attacking, he began a careful three-day reconnaissance of the Mexican positions. He soon learned that Mexican cannon occupied the high ground on both sides of the road. The first

obstacle was a trio of batteries sited on three promontories between the river and the road. Adjacent to the road and about a mile behind the promontories was a seven-gun battery, well placed to clear the road of any troops that approached. Back another 800 yards and across the road rose Telégrafo—600 feet high and well fortified with a four-gun battery. A frontal attack along the road, such as the assault Twiggs had ordered, would have been suicidal.

On the Americans' left, the Río del Plan ran through a gorge 500 feet deep, which made an advance in that direction impossible. Scott's best hope was to find a way to attack on the right—the weak side of the Mexican position that engineer Robles had tried to warn Santa Anna about. To blaze this trail, Scott turned to his engineers.

This doughty band—which included three future Civil War leaders, Lee, Beauregard and McClellan—were as often pathfinders as builders. The engineers' West Point-trained officers understood the limits of men and horses in dragging artillery across rough terrain; they also knew how to make the impassable passable. Being an engineer in wartime was hazardous duty, demanding courage, intelligence, coolness under pressure, physical stamina and judgment. Engineers often forayed beyond their own pickets and penetrated enemy lines. Even coming back into camp to report could be dangerous. One night at Veracruz a nervous American sentry fired point-blank at Lee and Beauregard as they returned from a probe into Mexican-held territory. The bullet passed between Lee's arm and his ribs, singeing his uniform.

Scott had brevetted Chief Engineer Totten to brigadier for his work at Veracruz and detailed him to personally carry news of that victory to President Polk in Washington. In Totten's absence, Captain Lee became commander of the engineers. Early on April 15, he set out to retrace and confirm Lieutenant Beauregard's reconnaissance of three days earlier and to enlarge it if at all possible. Beauregard had spotted a jungle-like undergrowth and a succession of rocky chasms that blocked the American right flank, but he believed that those obstacles could be penetrated; he also had noted an unfortified hill, which was called Atalaya, a half mile from Telégrafo and had suggested that it might be of critical importance in the attack.

Destined for fame in the Civil War, these young officers exhibited traits in the Mexican War that would mark each as a general: McClellan criticized his commanders; Lee ignored hardship and fatigue; Beauregard preached strategy to his superiors.

GEORGE B. McCLELLAN

ROBERT E. LEE

P. G. T. BEAUREGARD

Lee, checking on these findings, swung to the left of the Mexican lines; plunging into dense forest and scrambling through steep ravines, he soon outdistanced his small escort. At about midmorning, he stumbled onto a small spring ringed with ferns that had been trampled and surmised that he was well behind enemy lines. Suddenly there were voices; a party of Mexican soldiers was approaching. In an instant, Lee dropped behind a huge log near the water and slid far enough underneath it to be concealed by the ferns. The Mexicans drank from the spring, then sat down on the log, laughing and chatting. Ants and spiders began to chew on Lee; he lay motionless, hardly daring to breathe. More soldiers arrived. It was evening before the last one left. Finally Lee stood up, stiff and burning with insect bites, and made his way back to camp through the darkness. Late that night he reported to Scott: a trail probably could be cut through the undergrowth for men and cannon to outflank Santa Anna.

The next day, Lee retraced his steps along a path that led behind Atalaya and extended his reconnaissance almost to the Jalapa road. While Lee scouted, a working party began to clear a trail for infantry and light artillery. So confident was Santa Anna that no attack could come from that direction that he summarily dismissed his pickets' first report of chopping sounds in the woods. At the second report, he threatened to discipline the messenger for spreading falsehoods.

Basing his plans on his engineers' reconnaissance, Scott proposed a two-faceted attack for April 18. General Twiggs's division of regulars, reinforced by part of Shields's brigade, would cut the Jalapa road in order to trap the bulk of Santa Anna's army, just as the Mexican engineers had feared. At the same time, General Pillow's brigade would mount a diversionary attack designed to convince Santa Anna that the American main effort would come precisely where he expected it—against the three strongly defended prom-

An engineer's map traces the battle of Cerro Gordo. The Mexicans defended hills along the river and the road to Jalapa. The Americans circled north of these positions, then attacked across rough terrain.

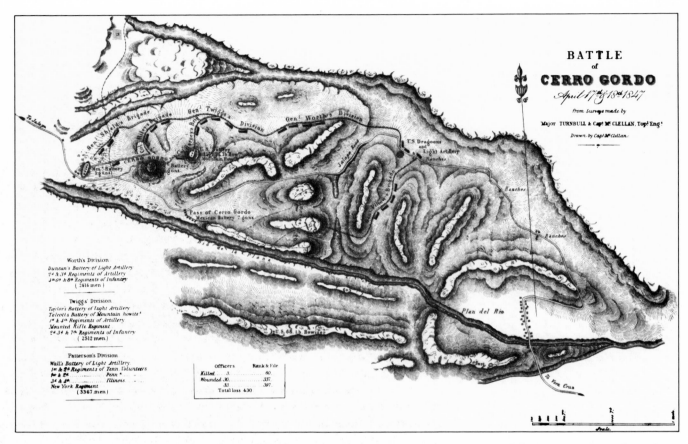

ontories between the road and the river. Worth's division, which had finally collected enough horses to leave Veracruz, was to support Twiggs.

Early on the 17th, the men of Twiggs's division followed Lee along his makeshift road, to position themselves for the next day's battle. Hauling cannon over the crude path was brutal work. Ulysses Grant noted that the sides of the ravines "were so steep that men could barely climb them. Animals could not." So the artillery was let down each steep slope on ropes and pulled up the opposite sides.

As the soldiers advanced toward the Mexican lines, moving silently to avoid detection, tension began to build. There was a ripple of laughter when a soldier slipped on a rock and rattled his musket against his canteen. A captain who was known sarcastically to his men as Blunderbore rushed with drawn sword at the hapless enlistee and bellowed, "You infernal scoundrel, I'll run you through if you don't make less noise." No harm was done; the rugged terrain served to keep

the Americans out of the Mexicans' sight and earshot.

And then a rifle company, on a reconnoitering mission at the base of Atalaya, clashed unexpectedly with a troop of Mexicans.

Though Twiggs was under orders to wait until the next morning to attack, he sent part of Colonel William Selby Harney's brigade to rescue the rifle company. The flamboyant, red-haired Harney, at the head of his brigade, chased the Mexicans up one side of Atalaya and down the other toward Telégrafo. Far from defeated, the Mexicans counterattacked. Twice they slogged up the hill and twice the Americans beat them back. The third time, a handful of impetuous Americans followed Twiggs's advice to "Charge 'em to hell!" They chased the enemy troops down the hill, into the ravine, up the side of Telégrafo and straight into the teeth of 3,000 Mexicans—a hell indeed.

Outnumbered 50 to 1, the Americans were shattered by devastating fire that pinned them, crouched and bleeding, to the rocks. A lightweight mountain

This map of Plan del Río, where Scott camped for Cerro Gordo, accompanied a letter of condolence to the family of a soldier slain in the battle. He was buried under a tree 40 paces from the Jalapa road.

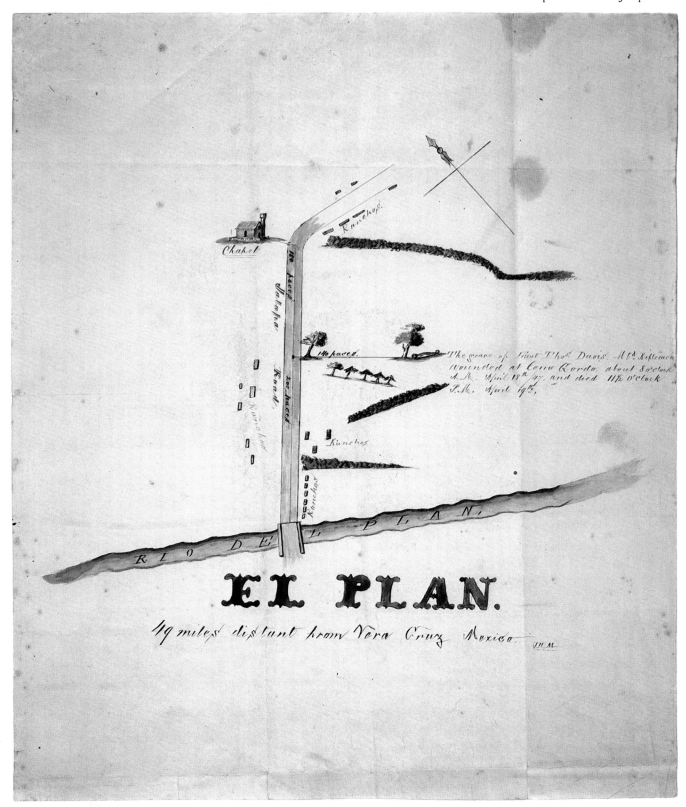

EL PLAN.

49 miles distant from Vera Cruz, Mexico.

A direct hit on an American gun emplacement scatters the crew. Under less pressing fire, gunners fought by General Scott's punctilious artillery manual, which told a man how to position even his fingernails.

howitzer, hastily dragged up Atalaya, kept the Mexicans at bay while a nine-man relief team started for the beleaguered Americans to help evacuate the casualties. Once darkness fell they were able to pull back to Atalaya with just enough men left whole to carry the injured. "It was a shocking sight," a private of the engineers wrote to his parents, "to behold the poor wounded riflemen and some artillery and infantry—about 100 in number—lying on the ground with legs shot off, arms gone, and cut in every part."

It was an inauspicious beginning, and Scott was certain that the premature attack had exposed his plan. His fears were groundless. Santa Anna still believed the attack against Atalaya was secondary to the main thrust that would come against the three promontories. Accordingly, during the night of the 17th, he reinforced Telégrafo with three additional guns.

A few hundred yards away, the Americans were busy dragging three more cannon up Atalaya. Their

task was unenviable; "the guns," wrote an officer in Shields's brigade, "were to be dragged up a steep rocky mountain side, without a road, a path or even a landmark." He continued: "A fire was kindled at the foot of the mountain, and taking this for the starting point we were to ascend in a perfectly straight line." At 9 p.m. 500 men manned the drag ropes of the 24-pounder, with additional teams of 500 following in relays to relieve them. "Many of our strongest men gave out. By the time the last gun was dragged up—I should judge about 3 in the morning—the track over which they had passed was strewn with tired, exhausted, and sleeping men from the top to the base of the mountain. I would have given every thing I possessed in the world to have the delicious sweet enjoyment of lying down to rest."

In the morning, Mexican reveille drifted across from Telégrafo. The same tired American officer, peering through a screen of bushes, saw what looked like the whole enemy army. "The lancers—the chivalry of

Mexico—were there, with their lances and streaming pennons," he wrote. The artillerymen were "drawn up beside their guns, and far down the mountain slope were assembled in groups, by hundreds and thousands, the Mexican infantry. Little did the men who held that height suppose that in one hour a 24-pounder and two 24-pound howitzers would open upon them from amidst the clouds."

At 7 a.m. the Atalaya battery fired its first round, and the Mexicans returned a dismaying barrage. "The grape and canister flew over our heads like hailstones, striking a few feet from us, tearing up the ground and cutting down the bushes and throwing the stone into the air in every direction," wrote the engineer private in his letter home. "I saw one ball strike into the body of mounted riflemen, killing six poor fellows."

The sound of firing from Telégrafo was General Pillow's signal to advance head on against the Mexicans. The diversion went awry from the start, basically because Pillow was a poor commander. Moving in a disorganized fashion along densely thicketed hollows, his men were late reaching their position. Then they attacked along a route that exposed them to fire from all three Mexican batteries at once, a nearly disastrous mistake. Pillow's plan called for Pennsylvania and Tennessee regiments under Colonels Francis Wynkoop and William Haskell to storm the heights first. But according to George McClellan's diary, before either was ready to attack, "General Pillow shouted out at the top of his voice—'Why the H--l dont Colonel Wynkoop file to the right?' I may here observe," McClellan went on, "that we had heard very distinctly the commands of the Mexican officers in their works. This yell of the General's was at once followed by the blast of a Mexican bugle and within three minutes after that their fire opened upon us."

The Tennessee volunteers were caught in cannon and musket fire at almost point-blank range. "The air

HEAD QUARTERS.

KNOW ALL MEN:

That Antonio Lopez de Santa-Anna, President of the United States of Mexico and Commander in chief of the mexican armies has been duly authorizel to make the following concessions to all and every one of the persons now in the American army who will present themselves before me or any of the commanding officers of the mexican forces, viz:

1.ˢᵗ Every soldier in the American army who appears before me or any of the commanding officers of the Mexican armies is to receive immediately *ten dollars* cash, if coming without arms, and a larger amount if he is armed, in order to cover the cost of the arms he may bring.

2.ⁿᵈ Every person who deserts the American army followed by 100 men is entitled to receive as soon as he presents himself with his men, $500 cash, besides the $10 to which every one of the soldiers is entitled, as well as the extra allowance in case they be armed.

3.ʳᵈ He who deserts with 200 men has right to claim and shall be paid immediately $1000 cash, and so on at the rate of $500, for every hundred men; or the proportional amount if the number be under one hundred; without including the $10 allowed to every soldier, nor the cost of arms and ammunitions, all of which will invariably be paid besides.

4.ᵗʰ All and every one of the soldiers in the American army who will desert and appear before mé or any af the Commanding officers of the Mexican forces, as aforesaid, besides the abovementioned gratifications in cash, are hereby entitled to claim and will immediately receive from me or any of the Commanding officers a document or bond by which the propriety of a grant of land consisting of 200 square acres will be ensured to them as well as to their families or heirs. The division of such grants will be made as soon as the present war is over.

5.ᵗʰ The Officers in the American army are not only entitled to the aforesaid document or bond but the number of acres in addition to the 200 allowed to the soldiers, will be computed in proportion to the respective grades they hold.

6.ᵗʰ Those who desert the American army and enter the Mexican service are to continue in it during the present campaign, and those of the same nation are to remain together if they choose and under the immediate command of their own officers, who will continue in the same grades they held in the American army.

7.ᵗʰ All those persons who come over to the Mexican armies shall be considered, rewarded and promoted in the same way as the Mexicans and according to their services in the present campaign.

The preceding articles shall be duly published in order that the Mexican Authorities may act in conformity thereto.

Head Quarters. Orizava the   April 1847.

Antonio Lopez de Santa-Anna.

Santa Anna's offer of cash and land to deserters after his defeat at Cerro Gordo lured few Americans to Mexican ranks.

was filled with the storm of iron, copper and lead," said Furber, the Tennessee cavalryman; "the trees and brush flew in splinters, the rocks were shattered on every surface; and the gallant command fell like leaves before the whirlwind." Eighty men fell in a few minutes and the others broke, some jumping to cover, some bolting for the rear. One of the wounded was Pillow, who described himself as "all shot to pieces." He had a flesh wound in the arm.

The main American attack, down the flank of Atalaya toward Telégrafo, progressed more satisfactorily. After a brisk artillery duel, Colonel Harney saw enemy reinforcements heading for the Mexican hilltop and ordered a charge. The brigade crossed the hollow between the hills and started up the steep slope of Telégrafo. "The officers were obliged to use their swords for canes to help them up the hill, as did the soldiers their muskets," wrote one trooper. Barna Upton, a Massachusetts volunteer, described what happened next: "We marched directly up to their breastwork, which was a slight one made of one thickness of timber, laid one above another and supported by stakes, and drove them to the rocks and behind another breastwork inside the first. We remained behind the breastwork to take a breath while we discharged ten or fifteen rounds."

In a few moments Harney, swinging his saber and shouting in a voice like a foghorn, had his men over the first breastwork and moving toward the hilltop. "Soon two of their guns were deserted," continued Upton, "and our whole force with a loud shout leaped the breastwork and met them at the point of the bayonet. Here for just one short minute ensued a kind of fighting which I hope never to see again. It seemed like murder to see men running bayonets into each other's breasts, but they soon turned and ran like a flock of frightened sheep down the hill."

Now the retreating Mexican infantrymen, their own cannon turned against them, saw part of Colonel Bennet Riley's brigade coming up another flank of Telégrafo. The Mexicans broke ranks and tumbled down the hill toward the Jalapa road below. The rest of Riley's troops, along with Shields's brigade, charged ahead to block the road. Santa Anna, realizing at last that he had been outflanked, descended from the heights and was on the road when his retreating troops reached it. He turned and lit out toward his headquarters at the village of Cerro Gordo, with Riley's men on his heels. The battery protecting Santa Anna's camp loosed one devastating charge of grape, then Riley's infantrymen were upon it with bayonets. Just then Shields's brigade burst from a thornbrake and charged the camp from the side. Shields, in the lead, took the first fire full in the chest. His men charged on without a pause, bayonets gleaming.

Meanwhile, the Mexicans who had routed General Pillow from the promontories saw their position on Telégrafo collapsing behind them and knew their line of retreat was lost. They surrendered.

The battle was all but over by a little after 10 a.m., though Shields's and Riley's troops, followed by Worth's division, pursued the shattered Mexicans for 10 miles to prevent them from regrouping. Late that night, Santa Anna rode into a distant village accompanied by only a handful of staff officers. He asked at a church for a fresh horse; the curate looked him over and closed the door in his face. The commander of all Mexico's armies rode into the night, scorned, defeated and sunk in depression.

General Scott, on the other hand, was elated. He began his report of the battle to Secretary of War Marcy, "Sir: The plan of attack was finely executed by this gallant army. We are quite embarrassed with the result of victory." Scott estimated that 3,000 Mexicans, "with the usual proportion of field and company officers," had been taken prisoner and another 1,200 killed or wounded. The Americans had suffered 431 casualties. General Shields recovered, despite a bullet in his lung. At a field hospital in Cerro Gordo, he was tended by a captured Mexican army surgeon, who drew a square of washed silk through the wound to clean out the debris.

Scott let all of the prisoners go; he had no means of feeding them and he hoped that word of his leniency would incline the Mexicans to be less tenacious in future encounters. He ordered their weapons dumped into the Río del Plan. Scott also called attention to a proclamation that Santa Anna had issued on hearing of the earlier United States victory at Veracruz. The Mexican leader had warned: "If the enemy advance one step more, the national independence will be buried in the abyss of the past." Concluding his report, Scott commented tersely, "We have taken that step."

149

Santa Anna glares imperially in this portrait done following the war.

A cocked hat and a false leg, both reputed possessions of Santa Anna, were among the war souvenirs taken home by American bluecoats. How the hat was acquired is unknown, but the leg was captured by Illinois volunteers when the general abandoned it in his carriage at Cerro Gordo.

Mexico's flawed, flamboyant leader of men

"Mexicans! Veracruz calls for vengeance—follow me, and wash out the stain of her dishonor." With rousing words like these, the popular General Antonio de López Santa Anna rallied his countrymen, rounded up his battered army and faced the Americans.

For all his charm and energy, Santa Anna was a failure in war. He was plagued by inept soldiers, some of them freed convicts, and he was distracted by sniping from political enemies in the capital. But basically his failures were rooted in his own shortcomings.

Like his uniforms, Santa Anna was often more show than substance. He loved the challenge of creating his army but drilling it to proficiency bored him. By all accounts, he was a courageous man—he lost one of his legs fighting the French in 1838 (he would later acquire the sobriquet Immortal Three-Fourths) and he had a horse killed under him at Buena Vista.

But such bravery was wasted on officers whom he treated so arrogantly that they hoped he would fail and on troops whom he lashed with his riding crop as they retreated. Less than two years after returning from exile in Cuba, Santa Anna had lost Mexico and sailed for Jamaica, an outcast.

Santa Anna draped his presidential figure in an elegant royal-blue cape worn over a tunic richly embroidered with gold thread. The left leg of the trousers, unfashionably baggy, was cut wide to slip more easily over Santa Anna's inflexible false foot.

Steaming against a river stronghold

In June 1847, as General Scott prepared to assault Mexico City, Commodore Matthew Perry's blockade of the Mexican Gulf Coast was about to lose two vessels in need of overhaul. "To give the officers and men of these two ships another opportunity of displaying their gallantry," Perry decided to steam up the Grijalva and take Villahermosa, which was a conduit for troops and supplies to Santa Anna.

The Americans casually called both the river and the city Tabasco, for the province in which they were located. Perry planned to attack Villahermosa with enough sailors and Marines to overrun defenses the Mexicans had built along the river and to hold the city. One of his officers, Lieutenant Henry Walke, chronicled the expedition in the lithographs on these pages.

Taking the city was easy enough. Its defenders, led by a corrupt officer who pocketed their pay to quench "an insatiable thirst for gold," simply evaporated before the American advance. Holding it, however, was impossible. Yellow fever, guerrilla attacks and a lack of reinforcements forced the Americans to retreat after five weeks.

Led by Commodore Matthew Perry's flagship, *Scorpion,* four shallow-draft steamers haul 47 boats abrim with 1,173 men and seven small cannon through waves breaking over a sandbar at the mouth of the Grijalva. Once across the bar, the ships refilled their coal bunkers, then headed upriver the same evening with the boats in tow.

153

Inching upriver, Perry's flotilla looses a fusillade at Mexican soldiers firing from a riverbank ambush. No Americans were hurt in the exchange, and one participant attributed most of the bullet holes in the flagship *Scorpion*—as well as a shot that ripped an officer's cigar from his mouth—to overeager Marines firing across the deck at the enemy.

Mexican sharpshooters spy on the American squadron as it steams through Devil's Bend, an S curve 45 miles up the Grijalva. The marksmen caused little trouble, but pilings sunk into the riverbed halted the ships at this point. Perry then decided to put his landing force ashore and to attack Villahermosa and the intervening fortifications on foot.

Leaving his ships to a subordinate, Perry leads the landing force ashore. In only 35 minutes the sailors and Marines had assembled and were marching with their artillery toward a Mexican breastwork, which gave up without a fight. In the meantime, the crews of the ships had dislodged the pilings with explosives, reopening the river to the flotilla.

Approaching Villahermosa, the *Scorpion* exchanges fire with Fort Itúrbide *(right)*, the city's last line of defense. The ships churned past the Mexican guns — which inflicted only minor damage — and overwhelmed the fort from the rear. Villahermosa lowered its flag without firing a shot, and four hours later Perry arrived to occupy the city.

5 | The cost of war at home

Most Americans responded enthusiastically to the trumpets of war in 1846 when the country rang with slogans such as "Mexico or Death" and "Ho, for the Halls of Montezuma." Even the gentle poet Walt Whitman thundered, "Yes, Mexico must be thoroughly chastised!"

But as the war dragged into its second year and mounting death tolls became a painful reality on both sides, the initial enthusiasm dwindled. As Scott's doughty expeditionary force, victorious at Cerro Gordo, gathered itself for the ultimate assault on the ancient citadel where Aztec emperors once ruled, voices raised against an "unjust, unholy war of agression" began to be heard in the United States. Although always a minority, the antiwar faction boasted a fiery and articulate array of intellectuals, clergy, abolitionists and pacifists of every sort.

But many Americans were turned against the war by subtler means — like the sentimental paintings on these pages or by poems like John Greenleaf Whittier's "The Angels of Buena Vista." In Whittier's verse a Mexican woman impartially nurses the wounded of both armies and laments over a dead U.S. soldier: *"A bitter curse upon them, poor boy, who led thee forth/From some gentle, sad-eyed mother, weeping lonely in the North!"*

The latest news from the Mexican battle-front produces astonishment and concern among some townsfolk on the porch of the American Hotel in this work by Richard Caton Woodville, a Baltimore-born artist.

The persistence of war is symbolized in this Woodville painting of a wounded young officer describing his experience to his Southern family and their household slaves. The grandfather, a veteran of the American Revolution, still wears the knee britches popular a half century earlier.

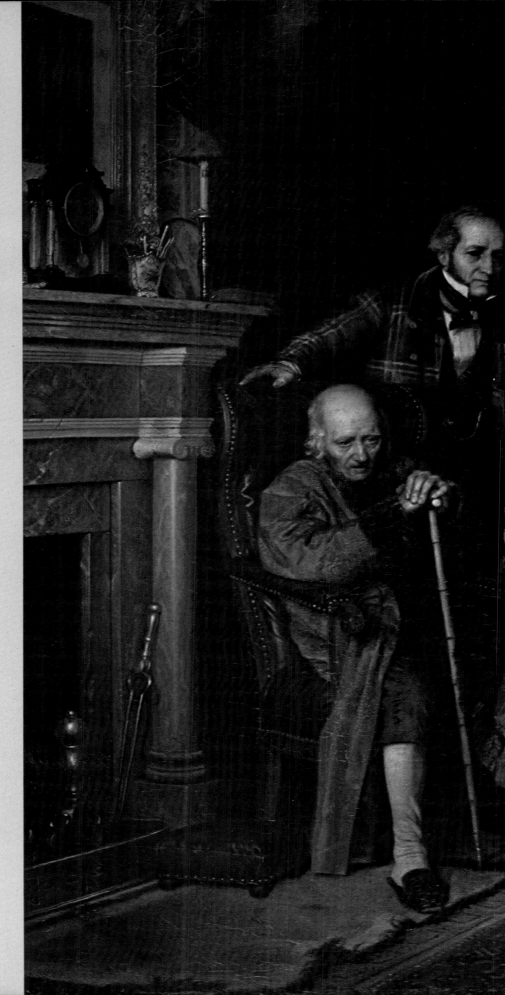

The poignant moment when a young wife and mother learns of the death of her soldier husband is dramatized in this painting of a Scottish-American family by John L. Magee. The little boy at right, too young to comprehend the tragedy, is pointedly shown playing with a sword and drum.

A resolute advance "with naked blade in hand"

The hardest part of the war began just when Americans thought that peace had come within reach. Major General Winfield Scott's resounding victory at Cerro Gordo on April 18, 1847, had smashed the only enemy army between him and the Valley of Mexico, which lay 180 miles away. The Americans hoped that Santa Anna would send negotiators to seek peace terms or, at worst, that he would scrape together another green army and come out to fight a last, decisive battle.

But nothing of the sort happened. In Washington, hope for a quick end to the war faded as the months passed without bringing a shred of dramatic news from the front. Senator Daniel Webster of Massachusetts had predicted: "Mexico is an ugly enemy. She will not fight—and will not treat." And so it seemed.

The interminable weeks after Cerro Gordo put American morale to a severe test. In miserable camps and hostile towns deep inside Mexico, soldiers grew restless and surly. Discipline faltered at every level; even ranking officers, their judgment impaired by nerves worn raw, ignored routine regulations, bridled at reprimands, quarreled and laid mutinous plots.

In the United States the lengthening hiatus brought the war home to civilians as their prowar rallies and victory celebrations had never done. Disappointment gave way to frustration and anger. Nowhere was the disaffection for the war more apparent than in the schisms created within the two major political parties. By the summer of 1847, differences in the Whig Party centered on two plans. One, endorsed by conservative Whigs, held that the United States should not acquire any territory as a result of the war; the other, supported by the party's radical wing, insisted that slavery be forbidden in any territory that was acquired. The Democratic Party was similarly divided into those who supported the expansionist plans of President Polk and those who became more strongly antislavery as that issue loomed larger in the debate over the war.

Whatever their political leanings, many Americans were calling for peace. Senator John C. Calhoun of South Carolina, an influential Democrat, broke with the mainstream of his party in the spring of 1847 to urge a unilateral withdrawal to the Rio Grande. Fearing that the war was escalating into the conquest of all Mexico, Calhoun warned, "Mexico is to us the forbidden fruit; the penalty of eating it would be to subject our institutions to political death."

Horace Greeley, no less unhappy with the war, nevertheless argued for finishing it conclusively. "We are in the predicament of a man who has a wolf by the ears," he wrote in the New York *Tribune.* "It is dangerous to hold on, and it may be fatal to let go."

Nor was it politically safe to denounce the war. One Whig politician who did so, an inconspicuous freshman Congressman named Abraham Lincoln, was reviled at home in Illinois as "the Benedict Arnold of our district" and was later denied his party's renomination.

The debate over this "endless war" was essentially a clash between American idealism and pragmatism. The issue of slavery, once raised, could not be turned away; like an impending storm, it would darken the American political horizon until its final resolution almost two decades hence. Abolitionism, strongest in the northeastern states, found effective spokesmen among prominent Whigs, who considered the issues of war and slavery inseparable. And no Whig made the case against slavery with greater fervor and conviction than former President John Quincy Adams, then 80

This sword with its elegant hilt attests to the high price of glory in the climactic summer of the war. South Carolina awarded it to Colonel Pierce Butler—posthumously.

An antiwar cartoon, published in *Yankee Doodle* in 1847, draws a bitter contrast between the well-dressed, battle-eager recruit and veterans who were beginning to return from Mexico, ragged and maimed.

GOING TO AND RETURNING FROM MEXICO.

years old and serving in the House of Representatives.

Adams was one of the Immortal Fourteen, as their adherents called them—a group of Congressmen who had refused to support the initial war bill in May of 1846. Adams argued that the Polk administration was dominated by slave-state Democrats who supported the war in order to acquire new territories, which would enhance Southern power when they entered the Union, creating "a nation of slave-owners and slave-breeders." Polk's administration did have a Southern tilt but Polk, himself a Tennessean, insisted that Adams' argument was fallacious. "There is no probability," he wrote, "that any territory will ever be acquired from Mexico in which slavery would ever exist."

The slavery question had been linked to the war as early as August of 1846 when the administration sought to put through Congress a two-million-dollar appropriation for war expenses. Congressman David Wilmot, a dissident Pennsylvania Democrat, tried to amend the bill: "Provided, That, as an express and fundamental condition to the acquisition of any territory from the Republic of Mexico by the United States . . . neither slavery nor involuntary servitude shall ever exist in any part of said territory." The so-called Wilmot Proviso divided both parties down sectional lines, and Southern Whigs joined Polk Democrats in an effort to defeat it. Nonetheless, it passed in the House and was sent to the Senate, where it died when Congress adjourned. Similar antislavery amendments delayed, at least temporarily, the passage of almost all subsequent war appropriations bills.

The entwined debates over slavery and war raged from the pages of literary magazines and pulpits as well as in the daily press. Massachusetts, the "cradle of liberty," was also the cradle of the abolitionist movement. Congregationalist minister Theodore Parker of West Roxbury ignored prowar hecklers to tell audiences that if "war be right then Christianity is wrong, false, a lie. But if Christianity be true . . . then war is the wrong, the falsehood, the lie." The platform of the militant abolitionist William Lloyd Garrison was *The Liberator,* a periodical so extreme that it accused legislators who supported abolition of being politically motivated, and thus destructive to "genuine antislavery activity." *The Liberator* proclaimed itself in sympathy with the Mexicans, declaring, "Every lover of Freedom and humanity throughout the world must wish them the most triumphant success." To General Scott the message went, "We wish him and his troops no bodily harm, but the most utter defeat and disgrace."

Yet none of the abolitionist writing, vitriolic as some of it was, did as much for the antiwar cause as a single phrase coined in the Boston *Atlas.* The *Atlas* gave dissenters of all parties a focus and a whipping boy when it contemptuously described the conflict in Mexico as "Mr. Polk's War." The President had been little known before his election, and his popularity had not been improved by a penchant for secrecy and a lack of candor. To attack him personally was easier, more amusing and certainly less controversial than to attack the war itself. People saw James Polk as a small man of limited resources. "That little mole," one critic called him, and his Cabinet became known as the "little fellows." It was not surprising when an opponent linked Polk to the famous show-business dwarf of the day, calling him "Tom Thumb's cousin, Jim Thumb."

The successful attacks on Polk and his conduct of the war made him a millstone around his party's neck. By the summer of 1847, Democratic leaders were defending him only weakly. Some, deciding to jettison him as a candidate for re-election, were maneuvering to win the nomination for themselves.

Whig Party candidates also had been looking ahead to the Presidential election, now little more than a year away. They found it increasingly hard to straddle the issues that threatened to rupture their minority party. Daniel Webster, already twice a candidate, sought the nomination with a late and rather transparent bid for abolitionist support in his native New England. Senator Thomas Corwin of Ohio, who had crossed party lines to support administration war bills, caused a sensation by changing his mind and enjoining the President: "Call home your army—I will feed and clothe it no longer." Corwin enjoyed a brief period as the leading Whig candidate but faded when he could not rally the support of party conservatives. Desperate to regain the White House, the Whigs turned more and more to a political innocent, Zachary Taylor. Although a slaveholder, Taylor won the nomination—and the election of 1848—not just because he was a war hero but because his political views were unknown.

If any segment of the troubled population was nearly unanimous in its view of President Polk and the great debate, it was the Army, languishing exposed and impatient in Mexico. The soldiers in general, and General Scott in particular, felt that Polk and his administration were letting them down by failing to provide the matériel and man power they needed to win the war with dispatch. Reports of Whig opposition to the war infuriated them. When news arrived that Senator Corwin had come out against further appropriations, one group of soldiers burned him in effigy in a Mexican uniform. The maneuvering toward the 1848 election was another sore point with the troops. Secretary of War Marcy had given a fair accounting of their exasperated reaction: "In the name of God, will the politicians of our country never cease gambling for the Presidency upon the blood of their countrymen?"

On April 19, 1847, the day after the great victory at Cerro Gordo, the American Army moved on to the picturesque hill town of Jalapa, about 13 miles beyond

the battlefield. There the Americans posted Scott's General Order Number 20, which declared martial law; they set up a headquarters and a hospital and went into bivouac nearby. In Scott's plan, Jalapa was to be one of the two principal way stations on the 240-mile road that led from Veracruz to Mexico City. From this collection point he would move his army in stages to the second-largest city in Mexico, Puebla, 90 miles ahead. Puebla would become the marshaling area for the final leg of his march to the Mexican capital city, another 70 miles beyond.

Scott was satisfied with his progress. The battle at Cerro Gordo had cost him only light casualties, and the results, as he wrote enthusiastically to General Taylor, were that "Mexico has no longer an army." The main body of his own force—almost 10,000 troops—was now safely established in the healthful highlands before the yellow-fever season began on the sweltering coastal plain. Moreover, Scott presently received a War Department promise of enough reinforcements to bring his

U.S. volunteers in Mexico "see the elephant"—with death riding its howdah. The elephant expression referred to any great experience, but it became—as in this antiwar cartoon—slang for "combat."

total strength to 20,000, and he knew for a fact that 4,000 fresh volunteers already had orders to Mexico. With 20,000 men he could confidently attack Mexico City if peace negotiations did not begin in the meantime. So, in hopes of pressing his advantage, Scott ordered General Worth to move his 1st Division of regulars 30 miles west to the next stop, Perote.

Worth started out at once. From Jalapa, itself nearly a mile high, the mountain road climbed up the rugged Sierra Madre, the soldiers hiking along through the clouds. Santa Anna's shattered army had not entirely disappeared. Worth reported that some 2,000 enemy troops sifted by his column in small, disorganized groups. A 1st Division man wrote of finding Mexican "waggons loaded with dead bodies, some rapped in blankets and others almost naked; some with swollen legs, arms & heads &c., & c., being mostly wounded and broken down soldiers who were left to die."

Worth reached Perote on April 22. The old Spanish fort there had been abandoned, leaving the Americans 54 cannon and a cache of supplies. Worth paused to await Scott's next orders. It would be a long pause.

In Jalapa problems were shaping up that would haunt Scott for the rest of his campaign. Though he could buy food and forage locally, he lacked wagons and horses to bring up the tons of military supplies from Veracruz; the few skimpy wagon trains that did head inland were attacked on the road by bandits and groups of belligerent civilians. Just to get messages through this guerrilla blockade, Scott's inspector general, Colonel Ethan Allen Hitchcock, had to hire a robber band headed by a cutthroat named Manuel Domínguez to serve as couriers.

It was impossible to guard the whole stretch of road against hit-and-run attacks. And when cavalry units were used as escorts, the troopers and their mounts

Throughout the war, New England flowered with literary protest. Poet Ralph Waldo Emerson and the up-and-coming politician Charles Sumner published articles attacking the conflict as a trumped-up land grab. An angry hermit named Henry David Thoreau went to jail in symbolic protest and even wrote, "It is not too soon to revolutionize." But the most effective literary dissenter was critic James Russell Lowell. Writing satiric doggerel in a Yankee dialect, Lowell said, "Ez fer war, I call it murder," and "They just want this Californy/So's to lug new slave-states in."

HENRY DAVID THOREAU

CHARLES SUMNER

RALPH WALDO EMERSON

JAMES RUSSELL LOWELL

were worn to a frazzle. The only real solution was to delay each wagon train until a large force of Jalapa-bound soldiers had been assembled to march along as guards. There was no sign of the new volunteers promised by the War Department.

To make matters worse, Scott was having trouble with the soldiers already at Jalapa. Many of the troops had not been paid for months; they were growing restless in their crude bivouac, which they sourly named "Camp Misery." Though the regulars generally behaved well enough, a number of unruly volunteers roamed about unchecked, pillaging the countryside. Mexican civilians lodged a flurry of real and invented complaints; Scott's officers in charge of military government made an example of several American malefactors, disciplining them with 30 lashes. Many soldiers got hold of locally made alcoholic beverages and went on binges. Dr. John Campbell, a young surgeon at

the hospital at Veracruz, later treated hundreds of dysentery victims, many of whom fell ill because, Campbell complained, they kept on "drinking wine and liquor and swilling fruits in spite of what I say."

Scott's most serious problem involved some 3,700 volunteers who had enlisted for only one year. Their hitch was nearly finished, and it made no sense to send them forward if they were going to opt for returning home. Scott passed among the regiments that would soon become eligible to leave Mexico and offered the men various re-enlistment inducements that had been authorized by Congress. More than 90 per cent of these veteran soldiers refused to sign up again; they had had enough of bloodshed and disease, enough of marking time and going without pay, and more than enough of Camp Misery.

A number of the "short-timers" announced that they had no quarrel with General Scott—that their grudge was against the government. In any case, Scott ordered the men to get ready to leave Jalapa in a hurry; he wanted them to ship out of Veracruz before the yellow-fever season peaked. On May 6 and 7, seven regiments—soldiers from Illinois, Georgia, Alabama and Tennessee—marched away, cheering and grinning, the envy of those who had to stay behind. Their departure reduced Scott's army to only about 7,000 men, more than half of them with Worth at Perote.

On May 7, Scott finally sent marching orders to Worth's 1st Division. But almost three weeks had been lost since Cerro Gordo. By then Santa Anna had regained his invincible optimism and gathered the remnants of his vincible army. He hurried to Puebla to quell political rivals there, to demand more troops and supplies and to exhort its people to defend their city. But the citizens had no desire to fight for Santa Anna. They considered him a despot and hated him more than they feared the Americans, who were pictured as frightful in their "ferocious prowess—their gigantic stature—their cannibal propensities."

Santa Anna, divining that Puebla would submit to occupation without a fight, rallied his tattered dragoons and on May 14 headed east to intercept Worth on the road from Perote. Some 2,000 dragoons followed Santa Anna dutifully, but their hearts were not in it. Nor did Santa Anna have any real plan of attack; when he caught sight of the Americans, he merely hurled his horsemen at them.

Worth had halted his division at a small town 11 miles from Puebla; he wanted to let his lagging baggage train catch up and to allow his troops to spruce up for an impressive entrance into Puebla. Then, all of a sudden, the Americans saw Santa Anna's ragtag cavalry racing toward them. Gun crews quickly unlimbered their artillery, and grapeshot emptied a few Mexican saddles. The dragoons sheered off and rode past, colliding with Brigadier General John Quitman's brigade two miles beyond. At last the Mexicans galloped away. Santa Anna turned and headed toward Mexico City to repair his damaged political fortunes and to try to raise yet another army.

Early the next morning, officials from Puebla came out to learn what terms of occupation the American general would impose on them. At that point, Worth blundered. He foolishly disregarded Scott's orders to institute martial law and agreed instead that the Mexican courts should retain authority over Mexicans who committed offenses against the Americans. This concession, suggesting to potential troublemakers that Mexican judges would deal with them leniently, if not patriotically, was practically an invitation to civilians to commit larceny, or worse.

At 10:00 that morning about 4,200 American troops paraded up to Puebla. "With our colors displayed and our bands playing," wrote Captain Kirby Smith of the 5th Infantry, "we marched into the city over a fine macadamized road." Most of Puebla's 80,000 fearful citizens lined the streets leading to the main plaza. The Mexicans were encouraged to discover that the frightening Americans were only human after all. In fact, they were plain careless about stacking their arms in the plaza and going off to drink at the fountain and stroll through the marketplace. Watching this casual takeover, more than one local patriot concluded that Mexico might yet prevail.

Both Worth in Puebla and Scott in Jalapa realized their problems had been compounded by the 90 miles now separating them: neither could help the other in case of a surprise Mexican attack. The risky isolation, coupled with the long and frustrating delays, strained Worth's nerves. On the vaguest report of Mexican troops, he repeatedly called his whole division to arms; these false alarms became known as "Worth's scarecrows." He got the notion Mexicans were trying to poison his men. His failure to impose martial law left him powerless to punish Mexicans who robbed and sometimes knifed his men. His troops' morale sagged.

Scott, however, had figured out a single bold answer to the perils of his divided command and the problems of his unproductive supply line. "We had to throw away the scabbard," he wrote later, "and to advance with the naked blade in hand." At the end of May, accompanied by a cavalry escort, Scott moved his headquarters from Jalapa to Puebla, and on June 3 he sent orders to his garrisons at Jalapa and Perote to join him. "I resolved no longer to depend on Veracruz or home," he said, "but to render my little army a *self-sustaining machine.*" With his army so dangerously small, and with his reinforcements so meager and slow to arrive, he could not afford to use soldiers as wagon-

train escorts or municipal policemen. He needed all the men he had for the hard campaigning that lay ahead. Henceforth, they would have to get the weapons and munitions they needed from the Mexicans.

Scott's decision was a faultless piece of military logic, yet it struck the outside world as sheer lunacy. Polk called it "a great military error." London newspapers compared it with Napoleon's disastrous attempt to live off the land on his march to Moscow. Napoleon's eventual conqueror, the Duke of Wellington, said flatly, "Scott is lost! He can't take the city and he can't fall back upon his bases. He won't leave Mexico without the permission of the Mexicans."

Scott immediately took steps to remedy the chaotic conditions he found in Puebla. He imposed martial law, stopped the pointless calls to arms and censured Worth for his conduct of the occupation. That ended their long friendship. Worth confided his indignation to an ambitious young admirer, the recently brevetted

Lieutenant Colonel James Duncan of the artillery. Eventually the two officers would join the incompetent General Gideon Pillow in a plot to discredit Scott.

By now Scott's nerves were also on edge, thanks in large part to the appearance of a peace negotiator whom Polk had dispatched from Washington in mid-April. The envoy was Nicholas Trist, a Spanish-speaking State Department official trained in law and experienced at diplomacy. But Trist had been distinctly undiplomatic when he landed at Veracruz on May 6; he instantly antagonized the thin-skinned general by sending him peremptory instructions to convey a sealed peace proposal to the Mexican government. Scott balked. He was convinced, to begin with, that President Polk and his Democratic administration had been harassing him for being a member of the Whig Party; now they had sent him a civilian who arrogantly superseded his military authority with unexplained peace proposals that might jeopardize the American Army.

women and an ample marketplace. After consuming its fruits and sugarcane brandy, 1,000 U.S. troops fell ill with dysentery and fever.

Trist caught up with Scott at Jalapa on May 14 and followed him to Puebla; neither man would speak to the other and each denounced the other in bitter letters to Washington. Scott, brooding over Trist and upset by his clash with Worth, reached a breaking point. On June 4 he wrote to Secretary of War Marcy that his "cruel disappointments and mortifications" were such that "I beg to be recalled." Militarily, a change in command at this juncture was unthinkable, though Polk, too, had thought of it and regretfully discarded the notion. Instead, the President ordered the two belligerents to end their quarrel.

His orders proved unnecessary. By the time they arrived, Trist had shown Scott the documents that explained his mission. Scott, acting on impulse when Trist fell ill, sent him a box of guava marmalade as a gift. Soon the two men were warm friends and wrote letters asking that their earlier denunciations of each other be expunged from the record. To cap the episode,

when Trist, working through the British Ambassador, finally informed the Mexican government of his mission, he learned that Mexico would not negotiate.

Meanwhile, Scott's spirits and the morale of his command began to perk up with the arrival of 4,000 long-awaited reinforcements; these included five regular infantry regiments plus individual replacements for the understrength old regiments. The replacements were sorely needed; in a typical case, recruits now filled out almost half of Kirby Smith's company.

While officers struggled to whip their recruits into battle-ready soldiers, Scott learned that 2,500 more recruits had arrived in Veracruz and were forming up for the trek inland. They were under the command of Brigadier General Franklin Pierce, a former Democratic Senator from New Hampshire and one of the many political appointees the Polk administration had foisted on Scott. But Pierce, who in five years would be elected President of the United States—defeating

Winfield Scott—proved to be an effective military leader. He organized his men with minimal losses to yellow fever and brought them through six stiff guerrilla attacks in good order.

Pierce's brigade arrived in Puebla on August 6. It was the last outside help Scott could expect. It brought his total strength to about 13,000, of whom 2,200 were sick and unfit for duty. Scott had no illusions about what lay ahead. With negotiations ruled out by the Mexicans, he must march against an enemy capital of 200,000 citizens, now defended by some 30,000 men. Scott finally gave the order every soldier was waiting tremulously to hear: prepare to advance!

The men sensed the gamble that Scott was taking, and their last letters from Puebla spoke of their mortal risk. Captain Kirby Smith wrote to his wife: "I almost despair when I reflect upon the destitute situation in which you will be left, with the three children dependent upon you, should I fall in the coming battle." Barna Upton, a young Massachusetts veteran of the charge at Cerro Gordo, wrote home: "I hope that I shall yet live to return to my Father's house, but if not, I hope to meet you all in heaven."

By Scott's final tally, exactly 10,738 American soldiers were ready on August 7 for the march to the Valley of Mexico. Twiggs's division led the way, departing Puebla with a mighty shout. The other divisions—led by Quitman, Worth and Pillow—left successively at one-day intervals. It was a hard, chilly, uphill march, but at last the waiting was over.

Scott's vanguard topped a rise on August 10 and saw for the first time what they had come so far to conquer. Below them, 20 miles across the bowl-like Valley of Mexico, lay the capital city, its spires and domes glinting in the sun, its dense, walled mass dominating a wide landscape of lakes, marshes and satellite villages. The dazzling panorama caused several Americans to think of a dramatic moment in history more than three centuries past. Just as General Scott had figuratively burned his bridges behind him, so the conquistador Hernan Cortés had, in 1519, actually scuttled his ships to force his little army to stay in Mexico and triumph. The Americans felt the same heady combination of awe and exhilaration that had come over Cortés when he reached this very spot. His comrade Bernal

Díaz had written: "We didn't know what to say or whether it was real, with all the cities on the land and in the lake, the causeways with bridges one after another, and before us the great city of Mexico. . . . What men have ever in the world shown such boldness?"

The appearance of the would-be conquistadors of 1847 was instantly observed in Mexico City. A cannon boomed in the central Plaza de la Constitución, announcing the invaders. "Mexico was agitated," a chronicler in the city wrote. "The rough bugle of war had interrupted her mournful silence. All was commotion, all was borne down before the grand signal that precedes a great conflict of a people. Families, trembling and in fear, fled as if from a burning city."

Yet the capital seemed secure enough. Cortés' Spanish and Mexican successors had greatly expanded and improved its defenses. A series of strongholds and complex fortifications guarded each road into the city, and between the roads were great tracts of marshland that artillery and supply wagons could not cross. The Americans would have to run a gauntlet of forts on whichever route their commander chose.

General Scott came to grips with the choice on August 11 as his army drew up at the village of Ayotla, 15 miles east of the capital. There were four possibilities. He dismissed one, a road running north of Lake Texcoco, as being impractically long, and sent out his trusted engineers to reconnoiter the other three. Dead ahead, blocking the main road to Mexico City, stood El Peñón, a lofty, fortified hill where Santa Anna himself lay in wait with 30-odd cannon and about 7,000 of his best troops. The estimate of El Peñón's strength came from Captain Robert E. Lee; it suggested to Scott that he would suffer "a great and disproportionate loss" if he tried taking the stronghold by storm. Scott dismissed that route as too costly. Lieutenant P. G. T. Beauregard interested Scott in a route that led along the north shore of Lake Chalco to a stronghold called Mexicalcingo. But the fourth route, a soggy trail leading south of Lake Chalco to the village of San Agustín, was undefended for 20-odd miles. When Lee and others reported that the ground was solid enough to support guns and wagons, Scott decided on it.

He swung his army south, leaving Twiggs's division at Ayotla to mask his move. Santa Anna was disconsolate when he realized that the Americans had declined to challenge his deadly hill. But he quickly began shifting troops from El Peñón southwestward to counter the new threat.

The Americans had a little trouble on their march south of Lake Chalco and past Lake Xochimilco. It was, an officer wrote, "mud, mud, mud" all the way, and the soldiers had to drive off Mexican skirmishers lurking in a roadside barley field. But in two days the army completed its 25-mile trek and drew up at San Agustín less than nine miles south of Mexico City.

Scott now confronted the problem of San Antonio, a heavily fortified hacienda that blocked the road north about two miles above San Agustín. The engineers reported that San Antonio was unflankable and would have to be taken by frontal assault: off the road to the Americans' right, the marshes were impenetrable; to the left, the terrain was even worse. There lay the pedregal, an ancient lava field about five miles wide. The Americans variously described this geological nightmare as "hell with the fires out," as a tempest-tossed sea "which had suddenly been transformed into stone," and—more factually—as "a vast surface of volcanic rocks and scoria broken into every possible form, presenting sharp ridges and deep fissures, exceedingly difficult even in the daytime for the passage of infantry and utterly impassable for artillery, cavalry or a single horseman."

On the morning of August 18, Scott sent a small force of dragoons and infantry to probe the defenses of San Antonio. "The dragoons in our front," wrote Kirby Smith, "pushed forward rapidly and were a few hundred yards in advance of us when a heavy piece of artillery was discharged at them." The solid iron ball mangled Captain Seth Thornton, whose clash with General Torrejón's lancers on the Rio Grande had triggered the war. Soon the probers returned to their line, having proved that San Antonio would indeed be a difficult objective to take. They reported that any attempt to crack it would have to be made by infantry alone, without the support of cavalry or artillery. "I think we shall try it tomorrow," Smith wrote, "and we may have a bloody day."

General Worth, always impatient, counseled an immediate attack. Scott agreed, but first he wanted to make sure the pedregal was really impassable. If his men could cross the lava field in force, a local road on the far side would bring them to the rear of San Antonio, giving them a chance to take the hacienda cheaply, by surprise. Scott entrusted the exploration of the pedregal to Captain Lee.

Lee set out that afternoon with a small escort of dragoons and infantry. The men slowly picked their way across the sharp black rocks to a high volcanic hill called Zacatapac. Lee climbed the hill to take a look around. Just then musket fire broke out. Dragoon Lieutenant Richard Ewell (later a corps commander in the Confederate Army) said that "about 200 Mexicans, stuck away in the cracks & behind rocks, began firing upon us, quite to my surprise, for it was the first time I had been under fire."

The Mexicans soon withdrew, and so did Lee; he had learned what he wanted to know. The pedregal could indeed be penetrated in force. Moreover, it was clear that a large Mexican force, with many cannon, had taken position on a hill beyond the western edge of the lava field, between the villages of San Gerónimo to the north and Contreras to the south, and it was in an exposed position.

The force that Lee discovered was the Mexican Army of the North, now commanded by the ambitious veteran General Gabriel Valencia. When Santa Anna began deploying his 30,000 troops against the expected attack through San Antonio, he had sent Valencia's army of more than 5,000 men to the far edge of the pedregal to protect his western flank. But Valencia, who aspired to overthrow and succeed Santa Anna as dictator, refused to settle for an inconspicuous supporting role and had advanced about four miles south of his assigned position. Valencia's army was out on a limb, and Scott decided to saw the limb off.

Scott ordered Pillow's division of volunteers to build a crude road across the pedregal to pave the way for his artillery. Twiggs's division was to go along to do the fighting if an emergency arose. Scott left Worth's division in front of San Antonio and Quitman's division at San Agustín, guarding the rear.

On August 19, Pillow's men went to work under Lee's guidance. They pickaxed and shoveled their way into the pedregal, carving a narrow roadbed over which the struggling artillerymen dragged their guns. By early afternoon two rifle companies had reached the western edge of the lava field, about 1,000 yards from Valen-

L A K E

T E Z C U C O

LAKE XOCHIMILCO

CHURUBUSCO

SAN ANTONIO

PEDREGAL OR FIELD OF LAVA

CONTRERAS

SAN AGUSTÍN

Scott's Advance

The battles of August 20, 1847, are outlined on an old Mexican map. American units, having reached San Agustín, found the route north blocked by a fortified hacienda at San Antonio. They blazed a trail west through the pedregal, a lava field, and routed Valencia's army near Contreras. These units merged with others that raced through San Antonio, now abandoned, and stormed Churubusco.

cia's hill, and were joined there by Captain John Magruder's artillerymen, who began peppering the enemy with their field guns and mountain howitzers. The Mexicans were astonished to find that a large number of Americans had made it through the pedregal, but they quickly opened up with their own 22 cannon. After a brisk duel, the outgunned American crews were forced to pull back into the lava field.

Scott, not intending to fight this day, had remained in San Agustín. General Pillow, who had recently been promoted to major general by his friend President Polk, outranked the more experienced Twiggs and was in charge at the pedregal. And Pillow, the inglorious lesson of Cerro Gordo already forgotten, decided to prove he was a brilliant strategist.

He concocted an attack plan using four brigades— about 3,000 of his and Twiggs's infantrymen. General Bennet Riley's brigade, followed by George Cadwalader's, would veer right across the pedregal, cut off Valencia and attack from the north. Smith's brigade, supported by Franklin Pierce's, would attack Valencia head on. It was a good plan—as far as it went.

It soon became apparent, however, that Pillow had not taken into account Santa Anna's likely reaction to the situation. The Mexican commander had deployed the bulk of his 30,000 men behind San Antonio, expecting Scott to storm the hacienda. But Valencia's isolated position had worried Santa Anna, and he had moved a large force—estimated at anywhere from 5,000 to 12,000 men—southwestward to support him. These reinforcements occupied a height overlooking the town of San Gerónimo. Not until the American advance brigades under Riley and Cadwalader reached San Gerónimo and saw Santa Anna's army spread out on the high ground above them did they realize that Pillow's enterprise had put about one third of the American Army in a fine position to be crushed between two much larger Mexican forces—Santa Anna to the north and Valencia to the south.

Presently, more American heads were put in the vise. Persifor Smith, whose advance directly against Valencia had been stopped by a ravine, changed course and followed Riley and Cadwalader to San Gerónimo. Cadwalader was relieved to see Smith, who was his senior. "I suppose, sir, you assume the command here?" he asked. Smith replied, "Certainly, with plea-

sure." Then, unimpressed by the odds against them, Smith added, "Let us look at our position, and at that fellow Santa Anna's, whilst my brigade is coming up."

By 4 p.m. the sound of the artillery duel in the pedregal had brought General Scott hurrying over from San Agustín. At a command post on Zacatapac hill, Pillow briefed his commander on his unauthorized battle plan. Scott decided he had no choice but to make the best of a dangerous situation. He approved Pillow's deployment of the troops.

Fortunately for the Americans, Santa Anna did not want to fight at the pedregal any more than Scott originally had. His only thought was to get Valencia to fall back to the town of Churubusco, two miles north of San Antonio on the main road to the capital. Churubusco was the last stronghold of Mexico City's outer defenses; its guns and powerful fortifications offered the best chance to break the American Army. As darkness fell and a cold, pelting rain began, Santa Anna sent a messenger to Valencia, ordering him to withdraw under cover of night. Valencia, however, decided that the Americans' failure to attack him that day constituted a victory, and that Santa Anna was selfishly trying to deprive him of a chance for greater glory on the morrow. He returned the order with a disdainful refusal. Santa Anna was so enraged at his insubordinate general that it never occurred to him to attack the vulnerable Americans west of the pedregal—an attack that might well have ended Scott's campaign.

While Valencia celebrated his imaginary victory, Persifor Smith set up headquarters in a church in San Gerónimo. He was pondering his battle tactics for the morning when Lieutenant Zealous B. Tower arrived. The engineer told Smith he had explored a ravine that led from San Gerónimo up into the hills and curved around behind Valencia's camp. The ravine could be a godsend—a hidden avenue for a surprise attack, which might help overcome the Mexicans' superior numbers.

Smith responded decisively: "We will attack before daylight." For the troops to be in position for an attack at dawn, they would have to start up the ravine by 3 a.m. And to keep the Mexicans' attention until the Americans burst from their hiding place, Smith would need a simulated attack on Valencia's front. Robert E. Lee volunteered to carry Smith's proposal to Scott.

Scott's march toward Mexico City is illustrated in detail in these paintings by James Walker, who traveled with the Army. Setting out

In this Walker painting, the Americans begin their attack on the Mexican camp (*center rear*) outside Contreras. A light-artillery battery

from Puebla *(left)*, the Americans struggled around marshy Lake Chalco *(center)* before sighting the enemy near Contreras *(right)*.

opens fire from the high ground at left and crouching skirmishers move forward while a mounted officer holds his main force in wait.

Whether their patients were Americans or captive Mexicans like the trio in this grisly cartoon, U.S. Army surgeons regularly resorted to amputation as the surest way to prevent sepsis, or bloodstream infection.

A NEW RULE IN ALGEBRA.

Five from Three and One remains!!

or

"The Three Mexican Prisoners, having but one leg between them all".

Series Nº 2.

For Lee, it was the beginning of a sleepless night.

With a few men, Lee set out in the driving rain at about 8 p.m. He climbed toward the pedregal, guided only by the hill of Zacatapac, which was outlined by occasional lightning flashes. Soon Lee bumped into Shields's brigade, on its way to reinforce Smith; Lee detailed a man to lead Shields to San Gerónimo. He then pressed on across the slippery lava field to Zacatapac and climbed the hill to Scott's command post, only to discover that Scott had gone back to San Agustín. Lee scrambled out of the pedregal, and at about 11 p.m. delivered Smith's message to the General in Chief at San Agustín. Lee then joined General Twiggs to help organize the diversionary attack. At about 1 a.m. on August 20, he collected the troops who would stage the mock assault and led them back through the pedregal, into position under Valencia's guns.

General Shields, now the senior officer of the 4,000 Americans at San Gerónimo, had waived the right to lead the attack on Valencia; instead, he took on the seemingly impossible task of defending Persifor Smith's rear against Santa Anna's army on the heights above. At 2:30 a.m. Smith's men were awakened and informed that they would attack at dawn, using bayonets because, as one lieutenant explained, "our arms were not to be relied upon in the tremendous rain." The officer went on: "Our men were formed in silence and we moved on, led by Lt. Tower of the Engineers. The night was so dark that 'twas scarcely possible to see the hand before the face & the path was muddy and slippery. We wandered about for hours not knowing where we were. At length we got upon the right trail and succeeded in reaching the rendezvous."

Crouched in the ravine behind Valencia's position, the men drew the wet charges from their muskets and reloaded. Lieutenant William Gardner wrote, "When it was broad daylight we formed columns of attack. Just imagine to yourself 900 men, for the columns of attack

Army surgeon John Campbell, traveling with General Patterson's troops from Veracruz to Jalapa, was shocked to find no transportation for the sick, though the general had 14 wagons for his own baggage.

did not contain quite that number, attacking an entrenched camp with 27 pieces of ordnance and at least 8,000 Infantry, to say nothing about *lancers*. I thought that at least two thirds of our numbers would be swept down before we could use our bayonets."

The attackers moved undetected to the edge of the Mexican camp. The diversionary attack from the pedregal began at about 5 a.m., drawing the attention of Valencia's men. "General Smith slowly walking up, asked if all was ready," an officer reported. "A look answered him. *'Men, forward!'* and we *did* 'forward.'" The battle had begun.

"We saw a devil of a hubbub in their camp," Lieutenant Gardner resumed, "the men running to arms, the mounting of horses & c. It was a complete surprise. We received a volley from the enemy's infantry thrown hastily out to oppose us. We did not return a shot but stood up as if they were throwing apples instead of lead at us. We marched towards them still under heavy fire of musketry, for some twenty or thirty yards, then halted. During all this time we had not fired a shot and men were dropping in our ranks at every moment. I admire the coolness of our men during this trying time even more than their headlong impetuosity after the word *charge* was given. When we had deployed into line of battle, we gave them a volley, and then made a head long rush."

"Cheers arose as you never heard," another officer wrote. "The men rushed forward like demons, yelling and firing the while. The carnage was frightful."

The Mexican troops had whirled to face this sudden apparition bursting from the woods at their backs and panic swept their ranks. The gunners frantically began swinging their cannon to the rear. Only a few managed the turn before the Americans were among them, charging with desperation, knowing that, outnumbered, they must prevail swiftly or fail. The Americans ran in with their bayonets level, stabbing and ripping, then reversing their weapons to smash faces with butts. Blood sluiced down uniform fronts. Men were stumbling, collapsing, screaming with pain and terror.

After 17 minutes of this savage work, Valencia's army collapsed and ran. American gunners turned the Mexican cannon again and hurled round after round into the fleeing Mexican force until American pursuers got so close that no more firing was possible.

Inexplicably, Santa Anna's force on the height overlooking San Gerónimo began a swift withdrawal. Many of Valencia's men joined Santa Anna's retreat. Hundreds of others came back toward the Americans and, as a South Carolina volunteer described it, "almost in a state of nudity, they would fall upon their knees and with their hands thrown up beg for quarter," shouting that they were not even soldiers— *"No hay soldado, no hay soldado!"* Indeed, many of the Mexicans were soldiers in name only; they were conscripts forced into service within the month. They had tried to fight without training a competent leadership, and they knew they were lucky to be alive.

While the American brigades reassembled, Persifor Smith sent Beauregard across the pedregal to report the results of the morning. Beauregard met Scott and his staff as they rode toward the front. The officers greeted his news with cheers, and Scott exclaimed, "Young man, if I were not on horseback I would embrace you." Then the general, whose artillerymen had

An evolution in accuracy for weapons of war

The Mexican War was a testing ground that brought radical changes in firearms. The smoothbore musket, which was used by most of the troops on both sides, was much less accurate than the American frontiersman's ri-fle, whose spiral-grooved bore spun the bullet and thus stabilized and lengthened its flight. But because the musket was less expensive to manu-facture and simpler for untrained re-cruits to use, the U.S. Army was slow to adopt the rifle-barreled gun.

The early rifles also had shortcom-ings. They produced less fire power than muskets because it took longer to ram their close-fitting bullets into the long, grooved barrels. The load-

ing process was speeded up by the U.S. Hall rifle *(below),* which was loaded at the breech end of the barrel.

Both rifles and muskets were flintlock weapons fired by a spark, and they were unreliable when rain wet the flint and powder. This problem was solved by the watertight percussion cap, which held powder that could be ignited by a blow rather than by a spark. From these improvements came the U.S. Army's 1841 percussion rifle, the most reliable and accurate firearm of the time.

Mexico, having no small-arms factories of its own, equipped its soldiers with European guns. Most of these were obsolescent discards like

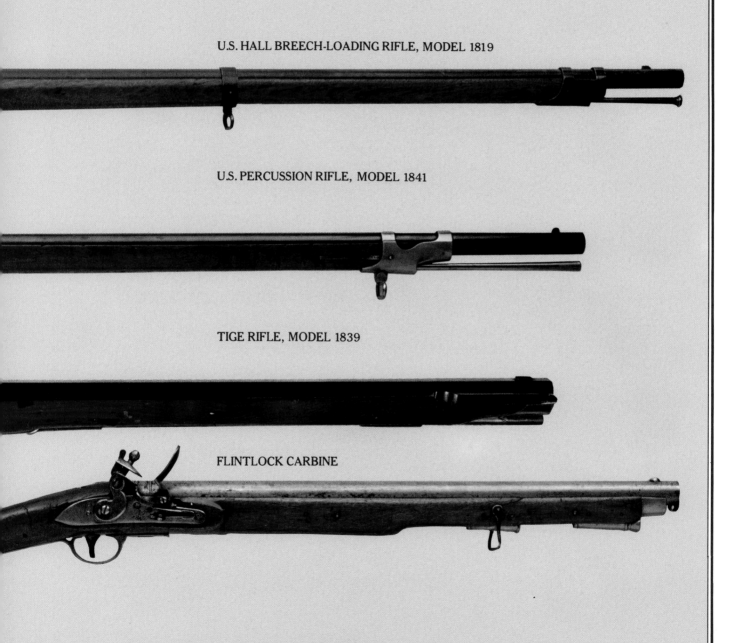

U.S. HALL BREECH-LOADING RIFLE, MODEL 1819

U.S. PERCUSSION RIFLE, MODEL 1841

TIGE RIFLE, MODEL 1839

FLINTLOCK CARBINE

the two at bottom on the previous pages. The 1839 Tige rifle, produced as a flintlock in Prussia, was later improved with a percussion firing mechanism. The carbine, short-barreled for convenient use by mounted troops, was used at close range with reasonable accuracy.

The American pistols shown below were also short-range weapons. One, the Army-issued flintlock pistol, was primitive. But the other two, ordered by officers at their own expense, paralleled the evolution of the rifle. By the end of the war, a few Americans were using a more formidable handgun with a short range but a long future: the first Colt revolver.

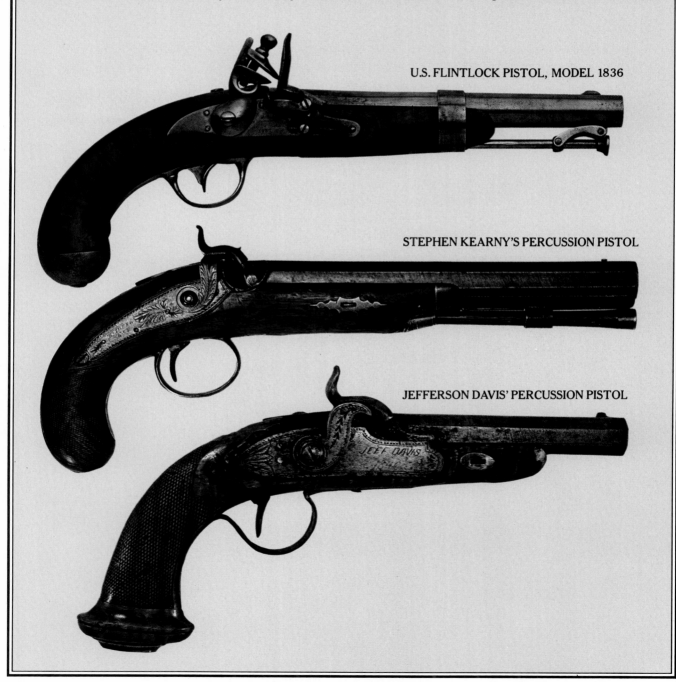

U.S. FLINTLOCK PISTOL, MODEL 1836

STEPHEN KEARNY'S PERCUSSION PISTOL

JEFFERSON DAVIS' PERCUSSION PISTOL

dragged their guns 240 miles from the coast only to see infantrymen win the battle without their supporting fire, said jubilantly: "I am an idiot to bring artillery so far, and at such expense, when I have such soldiers."

Santa Anna, trying to stabilize his situation, positioned part of his force to delay the victorious Americans and ordered his garrison at San Antonio to retreat to Churubusco. Now Scott unleashed Twiggs, Pillow and Worth for the delayed assault on San Antonio. The hacienda's defenders, following Santa Anna's orders, withdrew up the road toward Churubusco with American units in hot pursuit. At the same time, the Americans who had fought against Valencia's men brushed past Santa Anna's rear guard and also streamed up the local road toward Churubusco.

With American forces converging headlong on Churubusco, Scott took direct field command of his army. He decided to press his advantage without pausing for reconnaissance, an uncharacteristic move for him. Hastily he roughed out a plan of attack and trusted that it would suffice. Twiggs's division would storm the town's main stronghold, to the left of the road; this was the massive walled convent of San Mateo, which was defended by seven cannon and about 1,800 troops, including the San Patricio Battalion with its contingent of American deserters *(page 209)*. Three hundred yards beyond the convent and connected to it by low earthwork stood a second powerful complex: a fortified bridge that continued the high road across the Churubusco River toward Mexico City. The bridge was defended by three cannon and by several thousand Mexican troops deployed along the far riverbank. It would be attacked in a pincers movement; Worth's veteran division would strike the bridge from the south, while Shields's and Pierce's brigades would ford the river west of town and storm the bridge from the north.

The attacks on the bridge and the convent began shortly after noon, and they soon foundered. The Mexicans in both strongholds, superbly led and fighting with a gallantry born of desperation, held fast. A huge, murky battle developed, and it ebbed and flowed for four hours, with the Americans almost constantly on the verge of defeat.

In the end, the battle would turn on the success or failure of General Worth's attack on the bridge.

Twiggs's men were battering themselves hopelessly against the convent walls when Worth's division, racing up the road from San Antonio, came under fire from both the convent and the bridge. The Mexican guns thundered and rolled, slashing into the Americans and pinning them down. Worth sent his men off the road away from the convent, into a marshy cornfield on the right where they were greeted with musket fire from Mexicans in ditches and corn rows. Captain Kirby Smith of the 5th Infantry was there, face down in the muck. With enemy fire chopping corn all around him, Smith — like hundreds of others — endured the ultimate test of his courage and will.

"It must have been about half-past twelve," Smith later wrote. "Immediately in front of us, at perhaps five hundred yards, the roll of the Mexican fire exceeded anything I have ever heard. The din was most horrible, the roar of cannon and musketry, the screams of the wounded, the awful cry of terrified horses and mules, and the yells of the fierce combatants all combined in a sound as hellish as can be conceived." Smith's men were fighting blind. "We could not tell what was before us — whether the enemy were in regular forts, behind breastworks or delivering their fire from the cover afforded by the hedges and ditches which bordered the roads and fields — all was hidden by the tall corn."

Gradually, the Americans in the cornfield coalesced into small units and started back toward the road. "We soon came out into a crossroad near some small houses where we were exposed to a dreadful cross fire which could scarcely be resisted," Smith wrote. "Many had fallen and the battalion was much scattered and broken. The grape, round shot and musketry were sweeping over the ground in a storm which strewed it with the dead and dying. I found it extremely difficult to make the men stand or form, but finally succeeded with my own company which was at once ordered to charge under my brave Lieutenant Farrelly.

"I was occupied reorganizing the three other companies when arose the most fearful time of the battle. My men were just formed and I had ordered the charge which I was about to lead, when the dreadful cry came from the left and rear that we were *repulsed*. A rush of men and officers in a panic followed, running over and again breaking my little command. I, however, succeeded in disentangling them from the mass, composed

After the fall of the fortress-convent of San Mateo at Churubusco, U.S. troops *(left)* march over the bodies of its defenders in this vivid oil by James Walker. Other Americans *(right foreground)* tend their own dead and dying.

of a great portion of the Eighth, Sixth and Fifth Infantry with some artillery. I shouted that we were *not* repulsed—to charge—and the day would be ours. Our colonel, C. F. Smith, now joined us and the cry throughout was 'Forward!' "

That hopeful note was sounded at about 3 p.m. Worth's scattered forces reformed and began to push back the Mexican skirmishers. Some units worked out toward their right, eastward along the riverbank, trying to outflank the Mexican line on the other side. Kirby Smith drove his men back onto the deadly road. They were joined by more men of the 5th Infantry and a large part of the 8th and began to advance toward the bridge. But so far, after suffering two and a half hours of carnage, they had done little to damage the Mexicans.

Twiggs's attack on the convent was not doing any better. The Mexican cannon fire was devastating. So was the musket fire from the walls of the convent and the roof of the church nearby; the Mexicans kept up "such rapid volleys," said Lieutenant Isaac Stevens, "that for three hours the sound of their firing was one continuous roll." One battery of American artillery fought back for an hour and a half under a terrific mixed barrage of grapeshot, canister, musketry, round shot and shell, which took a toll of 24 men and 13 horses. The gun crews finally had to withdraw.

At 3 o'clock, Shields's men across the river were also in deep trouble. They had made their way behind the Mexican defenders, but on their initial assault the Mexicans had turned and dealt them a fearful blow. Shields was reinforced by riflemen and dragoons, but each time his men advanced they were driven to cover by storms of deadly metal.

Colonel Pierce Butler, commanding the South Carolina Regiment in Shields's brigade, was wounded in the leg and his horse was shot from under him but he remained in the fore until a second, deadly bullet struck him in the temple. Only that morning he had told the adjutant, "I am laboring under a presentiment that I cannot shake off that I shall be killed today."

Carrying the American flag in advance of the New York Regiment, Sergeant Major James O'Reilly was hit twice but staggered on until a third and fatal bullet knocked him to the ground. A corporal seized the colors but was instantly killed. As he fell, a sergeant saved the flag. The New Yorkers were pinned behind the walls of a hacienda, and when the order came to charge, they faltered. To rally them, Captain Francis Page strode forward nearly 100 yards carrying the Stars and Stripes. This gallant act later earned Page a promotion to major, but when the order was given to follow him, it was disregarded.

Then, soon after 3 o'clock, with the battle hanging in the balance, Worth's battered men began to make their presence felt. Part of the division, far out on the right, crossed the river and drove toward the bridge, rolling up the line of Mexican defenders along the way. The 5th and 8th infantries, Kirby Smith among them, came charging up the road into the mouths of the Mexican cannon at the bridge. The guns fired their last blasts of grapeshot point-blank into the American ranks. The men who survived came over the parapets with bayonets fixed, driving the enemy across the bridge in full flight toward Mexico City.

Now American gunners took a four-pound cannon on the bridge and turned it against the convent. American artillerymen outside the convent, no longer pinned down by enemy fire from the bridge, wheeled their batteries up close to the walls and blew the defenders back with rounds delivered as rapidly as musket fire. As U.S. infantrymen flowed over the walls into the fortress, many defenders went over the opposite walls, trying to cross the bridge before they were cut off.

On the other side of the river, tremors of dismay ran through the Mexican force pinning down Shields's brigades. Now Shields got his men on their feet and went sweeping recklessly forward. "As soon as the enemy was observed to waver," an American report said, "the order to charge was given, and the men rushed upon him with the bayonet, broke his ranks, and put him to the rout, just as the fugitives from Churubusco came wildly up the road, closely pursued by the head of Worth's division. All now was confusion. The Mexican cavalry, putting spurs to their horses, fled panic-struck while the infantry scattered in all directions."

Into this boiling melee rode the impetuous Phil Kearny, a captain of dragoons, high in the stirrups, saber flashing, leading a charge that carried him onward toward Mexico City itself. The recall sounded but Kearny, far in the lead, never heard it—or so he said later when there was time to ask questions. One by one the squadrons behind him dropped off as the recall

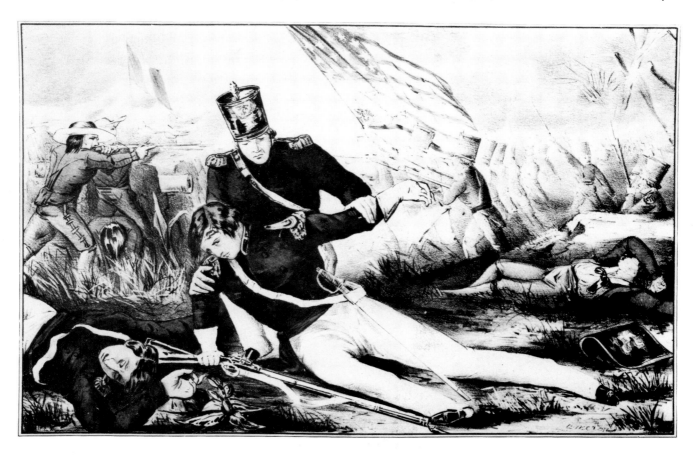

message got through, but Kearny and his lieutenant, Richard Ewell, rode clear to the city's gate. The Mexican cavalrymen they were chasing leaped off their horses and scrambled over the barriers. Kearny dismounted, yelled for his men to follow and jumped over after them. It was then that Ewell looked around and "to my horror, I found the Dragoons retiring some distance in the rear. Colonel Harney had ordered the recall to be sounded." Ewell began struggling to extricate his captain from the enemy capital. He finally succeeded, but not before Kearny suffered wounds that cost him an arm later that night.

On this note the fighting of August 20, 1847, ended. For the Americans it had been a day of great and sobering victories; they had suffered more than 1,000 casualties—133 killed, 865 wounded, 40 missing. Santa Anna had lost about one fourth of his army—roughly 4,000 killed or wounded and 3,000 taken prisoner—but the Mexicans had shown that

they would fight fiercely to block the last miles of Scott's path to the capital.

Kirby Smith, exhausted, went back to the cornfield where victory had risen from the ashes of defeat. "The field," he said, "presented an awful spectacle—the dead and the wounded were thickly sprinkled over the ground. How sickening was the sight after all the excitement of the contest was past!" General Scott, too, had grim thoughts to ponder. His generals' performance this day was cause for concern. Twiggs had squandered men in persistent unplanned charges. Shields had deployed his soldiers poorly. And Scott himself had temporarily lost control of his far-flung forces.

But ah, the men! The troops of the line—recruits and veterans alike—had exceeded Scott's fondest hopes. They had endured terrible poundings, had been forced to stagger backward many times and had nearly panicked, but had rebounded time and time again. The American soldiers had covered themselves with glory.

6 | Proud flags to rally 'round

Both armies went into battle with banners flying. Each unit's colors became a rallying point and a proud symbol.

In December of 1846, a company of untried volunteers from Danville, Pennsylvania, went off to war under the flag below. Nine months later they marched triumphantly into Mexico City. Near them flew the eagle of the U.S. 6th Infantry, whose banner (*opposite, center*) reads like a road map of the bloody advance through Mexico.

Following the colors was not enough for some men: they took their own personal flags to war (*pages 196-197*). Others achieved momentary glory by capturing the enemy's flag or by saving their own (*page 199*). In any case, the colors became a lasting tribute to the memory of those men who fought and died beneath them.

Pennsylvania's coat of arms adorns the flag of Columbia County volunteers who fought their way from Veracruz to Mexico City.

Mexican women of Santa Fe reportedly gave this silk flag to men of the St. Louis Battery of Light Artillery. The lower left portion was reserved for battle honors.

The illustrious U.S. 6th Infantry's flag is crowded with battle names. But only one member of the regiment fought at Palo Alto and Resaca de la Palma—its nominal commander, General Zachary Taylor.

The precision-drilled batteries of the flying artillery fought from Palo Alto to Mexico City beneath the crossed cannon-barrel insignia of the U.S. 3rd Artillery Regiment.

National symbols abound on the personal flag carried by Augustus Gates, a volunteer from Vermont. A fellow soldier may have painted the cotton flag for him.

Lieutenant Colonel John Charles Frémont's personal flag, designed by his wife, Jessie, was first planted in Mexican territory on Frémont's 1842 Rocky Mountain expedition. He later carried it through the California campaign. A peace pipe in the eagle's claw was intended to persuade Indians of Frémont's peaceful intentions.

A Mexican guerrilla lancer carried this grim guidon at the battle of Sacramento, where the banner was taken. In Spanish on its reverse side was "Liberty or Death."

Though lacking a specific unit identity, this banner, with a hand-painted panoply of arms beneath the snake-and-eagle emblem, was a variant of the Mexican national flag. Americans captured it in 1847.

VIVA LA REPUBLICA MEXICANA.

Flame streams from a bursting bomb on a Mexican infantry battalion's guidon. A soldier of the U.S. 3rd Artillery Regiment captured it in the battle at Churubusco.

This battalion color was saved from capture at Molino del Rey when a Mexican sublieutenant pulled the bullet-riddled banner from its standard and tied it around his body. He was killed during the battle.

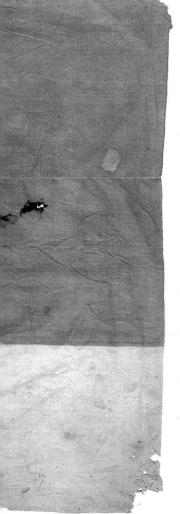

After 25 years of Mexican independence, the Spanish royal crest still adorned this banner of a provincial infantry battalion. The fragment—possibly part of a trumpet banner—was captured at Cerro Gordo.

The climactic assault on Montezuma's Halls

After the desperate fighting at Contreras and Churubusco, the American Army was bruised and worn. But the Mexican army had been shattered once again. A river of demoralized soldiers streamed back into Mexico City, where all was confusion. Wounded men roamed the streets, crying out in panic, "Here come the Yankees!" For the moment, the capital was defenseless. "Everything, everything has been lost," wrote José Fernando Ramírez, a disillusioned government official, "except our honor. That was lost a long time ago."

With the Americans virtually at the gates, General Scott had good reason to believe that the Mexicans would at last be not only willing but also politically able to negotiate peace. But, in fact, many hundreds of lives would be lost — in bloody battles whose planning and execution would leave American soldiers seriously doubting their commanders' judgment — and long months of guerrilla warfare and frustrating negotiation would follow before the war would really be over.

General Santa Anna, "possessed of a black despair," reached Mexico City early on the evening of the battle of August 20 and called a council of war at the National Palace. The Mexicans sorely needed a respite, and they asked the British consul, Edward Mackintosh, to intercede. Later that evening Mackintosh drove out to Scott's headquarters at San Agustín, nine miles southeast of the capital. The visit was "ostensibly to ask for a safeguard for the English Minister and British subjects," wrote Colonel Ethan Allen Hitchcock of Scott's staff, "but really to prepare the way for peace."

No record was kept of the meeting between Mackintosh and Scott, but instead of continuing the attack the next day, the American general prepared to move into "battering or assaulting positions" that would enable him "to summon the city to surrender."

As Scott was moving his headquarters to Tacubaya, a village just two and a half miles southwest of Mexico City, he and Nicholas Trist, the American peace negotiator, encountered a handsomely polished carriage under a flag of truce bearing Brigadier General Ignacio Mora y Villamil. The Mexican officer carried letters from Foreign Minister Francisco Pacheco and the British Ambassador, and the verbal message that Santa Anna desired an armistice.

Santa Anna was a great gambler. Despite his desperate position, the letter from his foreign minister was calm and shrewd. It pronounced the Mexican government ready to hear American proposals provided they were consistent with Mexican honor. Specifically, the letter proposed a truce of one year for discussion of the "preliminaries of peace."

Naturally, Scott refused to consider such a long delay. But — and here was the heart of Santa Anna's gamble — the American general counterproposed the very respite that Santa Anna wanted. Scott, whose original intention had been to demand Mexico City's immediate surrender, sent a dispatch to Santa Anna that demonstrated again why letter writing was so hazardous an occupation for him. "Too much blood has already been shed in this unnatural war between the two great Republics of this Continent," Scott wrote as a preface to indicate his willingness "to sign, on reasonable terms, a short armistice."

Santa Anna seized on Scott's offer with relish. His prompt reply, in a note from his minister of war, took the position that Scott had asked for the armistice and that the Mexican government was willing to grant his

201

In this American cartoon exaggerating the Polk administration's territorial ambitions, U.S. emissary Nicholas Trist *(right)* shocks Mexican negotiators by demanding almost all of Mexico as the price of peace.

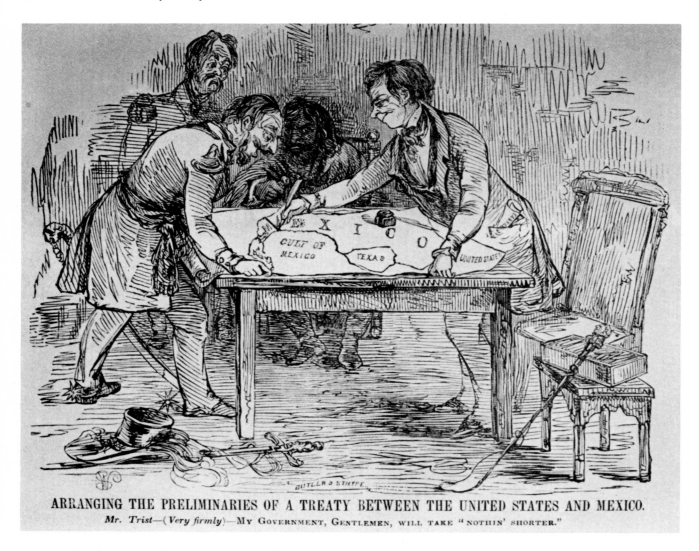

ARRANGING THE PRELIMINARIES OF A TREATY BETWEEN THE UNITED STATES AND MEXICO.
Mr. Trist—(Very firmly)—MY GOVERNMENT, GENTLEMEN, WILL TAKE "NOTHIN' SHORTER."

plea, since it too was interested in ending the war Scott himself had "characterized as unnatural."

The truce went into effect on August 24. As long as negotiations continued, hostilities would be halted. Each side promised not to improve its position or its fortifications, and the Mexicans agreed to sell supplies to the American Army. The armistice could be terminated by either side on 48 hours' notice.

The delay angered Scott's soldiers. They had won what Captain Kirby Smith called "a wonderful victory and undoubtedly the greatest battle our country has ever fought." But instead of taking the great city now at their mercy, they were to talk. "There was much muttering and grumbling throughout the army," Smith

wrote to his wife, "when it was known that these were to be the fruits of all our fatigue and fighting." Lieutenant Francis Collins, a West Pointer in the 4th Artillery, said the army was largely opposed to what it saw as a Mexican ploy to gain time and strength. Indeed, Captain Roswell S. Ripley of Pillow's staff later blamed the armistice for the loss of "1,652 men and officers killed and wounded."

The armistice lasted for two weeks and was perhaps the most controversial episode of the war. Many of Scott's officers objected strongly to the terms he had accepted. They had urged him to move his forces into a commanding position and especially to occupy Chapultepec Castle, which stood with threatening guns on

202

a hill just outside the city. But this condition—which in Ripley's opinion "would have insured the speedy conquest of the capital" in case negotiations failed—was one of the first items the Americans had given up in the initial negotiations for the cease-fire.

Scott had wanted to leave the Mexican republic something "on which to rest her pride, and to recover temper." He had agreed to stop in place, and thereafter he would do nothing to violate his pledge. So his men waited, increasingly sullen and apprehensive as the days rolled by. And the Mexicans, despite their own promise, steadily improved their defenses.

"During the armistice," young P. G. T. Beauregard wrote, "no reconnaissance was permitted by the General in Chief, although it was a notorious fact that the enemy was violating it day and night." Colonel Hitchcock of Scott's staff heard reports that the Mexican army was reforming—"the fragments of Santa Anna's army brought together make a force of some 18,000 men, more than double our army."

It was not a reassuring situation. The Americans were outnumbered, in hostile country, cut off from their supply base, encumbered by more than 1,000 sick and wounded men. Given these conditions, as Ripley said, retreat was out of the question. There was nothing but to take Mexico City or "perish in the attempt."

But Scott had his reasons for not pursuing the military advantages gained at Contreras and Churubusco. He had been warned, he said—by "intelligent neutrals and some American residents—against precipitation; lest, by wantonly driving away the government and others—dishonored—we might scatter the elements of peace, excite a spirit of national desperation, and thus indefinitely postpone the hope of accommodation."

Nevertheless, the negotiations went badly from the start, in part because Mexico no longer had a coherent national leadership. It was instead a galaxy of competing power centers whose pressures on one another were more immediate than those of the invading army at the city's gates. Though Santa Anna was still nominally in charge, his position was too insecure to allow him to seriously discuss a forced peace, even if he had wanted to. General Valencia had ignored Santa Anna's order to appear for a trial for insubordination at Contreras and was now trying to depose him. The members of Mexico's Congress refused to gather to discuss terms,

and the Mexican people, oblivious to the series of defeats, remained "indisposed to peace." Some outlying provinces actually threatened to secede if peace overtures were accepted.

The talks stumbled along until September 6, then collapsed. Scott sent Santa Anna a letter charging him with violations of the armistice and declaring that hostilities would be resumed at noon the following day "unless complete satisfaction should be made" by then.

Hewing to his word, Scott did not even begin reconnaissance efforts until midday on the 7th. Santa Anna, on the other hand, had been preparing for renewed fighting for several days. He cut off supplies to the Americans and reinforced Chapultepec's fortifications.

"Fatal credulity!" complained Kirby Smith. "How awful are its consequences to us!" Taking into account battle losses, illness and the necessity to garrison the area, Scott had fewer than 8,000 effective troops to mount an attack. Acutely aware of the Mexican preparations, his men were in a somber mood. Two weeks of enforced idleness had done nothing to improve either their efficiency or their morale. When Scott finally ordered the army into position for the coming battle, Kirby Smith remarked, "And now, alas, we have all our fighting to do over again."

Mexico City was a formidable objective. It was surrounded by marshes and approached by eight causeways. The causeways, flanked by ditches filled with water, each ended in a massive *garita*. More than just a gate, a *garita* included a large paved space and strong buildings where taxes used to be collected on goods entering the city. Now the *garitas* bristled with cannon laid to rake each roadway. El Peñón, the fortified hill to the east, and Lake Texcoco, on the northeast, protected the city from those directions. Thus the Americans would have to attack from the south, over three deadly causeways, or from the west, where two causeways leading to the Garita de San Cosmé and the Garita de Belén were protected by the guns of Chapultepec. The battle for Mexico City, as Lieutenant Francis Collins said, would "determine which was greatest, Mexican folly or Yankee impudence."

Scott's reconnaissance focused on the southern *garitas*. If the Americans could penetrate the defenses there, they could avoid Chapultepec, which loomed above the surrounding plain. As Scott probed, howev-

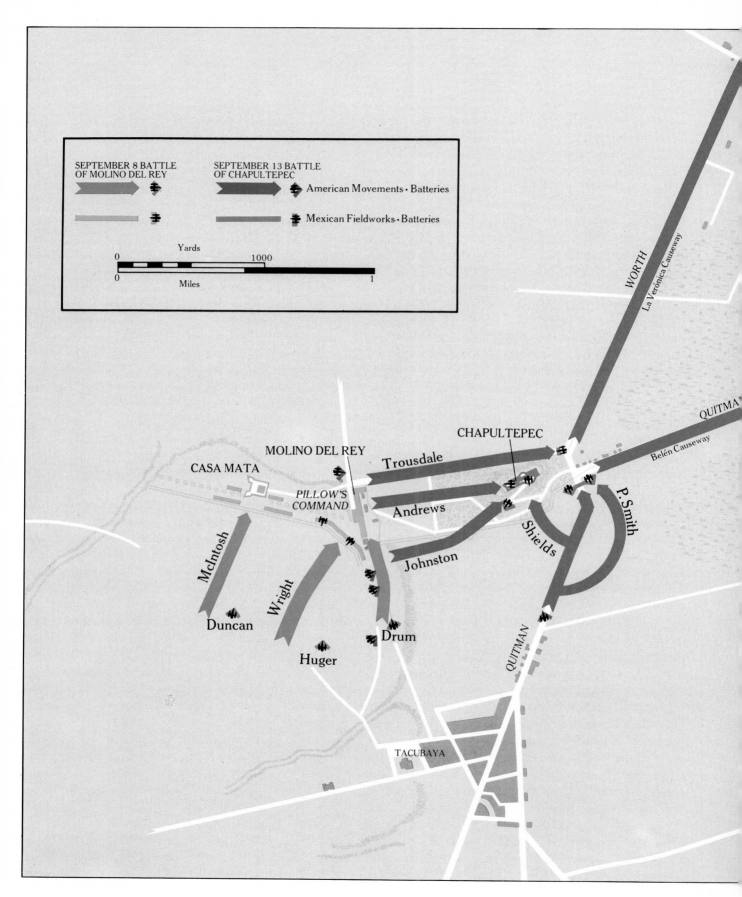

WORTH

La Verónica Causeway

QUITMAN

CHAPULTEPEC

Belén Causeway

MOLINO DEL REY

Trousdale

CASA MATA

P. Smith

*PILLOW'S
COMMAND*

Andrews

McIntosh

Johnston

Shields

Wright

Duncan

Drum

Huger

QUITMAN

TACUBAYA

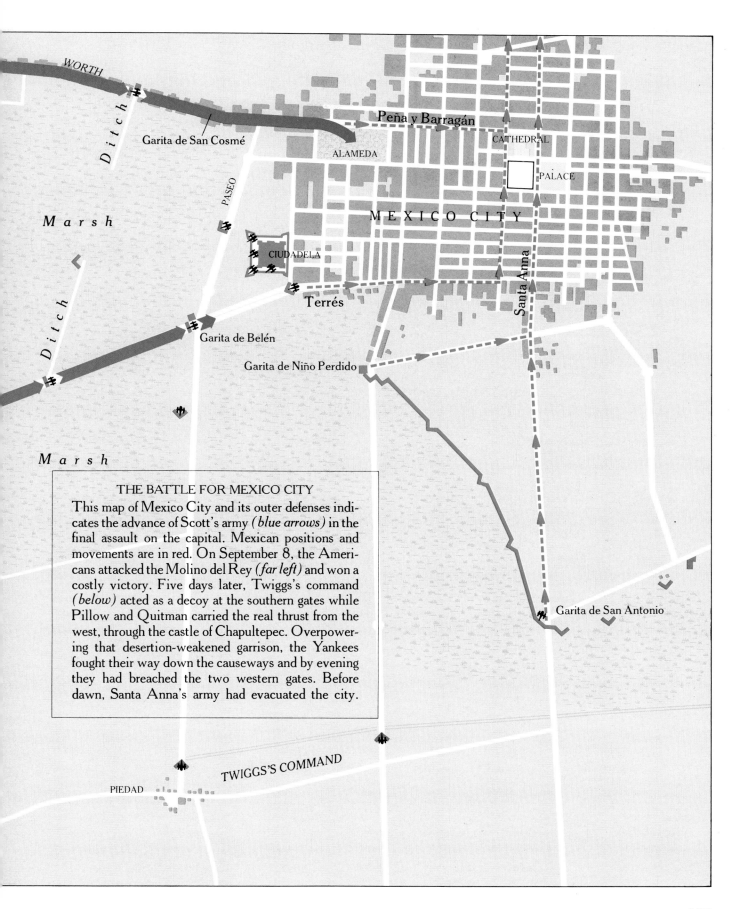

WORTH

Ditch

Garita de San Cosmé

Peña y Barragán

ALAMEDA

CATHEDRAL

PALACE

Marsh

PASEO

MEXICO CITY

CIUDADELA

Santa Anna

Terrés

Ditch

Garita de Belén

Marsh

Garita de Niño Perdido

THE BATTLE FOR MEXICO CITY

This map of Mexico City and its outer defenses indicates the advance of Scott's army *(blue arrows)* in the final assault on the capital. Mexican positions and movements are in red. On September 8, the Americans attacked the Molino del Rey *(far left)* and won a costly victory. Five days later, Twiggs's command *(below)* acted as a decoy at the southern gates while Pillow and Quitman carried the real thrust from the west, through the castle of Chapultepec. Overpowering that desertion-weakened garrison, the Yankees fought their way down the causeways and by evening they had breached the two western gates. Before dawn, Santa Anna's army had evacuated the city.

Garita de San Antonio

TWIGGS'S COMMAND

PIEDAD

er, he got a report that Mexican troops were moving in force to El Molino del Rey—the King's Mill. This array of stone buildings, within a mile of Scott's headquarters at Tacubaya, lay on the western edge of the great complex of Chapultepec Castle. Scott had been told that the *molino* was a foundry and that the Mexicans were hauling church bells there to be melted down and recast as cannon. Although this was unlikely—it was later speculated that Santa Anna himself had planted the information as a lure—Scott determined to attack the *molino* and destroy the reputed foundry.

Santa Anna, for his part, inferred from American activity and from Scott's challenging letter that once the truce ended, Chapultepec would be the object of a determined American assault. He moved his best troops to the *molino* and to the Casa Mata, a solid stone building used as a powder magazine about half a mile northwest of the *molino*.

Scott considered Molino del Rey only a limited operation; he was waiting for thorough scouting before planning his last attack on the capital. On the afternoon of September 7, he ordered Worth's division, some 3,400 men, to make a night attack, destroy any machinery and guns in the *molino* and be back at Tacu-

baya before dawn. The same day he sent a detachment of troops forward on the city's southern approaches—a feint that successfully distracted Santa Anna.

In the opinion of Ulysses S. Grant and others, Scott had given command of this operation to Worth in hope of patching their broken relationship. If so, the effort backfired. Scott and Worth would blame each other for what happened at Molino del Rey, and later disputes between them only made things worse. In 1840 Worth had named his only son Winfield Scott Worth, for his longtime friend; after the war he changed the boy's name to William.

Before attacking Molino del Rey, Worth asked for two modifications in his orders. Further scouting had convinced him that the job would be tougher than Scott envisioned and, because looking for a foundry in a strange set of buildings in the dark would be difficult and dangerous, he asked to hold off the attack until dawn. Scott agreed, but when Worth proposed expanding his assignment to include the capture of nearby Chapultepec, Scott turned him down.

As the hour of battle approached, Kirby Smith was full of foreboding. He was in temporary command of a light battalion in Garland's brigade, which would play

Attacking Molino del Rey at dawn, U.S. troops take heavy fire from a strong Mexican force defending the compound's walls. But by noon the Americans had seized the buildings and nearly 700 prisoners.

The Americans had two sound choices. They could blow the buildings apart with cannon fire, or, as Beauregard put it later, they could surprise the Mexicans "with the bayonet alone, a little before daybreak." They did neither. Later, heartsick over the results, Colonel Hitchcock mourned in his diary that had the buildings been bombarded properly, "we need not have lost perhaps a dozen men."

The precise number of Mexican troops facing the American line is not known, though there were surely far fewer than the 14,000 estimated by Worth. Occupying the mill's buildings were two brigades under Generals Antonio León and Joaquín Rangel, while General Francisco Pérez commanded about 1,500 regulars at the Casa Mata. Between these two wings of the Mexican army was deployed General Simeón Ramírez's brigade with seven guns. A mile west of Casa Mata, and separated from it by a ravine, were 4,000 cavalrymen under General Juan Alvarez.

Worth divided his force into three columns, holding Cadwalader's brigade in reserve. In the center was the principal assault column, 500 men picked from various units and led by Lieutenant Colonel George Wright of the 8th Infantry. Their assignment was to take a field battery found by reconnaissance on the previous day.

On the right Garland's brigade, supported by Simon Drum's two six-pounders—guns that had been lost to the Mexicans at Buena Vista and recaptured at Contreras—was to cut off any rescue force that might come from Chapultepec. Major Benjamin Huger's two 24-pounders, supported by the light battalion under Kirby Smith, were placed on the ridge to their left, about 600 yards from the *molino*. Facing the Casa Mata was a brigade led by Colonel James S. McIntosh, who had recovered from wounds suffered at Palo Alto. With him was another veteran of the war's first battle, Colonel James Duncan and his battery of flying artillery. Finally, on the extreme left was Lieutenant Colonel Edwin V. Sumner and three squadrons of dragoons, some 270 men; their assignment was to hold in check the 4,000-man Mexican cavalry.

As soon as the *molino's* low, white walls became visible in the dawnlight, Huger's cannon thundered, sending their 24-pound balls crashing into the central part of the complex. There was no response. The Mexican line was so quiet that the two engineers who

a central role in the attack, and he had turned over command of his company to Lieutenant Fred Dent, Grant's future brother-in-law. A little earlier Smith had written to his wife, "We have a rumor that a mail has arrived at Puebla, if so, I shall soon receive some of your delightful letters, shall again hear from my children. I wish I could be certain you will hear from me." Now, in a more somber mood, he wrote, "Tomorrow will be a day of slaughter. I am thankful that you do not know the peril we are in. Good night."

At 3 o'clock on the morning of September 8, the Americans began to move. By the first hint of dawn, wrote Worth, "they were as accurately in position as if posted in midday for review." The attacking troops were on a ridge, looking down on the line of grim stone buildings before them. The height of the position was unfortunate because it would compensate for the normal Mexican tendency to fire high.

The Molino del Rey was about three quarters of a mile west of Chapultepec Castle and within reach of its cannon. The mill's several main structures, linked with walls and courtyards, stretched a total of about 500 yards. Behind the *molino* was a walled park of cypress trees, the pleasant grounds of Chapultepec Castle.

had reconnoitered the area and were to guide Wright's assault column thought the Mexicans might have abandoned the positions they had held the day before. They advised Wright to advance. As a result, Huger's guns were stilled much sooner than had been planned.

But Ramírez was only waiting. When Wright and his 500 men ran down the slope, they met a furious storm of grape and canister that tore them apart. Wright fell; 11 of the 14 officers who made the charge and scores of soldiers were shot down. Despite the deadly hail, the remnants of the assault column drove the Mexicans from their guns. But Mexican troops kept firing from the *molino*'s parapets and the American column faltered and broke, nearly a third of them bolting in terror. Seeing how few Americans were left, the Mexicans launched a successful counterattack from Chapultepec. As the Mexicans reoccupied the battery, said Ripley, "they murdered every wounded man left on the ground except Captain Walker of the Sixth infantry and one private, both desperately wounded, and both doubtless believed to be dead."

Then Kirby Smith's light battalion and one of Cadwalader's reserve regiments swept down the hill. They poured through the exhausted men of the original attack force and drove the enemy back. Drum's artillery opened fire on the Mexican battery; and Kirby Smith led the light battalion in a charge that carried the enemy guns. But the assault was not without cost. Smith took a musket ball in the face and fell like a stone. He died three days later without regaining consciousness, his long letters finished, his fears for his wife and children left alone tragically realized.

The Americans were still exposed to a severe crossfire but, said Ripley, "in scattered parties they held their ground." The bulk of Garland's brigade had charged the other end of Molino del Rey, fighting through the buildings room by room, shooting through doors and then jumping in to finish each step of the advance with bayonets, until they were able to join the survivors of Kirby Smith's light battalion. There Ulysses Grant found Fred Dent unconscious from a bullet wound in the thigh, lifted him onto a wall to attract medical attention and ran on to rejoin his men.

The Mexican battery had been seized and now the fray became close combat. General León and several of his officers had been slain, but the Mexicans held onto the *molino* itself with fearful persistence, and the battle was far from decided.

On the left McIntosh's men were deployed to move on the square, stone Casa Mata. A ferocious fire from their right was silenced only when Duncan's guns bombarded the Mexican lines. But then, instead of turning the guns on the Casa Mata, Worth cut off Duncan's line of fire by ordering McIntosh's brigade to advance. Inside the Casa Mata and at the works in front of the building the troops under Pérez waited. When the Americans were just 100 yards away, the Mexicans opened fire, but the American advance kept moving. Then, 30 yards from the Mexican line, the hail of bullets took its toll. Both McIntosh and his second-in-command were mortally wounded. Men were falling "almost by platoons and companies," wrote Ripley.

Alvarez' cavalry began to advance on the American left flank. When the Mexican horsemen were within range, Duncan opened fire on them with two of his guns. Lieutenant Colonel Sumner, ignoring the destructive fire from the Casa Mata, now led his 270 dragoons in a fierce charge across the ravine at the 4,000 brilliantly arrayed Mexican cavalrymen. In about 10 seconds the Americans lost 44 men. But the Mexicans, cannonaded by Duncan's guns and a 24-pounder ordered up by Worth, retreated in disorder, "pursued by the riderless horses of Sumner's command." In a series of maneuvers and countermaneuvers, the drastically outnumbered American dragoons so confounded their opponents that the Mexican cavalry, as a Mexican observer later put it, soon became "cold spectators to the conflict."

At the Casa Mata the Americans were falling back in slow confusion. The Mexicans came after them but Cadwalader's reserves soon checked this movement, and Duncan's guns, their line of fire cleared by the American retreat, now turned again upon the enemy forces in and around the Casa Mata. Under this assault, Pérez was forced to abandon his position, for by now Molino del Rey had been captured and his communication with Chapultepec cut off.

But the Mexican retreat was not a rout. The troops withdrew in good order, and now Santa Anna appeared and rallied his forces along the road north of Chapultepec. Twice they surged and twice they were checked only by the prompt action of U.S. artillery.

Hard justice for a band of captured turncoats

As U.S. troops charged the castle of Chapultepec, 30 of their former comrades stood on mule carts beneath a scaffold on a nearby hill, watching the action with nooses around their necks, their eyes locked on a flagpole on top of the castle turret. The raising of the Stars and Stripes in place of the Mexican tricolor would be the signal for the executioner to motion the cart drivers forward and leave the prisoners dangling.

The condemned men were captured American deserters who—in an action unparalleled in the nation's history—had formed the backbone of a unit in the Mexican army and fought against the United States. They were called the San Patricio Battalion—however, they were never more than two companies strong (and not all of them deserters).

Though the story of the San Patricios has become shrouded in legend, it appears to have begun on a Sunday in April 1846 when Sergeant John Riley of Company K, U.S. 5th Infantry, swam the Rio Grande to desert from Taylor's army at Matamoros. In the months that followed, hundreds of men followed Riley's example. They were moved by boredom, drink, or by Mexican promises of land and money. Some were influenced by Mexican propaganda aimed at creating a rift between native and foreign-born American soldiers—and particularly between Irish Catholics and Protestants.

Many deserters were never heard from again; those who joined the Mexicans were first encountered as a unit at Buena Vista. Riley, now a first lieutenant, was the ranking American among the deserters. Their distinctive flag, decorated with a shamrock, a figure of St. Patrick and the harp of Erin, reflected Riley's national origin, though a substantial number of the men fighting with him were not Irish.

The San Patricios were cited for bravery after Buena Vista. Their impact was strongest, however, at Churubusco. The story is told that each time the Mexicans there tried to raise the white flag of surrender, the desperate San Patricios—knowing that, for them, capture meant death—pulled it down and continued the losing fight.

At least 65 of the San Patricios were finally taken at Churubusco, tried by court-martial and sentenced to hang. Major General Winfield Scott reviewed the sentences and commuted 11 of them, including Riley's, on grounds that these men had deserted before war was officially declared. Those who were spared received punishment that was harsh enough—50 lashes, the letter D branded on their cheeks and the grim job of digging graves for those to be hanged. Scott also pardoned four men who persuaded him that Mexicans had captured them and forced them to fight. He confirmed the others' convictions. They were executed in three groups, after occupying ringside seats at the American victory.

San Patricio Battalion members await hanging at the moment U.S. troops storming Chapultepec raise the American flag in victory.

Thus the battle of Molino del Rey came to a conclusion after two hours of intense fighting. The Mexicans had lost some 2,000 men, the Americans 787 killed and wounded, almost a quarter of those engaged. The 5th Infantry alone had suffered 38 per cent casualties, including Kirby Smith.

As they probed the buildings they had captured, the Americans began to realize how pointless the whole deadly exercise had been. There was "not a vestige of a foundry," no church bells being cast into cannon. A powder magazine was found at the Casa Mata, but in exploding it another dozen Americans were accidentally killed. Then, as a final straw, the fire-shocked troops were ordered to withdraw from the objective they had fought so hard to gain.

As the armistice was the great American political error of the war, so the attack on Molino del Rey was the great combat mistake. The soldiers took it badly. "There was deep depression among us," said Captain Daniel H. Hill of the 4th Artillery. The "fruitless victory" and the loss of so many competent officers and soldiers "in a great degree destroyed our confidence in our Commanders." Colonel Hitchcock was not able to fall asleep that night, telling himself that "a few more such victories and this army would be destroyed." Scott's army now was reduced to about 7,000 effective troops. Molino del Rey was an ominous way to begin the final strokes of a campaign that the Americans had to win just to survive.

Once the dead and wounded had been cleared from the battlefield, the Americans resumed their study of the southern approaches to the city. Surveys by engineers Lee, Beauregard and Tower revealed that the Mexicans were rapidly building up their southern defenses. The alternative — an attack from the west — meant first taking the guns on the towering hill of Chapultepec. If that could be accomplished, however, two routes to the city would be open: one causeway ran from the very foot of Chapultepec to the Garita de Belén, another headed north about two miles and connected with the causeway to the Garita de San Cosmé. At the city end of the causeways, a broad *paseo,* or promenade, studded with guns ran between the two gates.

On the morning of September 11, Scott called his commanders and engineers to a council of war in a picturesque chapel at La Piedad, less than two miles south of the Garita de Belén. The general declared himself in favor of striking from the west, through Chapultepec, but he wanted everyone's opinion on how best to use his already depleted army against the powerful defenses before him. Twiggs agreed with Scott. Lee and most of the other engineers, as well as Generals Quitman, Shields, Pillow, Cadwalader and Pierce, favored the southern approach.

Beauregard at first said nothing and eventually his silence was noticed. Scott snapped, "You, young man, in that corner, what have you to say on the subject?" The junior officer from New Orleans then took the floor and delivered a lecture straight out of a West Point textbook. He reminded his seniors of the importance of surprise and recommended a feint that would delude the enemy into expecting attack from the south, followed by a lightning stroke from the west. There was a thoughtful silence, and then General Pierce announced that he had changed his mind. Scott waited a moment, then stood. "Gentlemen," he said quietly, "we will attack by the western gates."

Thus the strategy for the final attack on Mexico City was set. The Americans would first have to take Chapultepec, then hurl themselves against the two western gates in one fluid motion.

Chapultepec had two distinct parts: the hill itself, which stood 200 feet above the surrounding plain, and the surmounting castle. In the Aztec language the name meant Grasshopper Hill, and the castle atop it once had been the resort of Aztec princes. Here at last were the Halls of Montezuma that in the years before and ever after so fired the American imagination. Chapultepec was not really a fortress; Spanish viceroys had used it for a summer castle, and since 1833 it had served as Mexico's military academy. But around it, supported by a huge retaining wall, was a broad terrace that made an excellent gun platform.

The hill was steep all around except on the west, where it sloped through the grove of cypress trees to Molino del Rey. The entire park was surrounded by a high stone wall four feet thick. An opening in the south wall was protected by a sandbag barricade, while a roadway that wound up to the castle had been fortified with sandbags and cannon. The obvious approach was from the west, but halfway up the hill lay a strong redoubt and beyond it the hillside was mined. Beyond that was a ditch, and then came the sheer retaining walls that men could climb only with scaling ladders, exposed to fire from above.

Scott wanted no repetition of the disaster at Molino del Rey. For a day before the attack began he ordered four batteries to bombard the castle. Scott hoped to persuade Santa Anna until the last possible moment that the real American attack would be from the south and that the attack on Chapultepec was the feint. To heighten this illusion, Quitman marched his division in broad daylight on the 11th to join Pillow, who along with Twiggs was covering the southern approaches. Then, under cover of darkness, Quitman and Pillow marched their men to take up positions for the attack.

Pillow's division reoccupied the battered Molino del Rey, ready to charge through the cypresses and up the slope with scaling ladders. Quitman's men were positioned to strike the southeastern end of Chapultepec hill and then to move immediately on the Belén gate. Worth's division was to support Pillow and, after Chapultepec's capture, was to make for the causeway that ran to the San Cosmé gate. Because Scott believed Belén to be much stronger than San Cosmé, Quitman's attack would also be a feint; Worth's strike at San Cosmé was to be the main assault.

For 14 hours, all through Sunday, September 12, Scott's cannon roared. Inside Chapultepec Castle, General Nicolás Bravo, a stalwart old commander who had been an insurrectionist against the Spanish and later a president of Mexico, sensed the attack that the ferocious bombardment foretold. That evening he called for reinforcements. But Santa Anna, who for several days had shifted men and matériel in a frenzy of anticipation, was still concerned about the southern approaches and merely replied that troops would be sent at the critical moment, if that moment came.

Chapultepec's apparent strength was deceptive. Lack of time, money and matériel had made adequate preparation impossible. The castle was vulnerable to the American bombardment. Two of Chapultepec's guns were disabled, and Bravo's disheartened soldiers quickly began to desert. He had fewer than 1,000 troops inside and immediately outside the building, barely half the number he needed. About 50 cadets, some no older than 13, insisted on remaining. The academy was training them to be soldiers, and never would there be a better time to serve their country.

That night Scott convened his officers and gave his final orders. The atmosphere of the meeting was grim. Afterward Hitchcock wrote in his diary, "At the close of the talk this evening, after all was arranged, General Worth said to me, 'We shall be defeated.'" Even Scott, when the others had left the room, confessed, "I have my misgivings."

Scott had ordered two storming parties of 250 men each, to be formed from the regular regiments and to be supplied with scaling ladders and pickaxes. One, led by Captain Samuel McKenzie, would carry the advance for Pillow's division from the west. The other, under Captain Silas Casey, would lead Quitman's attack up the Tacubaya road. Captain Hill on the 4th Artillery was among those who volunteered, but he was not optimistic. "As the leading storming party 'the forlorn hope' was expected to suffer very much," he wrote later. "Strong incentives were held out to induce us to volunteer." But even promises of promotions, of "pecuniary rewards" and of having one's name "borne on the regimental books forever" were not enough to dispel anxiety. "Affairs now looked dark and gloomily in the extreme," Hill wrote. "Chapultepec was regarded as impregnable."

When the bombardment resumed at dawn on Monday, September 13, the three prongs of Pillow's force were poised at the *molino*. On the American left, outside the northern wall of Chapultepec, two infantry regiments led by Colonel William B. Trousdale were posted to intercept reinforcements that might come out from the city. Supporting them was artillery under Lieutenant Thomas J. Jackson. A second party, led by Lieutenant Colonel Joseph E. Johnston, was to charge through the guarded entryway in the southern wall of the castle grounds.

Pillow himself was with a group behind the *molino* buildings waiting to charge enemy entrenchments at the far side of a watery field that lay between the *molino* gate and the cypress grove.

At about 8:00 a.m., the roaring cannon suddenly stopped and an eerie silence fell. This was the signal to attack, and a battalion of infantry led by Colonel Timothy Patrick Andrews burst out of the *molino* gate, yelling and running across the open field. In the fore-

U.S. infrantrymen scale Chapultepec Castle's walls near the climax of a four-hour battle, the last before Mexico City. From the parapets, the Americans streamed through the fort in a final bloody assault.

STORMING OF THE CASTLE OF CHAPULTEPEC, BY THE

AMERICAN ARMY UNDER GENERAL SCOTT, SEPT. 13, 1847.

Thomas J. Jackson entered the war as an artillery lieutenant fresh out of West Point. His rock-steady nerve under fire earned him the rank of major in 1847 and, 14 years later, the nickname "Stonewall."

front was the storming party under Captain McKenzie. The Mexicans rose to fire, but Johnston's troops on the right had already come through the southern wall and were into the park of cypress trees. Pinched between the two forces, the Mexican troops began to fall back. They gave way grudgingly, firing as they went from behind the shell-battered trunks of the ancient cypresses. General Pérez was mortally wounded while covering the Mexican withdrawal, but the troops were temporarily rallied by the arrival of reinforcements at the castle dispatched—too late—by Santa Anna.

Now the Americans were out of the trees and facing the mined hillside that led up to the great retaining wall of the castle terrace. Halfway up was the redoubt to which the retreating Mexicans were running. From the terrace came a murderous rain of grapeshot and musket fire. General Pillow was struck in the ankle and knocked down, yet forward movement was imperative and Pillow ordered the charge before letting Lee help him to get to shelter behind a tree. But the Mexicans in the redoubt and on the parapet let loose, in Beauregard's words, "as terrible a fire as I had yet seen!" and the American assault was checked.

Then Brevet Major Daniel Chase of the 15th Infantry leaped up with a wild yell. In an instant his men followed and the whole force flowed over the redoubt, pushing Mexican soldiers backward toward the castle. With friend and foe mingling on the hillside, the Mexican officer assigned to set off the defensive mines hesitated and his moment was lost; Americans severed the canvas powder trains that led to the mines and none of them exploded.

The Americans jammed up against the ditch at the base of the retaining wall. The men assigned to bring up the storming ladders had not yet arrived and the advance elements took what cover they could under the very muzzles on the Mexican cannon. With deadly accuracy they proceeded to pick off the Mexican gunners at their pieces on the terrace above. The rest of Pillow's command could only watch in trepidation for 15 heart-stopping minutes as their comrades huddled under a parapet that was often "one continued sheet of flame."

On the American right, Quitman's advance up the Tacubaya road had been severely hampered by a five-gun Mexican battery, part of General Rangel's command. In the lead were Captain Casey's storming party, 40 Marines under Captain John G. Reynolds and a mixed force under Marine Major Levi Twiggs. Casey and Twiggs fell wounded, the latter fatally, as Rangel's determined troops stopped the American advance 200 yards short of the guns. Three of Quitman's regiments left the road and, despite heavy fire, burst through the southern wall to link up with the storming party under the castle wall.

At last the long-awaited ladders reached the Americans. They leaped to the attack, using the ladders to bridge the ditch, then setting them against the wall. The Mexicans increased their fire, mowing down the men of the first wave. But so many ladders rose that 50 Americans could climb abreast. Finally, Captain John E. Howard gained the parapet unhurt, "and with a shout of victory, the great body of the troops rushed over" the walls and swept into the castle.

Soon the Americans on the terrace turned their fire on the Mexicans pinning the rest of Quitman's column. The Mexicans fell back and Quitman's men charged up the road to Chapultepec's main gates, where they met its defenders pelting down in mad retreat.

"Many Mexicans, in their flight," wrote Ripley, "jumped down the steep eastern side of the rock, regardless of the height." Remembering how the Mexicans had slaughtered American wounded at Molino del Rey, the Yankees were merciless. "It was not until the soldiers were satiated with revenge," Ripley said, "that the bloodshed was put a stop to."

The young cadets who had refused to desert their school fought to the end. One 13-year-old confronted an American bayonet charge. He shouted a command to halt and was trying to cock his musket when a bayonet ran through his body. Another cadet lowered the Mexican flag to keep it from American hands and ran across the roof toward a stairway. Struck by a

bullet, the youngster plunged off the roof to the rocks below, still clutching the flag. In all, six boys were killed, most of them, as an American correspondent put it, "fighting like demons" when they fell. Their countrymen would immortalize them as *Los Niños Heroicos* — the heroic children. Within minutes the American colors floated over the castle. In just over an hour after the first charge Chapultepec had fallen; the drive against the city itself could begin. Watching from a distance at Santa Anna's side, a Mexican officer muttered despondently, "God is a Yankee."

To the north, Colonel Trousdale's column had, in Scott's words, engaged in "some spirited affairs against superior numbers" of Mexicans led by General Peña y Barragán. In advance of the infantry, Lieutenant Jackson blazed away with his artillery at an enemy breastwork even after losing his horses, many men and a cannon. Later he was commended for showing the "highest qualities of a soldier — devotion, industry, tal-

ent and gallantry." Finally, Worth came up with Garland's brigade and the Mexican gun was taken, just as the general Mexican retreat from Chapultepec began.

Both Worth and Quitman pushed immediately toward the Mexican capital, Worth moving north along the Verónica causeway and Quitman directly east toward Belén. Down the center of both causeways to the city ran aqueducts supported on stone arches, with drainage canals flanking each side.

The Mexican soldiers abandoning Chapultepec fell back rapidly along the Belén causeway to a two-gun battery that stood well in advance of the *garita*. Quitman's column pressed forward in the face of Mexican fire that persisted despite the efforts of Simon Drum's guns to quell it. The column was led by a regiment of mounted rifles, fighting on foot, who finally surged forward and took the strongpoint, while the Mexicans fell back to the Garita de Belén.

The Americans reorganized and started forward against "a tremendous fire of artillery" from front and sides. "Here our loss was very great," an officer reported. "Slowly creeping from arch to arch, we lost many men by the batteries in front, while the fire from flanking batteries coming through the arches killed many who were safe from that in front."

Santa Anna, aware now that the main American attack was coming from the west, had visited the Garita de Belén earlier, then rushed on to prepare San Cosmé. At Belén, General Andrés Terrés watched in alarm as the Americans advanced. Though Quitman's attack was supposed to be only a feint, the headstrong Mississippian was pushing his column for all it was worth. Terrés' men began to desert and, as the Americans charged the battery at the *garita,* the Mexicans broke and fell back toward the *ciudadela,* a large barracks 300 yards to the rear, fortified with 15 cannon. At 1:20 in the afternoon Yankee troops, with the eager riflemen again in the vanguard, breached the Garita de Belén. "Brave Rifles," Scott saluted them later, "you have gone through fire and come out steel."

The Americans pushed to within 100 yards of the *ciudadela,* and there they were stopped. Santa Anna had returned to Belén in a rage. He slapped Terrés in the face, relieved him of command and directed a savage fire from the fortified barracks against the relatively exposed Americans at the *garita.* Drum's two guns were out of ammunition, but he turned the Mexican eight-pounder in the *garita* and returned fire. His men fell around him. Others who ran out of shelter to help were in turn cut down. Then Drum himself was hit, his legs torn apart; he bled to death in a few minutes. Finally, all ammunition was exhausted, and the American pieces fell silent. Quitman's entire staff and all of his artillery officers had been killed or wounded. There was nothing the impetuous commander could do but shelter his men and wait for nightfall.

After the capture of Chapultepec, Scott had followed Worth's division as it advanced on San Cosmé. Far in the lead rode Lee. Shaking with exhaustion after three sleepless nights and grazed by a bullet, he pressed on to reconnoiter the approach, then rode back to confer with Scott. Returning to the front, Lee broke at last—he fainted and toppled from his horse. His heroic part in the taking of Mexico City was over.

Worth's progress had been slow. He had reorganized his troops and replaced their ammunition; then he

GENERAL SCOTT REVELLING IN THE HALLS OF THE MONTEZUMAS.

had to beat off an attack by 1,500 Mexican cavalry. It was nearly 4 p.m. before his men could start down the San Cosmé causeway. Here the buildings clinging to the roadway held the Americans in the field of fire; casualties were severe until the attackers remembered the tactic they had used at Monterrey and began to break their way through the walls of the buildings, hauling their guns after them. From time to time they appeared on the roofs, sometimes dragging mountain howitzers into place and pelting the enemy.

The Garita de San Cosmé had not been well prepared, but its defenders fought hard. Rangel and Peña y Barragán put their limited resources to good use. But,

Late and Important from Mexico.

The City of Mexico is Ours!!

Arrival of the Steamer Jas. L. Day.

THE ARMISTICE AT AN END.

HOSTILITIES RE-COMMENCED.

Another Great Battle—Our Arms Victorious—The City of Mexico Bombarded by our Troops—The American Army in the Capital—Translation of Mr. Trist's Project of a Treaty—Besançon's Company and Lieut. Henderson's Command Safe—Mems from "Mustang," &c., &c.

said Ripley, the Americans working forward "from windows and roofs were pouring a stream of musketry and canister with accurate aim."

Ulysses Grant, meanwhile, had again escaped his assignment as quartermaster of the 4th Infantry. He discovered a church to the south of the road "which looked to me as if the belfry would command the ground back of the garita San Cosmé." Finding an officer with a howitzer and soldiers to operate it, Grant knocked on the church door and persuaded the reluctant priest who opened it "to see his duty in the same light that I did." After hoisting the gun in pieces up to the belfry and reassembling it, Grant began hurling shot upon the enemy below, creating "great confusion."

By 5 o'clock the rest of Worth's men had fought their way nearly to the *garita* and Worth ordered the barricade at its front captured with a light gun. "Lieutenant Hunt, of Duncan's battery, took it forward at a gallop," said Ripley, "under a fire which killed and wounded five out of nine men, and the piece was served on the enemy through the embrasure of the barricade." The Mexican commander, Rangel, was wounded and his biggest gun, a 24-pound howitzer, was disabled.

Now the American troops moving up through the houses popped out on the roofs in full force and delivered a powerful fire down into the redoubt at the *garita*.

An array of medals, for the winners and the losers

By the time an American soldier came home from Mexico he had probably seen enough medals pinned to Mexican uniforms to make him wonder who had won the war. The Mexican government, following European tradition, had medals struck to commemorate every major battle *(opposite)*, regardless of the outcome.

The United States Congress, however, was more conservative: valor under fire sometimes earned a certificate of merit for the enlisted man and often a brevet rank for an officer. Congressional medallions were struck only for Generals Taylor and Scott *(frontispiece, facing title page)*.

Medals did begin to appear on American chests in the decades following the war, but for the most part they were put there by veterans' organizations. The Aztec Club of 1847, founded by officers of the Army of Occupation, eventually issued badges to its members. They included such future Civil War leaders as Lee, Longstreet, Meade, Sherman and Sheridan.

The National Association of Mexican War Veterans awarded badges *(lower right)* to American enlisted men as well as officers. And some of the medals, like the one *(lower left)* bestowed upon Lieutenant Joseph Warren Revere for his service in California, came from sources so obscure that they can no longer be identified.

AZTEC CLUB

AZTEC CLUB

CONQUEST OF
THE CALIFORNIAS

MEXICAN WAR
VETERANS

PALO ALTO

BUENA VISTA

CHURUBUSCO

MOLINO DEL REY

CHAPULTEPEC

CHAPULTEPEC

219

The Mexicans broke and fled toward the *ciudadela,* dragging one of their two cannon. The Americans sprang over the parapets, spun the remaining cannon about and opened fire on the retreating soldiers.

Both *garitas* had fallen and there remained only the drive into the city itself. The Americans had lost 130 killed, 703 wounded and 29 missing; Mexican losses were estimated at 3,000, including 823 captured. But Santa Anna still had about 5,000 troops at the *ciudadela* and 7,000 more deployed elsewhere in the city.

All night the Americans worked preparing batteries to support the final assault on Tuesday morning. But Santa Anna had decided to evacuate his shell-shocked army from Mexico City in hope of resuming the fighting elsewhere. At 4 a.m. city authorities came to Scott's headquarters, hoping to negotiate. This time Scott refused; he had fought his way in and now he intended to have the city. At daylight he sent orders to both Worth and Quitman to advance "slowly and cautiously." Even before the order reached him, Quitman had received a white flag from the *ciudadela.* Sent to investigate, Beauregard and another officer found a lone Mexican officer who asked for a receipt for the matériel

within. Drawing himself up, Beauregard replied, "We gave our receipts with the points of our swords!"

Though Scott was angry at Quitman for the costliness of his attack on Belén the day before, he felt the Mississippian and his men had earned the honor of formally taking the city, and within hours he would appoint Quitman its military governor. Worth and his men were ordered to advance only as far as the Alameda, Mexico City's magnificent park, while Quitman's troops marched into the Grand Plaza, the city's heart.

The Americans hardly looked the part of a conquering army. The victorious General Quitman wore only one shoe as he walked at the head of his ragged, bloodstained troops. The streets of the city were silent, though lined with people. In the great square the Americans formed orderly ranks in front of the National Palace, and in a few minutes the American flag went up.

Then cheers were heard a few blocks away. Winfield Scott had arrived. Mounted on a heavy bay charger and escorted by a brigade of dragoons with drawn sabers, the general cut a magnificent figure. He was in full dress, epaulets gleaming gold against the blue uniform, white plumes flowing from his cocked hat. As he

Despite his placid appearance, Texas Ranger Samuel Walker *(below)* was an intrepid guerrilla fighter who helped design the Colt Walker six-shooter. Near the war's end, he was killed at Huamantla *(left)* leading a company of mounted rifles.

galloped into the plaza, the army's bands broke into "Yankee Doodle" and "Hail Columbia." Scott reined in the big horse in front of the troops who had come so far against such odds. He had cut them off from their base and put them on their own, to win or "to find a grave," and they had stood the test. Only about 6,000 of them remained on their feet, little more than half of those who had left Puebla. Now they greeted Scott with cheers that drowned the sound of the bands. The General in Chief listened another moment, then answered his men with a grand, sweeping saber salute. He dismounted and walked up the stairs into the National Palace of Mexico.

United States Marines were now patrolling the halls of Montezuma, yet peace remained elusive, and a final settlement would take months to achieve. Santa Anna resigned as president but retained command of the remnants of his army, which he had withdrawn to Guadalupe Hidalgo, a provincial town some 10 miles north of Mexico City. The always unstable Mexican government collapsed into chaos, and once more the Americans faced the frustration of trying to negotiate with a will-o'-the-wisp. Finally, toward the end of September, influential Mexicans shaped a tentative government under Manuel Peña y Peña, the aging leader who had recognized at the beginning that war with the United States would be "an abyss without bottom."

For Scott, the weeks and months after his dramatic entry into Mexico City were especially trying. With a small, battleworn and undersupplied army he had to garrison a populous capital, pacify the surrounding countryside and pressure the Mexicans into serious negotiations without shattering the tenuous control of the Peña government. Sniper attacks on the American troops in Mexico City broke out on the first day of occupation; they were the work of Mexican ex-soldiers and some of the 30,000 convicts whom the Mexicans had released from jail. Scott could ill afford further losses. He ordered the streets "swept with grape and canister" and had heavy guns "turned upon the houses whence the fire proceeded." Such tactics eventually quieted the city, but guerrilla warfare continued elsewhere in the country. Scott countered with what he called "disinfesting" action, but he was hampered even in this by the meager size of his army; no reinforcements reached him in the city until after the 1st of November.

At Puebla the small American garrison—only 400 effective troops—came under siege on the very day that Mexico City fell. Nearly a month passed before a column of some 3,000 men under General Joseph Lane came to its relief. On October 9, Lane encountered Santa Anna and about 1,000 men at Huamantla, 25 miles from Puebla. In the American vanguard was Captain Samuel Walker of the Texas Rangers, who had fought with distinction from the first moments of the war. Leading four companies of cavalry in a headlong charge, Walker was caught by a fierce counterattack led by Santa Anna himself; Walker and his men were trapped in Huamantla. Before the main body of Lane's infantry could catch up and settle the issue, Walker was mortally wounded.

General Lane retaliated for Walker's death by turning his men loose on the town in a rampage of pillage and destruction that was unmatched in the war. Three days later the Americans fought their way through to the beleaguered soldiers garrisoned at Puebla. Lane continued the pressure, conducting a series of antiguerrilla raids to clear the supply road to Veracruz.

221

Huamantla was Santa Anna's last stand. The Peña government, as the first test of its authority, ordered him to relinquish his military command and to prepare for an inquiry into his conduct of the war. The general was finally licked and he knew it; he quietly turned his troops over to a successor. The following January Santa Anna asked permission to leave Mexico and by April he was once again in exile.

With Santa Anna's fall from power and conditions in the capital relatively stable, Nicholas Trist was optimistic that peace negotiations could begin in earnest. But at this point the American representative received what to most men would have been a crushing setback. President Polk, under continued political pressure and out of patience with the whole Mexican adventure, decided to withdraw the proposal for a negotiated peace that Trist carried. In mid-November came orders canceling Trist's commission and instructing him to return home. But Trist was a remarkable individual. Both the Peña government and the British legation urged him to continue negotiations, fearing that any delay would sabotage peace efforts indefinitely. Trist decided to stay. He wrote his immediate superior, Secretary of State Buchanan, a 65-page letter as remarkable for its disrespect as for its length. He denounced Polk's decision as a "deadly blow to the cause of peace" and said he intended to arrange a treaty whether Washington liked it or not.

Fortunately for Trist, communication between the two capitals was slow, but he knew that his time was limited. On January 2, 1848, in utmost secrecy, negotiations at last began. Discussion turned primarily on drawing new national borders and deciding how much the U.S. government would pay for the land it acquired. As January drew to a close, the Mexicans were still haggling. Worried that any day he would receive fresh recall orders that he could not ignore, Trist issued an ultimatum: now or never. The Mexicans accepted, and on February 2, 1848, at the village that thus gave its name to history, the Treaty of Guadalupe Hidalgo was signed.

About two weeks later a copy of the treaty reached Washington. President Polk was surprised to learn that he had obtained essentially what he wanted. Though angry at Trist, he determined that the treaty should be judged on its merits and lost no time submit-

ting it to the U.S. Senate. There, after intense debate, it was ratified on March 10, 1848.

The heart of the treaty was the cession to the United States of more than half of Mexico's territory, an area larger than France and Germany together. The American boundary with Mexico would run from the Gulf of Mexico up the Rio Grande to the New Mexican border. From there it would continue west to reach the Pacific at a point one marine league, or just over three miles, south of San Diego. For its part the United States would pay Mexico $15 million in cash and would assume $3.25 million in claims of American citizens against the Mexican government. Great Britain's claim to Oregon had been settled by peaceful compromise in June 1846, giving the United States the Pacific Northwest to the 49th parallel. Thus—with a single small adjustment to come in the Gadsden Purchase of 1853—the borders of the continental United States were established. Westering Americans could pour unrestrained into the new land.

The United States continued to lurch toward its great Civil War. At most the Mexican War played an indirect part in bringing on that conflict. As Polk had foreseen, slavery did not move west, if only because it was impractical there. But the concern of the free states that the newly acquired territories would adopt slavery had sharpened the antipathies of both North and South and thus hastened the internal storm.

What did emerge from the Mexican War was an extremely competent officer corps for both sides in the Civil War. The two opposing commanders, Lee and Grant, formed their impressions of war on the hard road to Mexico City. They also formed impressions of each other. "The acquaintance thus formed was of immense service to me in the war of rebellion," Grant later wrote, noting that people tended to ascribe "almost superhuman abilities" to leaders of large armies. "A large part of the National army, for instance, and most of the press of the country, clothed General Lee with just such qualities," Grant said, "but I had known him personally, and knew that he was mortal."

Though Winfield Scott's all-too-mortal propensity for political squabbling robbed him of much of the credit he was due, he emerged as the pre-eminent American military figure of the fourscore years between the Revolution and the Civil War. The outspo-

ken Duke of Wellington, convinced of Scott's prowess at last, called him "the greatest living soldier."

But at home Scott's reputation was almost immediately tarnished by a bitter public dispute with his subordinates in Mexico over who deserved the most credit for the victory. Even before peace was ensured, the officers were arguing like rival schoolboys both in official reports and in letters printed in newspapers at home. At length Scott placed his severest critics, Generals Pillow and Worth, and the durable artilleryman James Duncan, under arrest for insubordination, only to be himself relieved of his command by Polk in February 1848. But his influence endured. The tactics that won the war—Scott's flexibility and imagination, his attention to reconnaissance, his tendency to

strike from an unexpected side—had been well learned by his juniors and were used again and again on the terrible fields of the Civil War.

After the Senate ratified the Treaty of Guadalupe Hidalgo, it was returned to Mexico City. On May 30, 1848, ratification documents were exchanged and the treaty went into effect. American troops began to leave Mexico City immediately, and on June 12 the last of them were ready to go. General Worth's division formed in the Grand Plaza, and gunners of both nations fired in salute as the Mexican tricolor replaced the Stars and Stripes over the National Palace. Commands echoed across the square and the American soldiers filed out of the city to begin the long journey home.

A MEMBER OF THE VOLUNTEERS

Faces of a generation tempered by war

The anonymous soldiers and sailors who are pictured in the gallery that begins on the opposite page are just a small number of the uncelebrated thousands of men who fought the American side of the war with Mexico. Their names and their fates are unknown. As a generation tempered by war, they and their comrades experienced a sweet moment of public adulation before they went on to fresh adventure in the nation they had helped so dramatically to expand.

After the fighting ended, some Americans stayed on to try their luck in Mexico or California, but most went home—to new assignments if they were regulars or to be mustered out if they were volunteers. Many volunteers, when they signed up, had been promised both a certificate redeemable for up to 160 acres of land and travel money to get them home from the point of discharge. One newspaper estimated that with these benefits, plus a bonus of three months' wages, a private in the Massachusetts volunteers was due at least $170. "No army ever mustered out of service," the newspaper stated approvingly, "was better paid than that of the United States."

Reality, however, did not always match the promise. Some volunteers were released in their regiment's home state and consequently got no travel pay. As one officer wrote to the Secretary of War, the denial of travel money meant that the men "will not be enabled to clothe themselves with decent clothing without disposing of their land scrip." Indeed, many cash-short veterans were fleeced out of their grants by unscrupulous speculators who paid half value or less to soldiers who were ignorant of the grants' true worth.

When the troops did reach home, they were feted as heroes. Parades were commonplace. Nashville threw a great barbecue. In Charleston, South Carolina, "a Grand Torch light Procession marched through the principal streets to the Gardens where a splendid display of Fire Works took place."

But such excitement did not last. Soon the men who had marched with Taylor and Scott, Frémont and Kearny went their separate ways—many to pioneer the recently enlarged West, and some to climb to new heights of glory and despair in the Civil War.

A CAPTAIN, UNITED STATES REGULAR ARMY

A LIEUTENANT, UNITED STATES REGULAR ARMY

A LIEUTENANT OF THE REGULAR ARMY

A PRIVATE OF THE VOLUNTEERS

A CABIN BOY, UNITED STATES NAVY

A SEAMAN, UNITED STATES NAVY

A CAPTAIN OF THE REGULAR ARMY

A GENERAL OF THE VOLUNTEERS

Chapter I: Particularly useful sources for information and quotes in this chapter: K. Jack Bauer, *The Mexican War 1846-1848*, Macmillan Publishing Co., Inc., 1974; Brainerd Dyer, *Zachary Taylor*, Louisiana State University Press, 1946; General Samuel G. French, *Two Wars*, Confederate Veteran, 1901; Ulysses S. Grant, *Personal Memoirs of U. S. Grant*, Charles L. Webster & Company, 1894; Holman Hamilton, *Zachary Taylor*, The Bobbs-Merrill Company, 1941; W. S. Henry, *Campaign Sketches of the War with Mexico*, Arno Press, 1973; Edward J. Nichols, *Zach Taylor's Little Army*, Doubleday & Company, Inc., 1963; John H. Schroeder, *Mr. Polk's War*, The University of Wisconsin Press, 1973; E. Kirby Smith, *To Mexico with Scott*, edited by Emma Jerome Blackwood, Harvard University Press, 1917; Justin H. Smith, *The War with Mexico*, Vol. I, Peter Smith, 1963. Chapter II: Particularly useful sources: Bauer, *The Mexican War*; French, *Two Wars*; Luther Giddings, *Sketches of the Campaign in Northern Mexico by an Officer of the First Regiment of Ohio Volunteers*, George P. Putnam & Co., 1853; Grant, *Personal Memoirs of U. S. Grant*; James Kimmins Greer, *Colonel Jack Hays*, W. M. Morrison, Pub., 1974; Henry, *Campaign Sketches of the War with Mexico*; John R. Kenly, *Memoirs of a Maryland Volunteer*, J. B. Lippincott & Co., 1873; E. Kirby Smith, *To Mexico with Scott*; George Winston Smith and Charles Judah, *Chronicles of the Gringos*, The University of New Mexico Press, 1968; Justin H. Smith, *The War with Mexico*; Walter Prescott Webb, *The Story of the Texas Rangers*, Encino Press, 1971. Chapter III: Particularly useful sources: Hubert Howe Bancroft, *The Works of Hubert Howe Bancroft*, Vol. XXII, The History Company, Publishers, 1886; K. Jack Bauer, *Surfboats and Horse Marines*, United States Naval Institute, 1969; Bauer, *The Mexican War 1846-1848*; Walter Colton, *Three Years in California*, Arno Press, 1976; Bernard DeVoto, *The Year of Decision 1846*, Houghton Mifflin Company, 1943; William H. Emory, *Notes on a Military Reconnaissance*, Wendell and Van Benthuysen, 1848; John S. Griffin, *A Doctor Comes to California*, California Historical Society, 1943; Robert Selph Henry, *The Story of the Mexican War*, Frederick Ungar Publishing Co., 1950; Werner H. Marti, *Messenger of Destiny*, John Howell-Books, 1960; Allan Nevins. *Frémont*, Vol. I, Frederick Ungar Publishing Co., 1955; Allan Nevins, ed., *Polk*, Capricorn Books, 1968; Josiah Royce, *California*, Alfred A. Knopf, 1948; George Winston Smith, *Chronicles of the Gringos*; Justin H. Smith, *The War with Mexico*. Chapter IV: Particularly useful sources: Bauer, *Surfboats and Horse Marines*; Bauer, *The Mexican War 1846-1848*; Charles Winslow Elliott, *Winfield Scott*, The Macmillan Company, 1937; Douglas Southall Freeman, *R. E. Lee*, Vol. I, Charles Scribner's Sons, 1934; George S. Furber, *The Twelve Months Volunteer*, J. A. and U. P. James, 1850; William Goetzmann, ed., "Our First Foreign War," *American Heritage*, Vol. XVII, No. 1, June 1966; George B. McClellan, *The Mexican War Diary of General George B. McClellan*, edited by William Myers, Da Capo Press, 1972; Winfield Scott, *Memoirs of Lieut.-General Scott, LL.D.*, Books For Libraries Press, 1970; E. Kirby Smith, *To Mexico with Scott*; George Winston Smith, *Chronicles of the Gringos*; Justin H. Smith, *The War with Mexico*. Chapter V: Particularly useful sources: Bauer, *The Mexican War 1846-1848*; Alfred Hoyt Bill, *Rehearsal for Conflict*, Cooper Square Publishers, Inc., 1947; Nathan Covington Brooks, *A Complete History of the Mexican War*, The Rio Grande Press Inc., 1965; Charles L. Dufour, *The Mexican War*, Hawthorne Books, 1968; Schroeder, *Mr. Polk's War*; E. Kirby Smith, *To Mexico with Scott*; George Winston Smith, *Chronicles of the Gringos*; Justin H. Smith, *The War with Mexico*, Vol. II. Chapter VI: Particularly useful sources: Bauer, *The Mexican War 1846-1848*; Grant, *Personal Memoirs of U. S. Grant*; Robert Selph Henry, *The Story of the Mexican War*; Ethan Allen Hitchcock, *Fifty Years in Camp and Field*, G. P. Putnam's Sons, 1909; Roswell Sabine Ripley, *War with Mexico*, Harper & Brothers, Publishers, 1849; Scott, *Memoirs of Lieut.-General Scott, LL.D.*; E. Kirby Smith, *To Mexico with Scott*; George Winston Smith, *Chronicles of the Gringos*; Justin H. Smith, *The War with Mexico*, Vol. II; T. Harry Williams, ed., *With Beauregard in Mexico*, Da Capo Press, 1969.

BIBLIOGRAPHY

Bancroft, Hubert Howe, *The Works of Hubert Howe Bancroft*, Volumes V and XXII. The History Company, Publishers, 1886 (Reprint).

Bauer, K. Jack: *The Mexican War 1846-1848*. Macmillan Publishing Co., Inc., 1974.
Surfboats and Horse Marines. United States Naval Institute, 1969.

Bill, Alfred Hoyt, *Rehearsal for Conflict*. Cooper Square Publishers, Inc., 1947.

Brooks, Nathan Covington, *A Complete History of the Mexican War*. The Rio Grande Press, Inc., 1965 (Reprint).

Callcott, Wilfrid M., *Santa Anna*. Archon Books, 1964.

Colton, Walter, *Three Years in California*. Arno Press, 1976 (Reprint).

Davis, Gherardi, *The Colors of the United States Army, 1789-1912*. The Gillis Press, 1912.

DeVoto, Bernard, *The Year of Decision 1846*. Houghton Mifflin Company, 1943.

Dufour, Charles L., *The Mexican War, A Compact History 1846-1848*. Hawthorne Books, 1968.

Dyer, Brainerd, *Zachary Taylor*. Louisiana State University Press, 1946.

Elliott, Charles Winslow, *Winfield Scott*. The Macmillan Company, 1937.

Ellison, William, "San Juan to Cahuenga," *Pacific Historical Review*, Vol. 27, 1958.

Elting, Col. John R., *Military Uniforms in America*, Vol. II. Presidio Press, 1977.

Emory, William H., *Notes on a Military Reconnaissance*. Wendell and Van Benthuysen, 1848.

Engelmann, Otto B., ed., "The Second Illinois In the Mexican War, Mexican War Letters of Adolph Engelmann, 1846-1847," *Journal of the Illinois State Historical Society*, Vol. XXVI, January 1934.

Finke, Detmar H., "The Organization and Uniforms of the San Patricio Units of the Mexican Army, 1846-1848," *Journal of the Company of Military Collectors and Historians*, Vol. 9, No. 2, Summer, 1957.

Freeman, Douglas Southall, *R. E. Lee*, Vol. I. Charles Scribner's

Sons, 1934.

French, General Samuel G., *Two Wars*. Confederate Veteran, 1901.

Furber, George S., *The Twelve Months Volunteer*. J. H. and U. P. James, 1850.

Ganoe, William A., *The History of the United States Army*. Eric Lundberg, 1964.

Giddings, Luther, *Sketches of the Campaign in Northern Mexico by an Officer of the First Regiment of Ohio Volunteers*. George P. Putnam & Co., 1853.

Goetzmann, William, ed., "Our First Foreign War," *American Heritage*, Vol. XVII, No. 1, June 1966.

Grant, Ulysses S., *Personal Memoirs of U. S. Grant*. Charles L. Webster & Company, 1894.

Greer, James Kimmins, *Colonel Jack Hays*. W. M. Morrison, Pub., 1974.

Griffin, John S., *A Doctor Comes to California*. California Historical Society, 1943.

Hamilton, Holman, *Zachary Taylor*. The Bobbs-Merrill Company, 1941.

Heitman, Francis B., *Historical Register and Dictionary of the United States Army*, Vols. I and II. U.S. Government Printing Office, 1903.

Henry, Robert Selph, *The Story of the Mexican War*. Frederick Ungar Publishing Co., 1950.

Henry, W. S., *Campaign Sketches of the War with Mexico*. Arno Press, 1973 (Reprint).

Hitchcock, Ethan Allen, *Fifty Years in Camp and Field*. G. P. Putnam's Sons, 1909.

Howden Smith, Arthur D., *Old Fuss and Feathers*. The Greystone Press, 1937.

Howell, Edgar M. and Donald E. Kloster, *United States Army Headgear to 1854*, Vol. 1. Smithsonian Institution Press, 1969.

Kenly, John R., *Memoirs of a Maryland Volunteer*. J. B. Lippincott & Co., 1873.

Lewis, Lloyd, *Captain Sam Grant*. Little, Brown & Company, 1950.

McClellan, George B., *The Mexican War Diary of General George B. McClellan*, William Myers, ed. Da Capo Press, 1972.

McCornack, Richard B., "The San Patricio Deserters in the Mexican War," *The Americas*, Vol. 8, October 1951.

Mansfield, Edward D., *The Mexican War*. A. S. Barnes & Co., 1848.

Marti, Werner H., *Messenger of Destiny*. John Howell-Books, 1960.

Mastai, Boleslaw and Marie-Louise D'Otrange, *The Stars and the Stripes*. Alfred A. Knopf, Inc., 1973.

Meade, George, *The Life and Letters of George Gordon Meade*, Vol. I. Charles Scribner's Sons, 1913.

Meltzer, Milton, *Bound for the Rio Grande*. Alfred A. Knopf, 1974.

Merk, Frederick, *Manifest Destiny and Mission in American History*. Vintage Books, 1966.

Nevins, Allan, *Frémont*, Vol. 1. Frederick Ungar Publishing Co., 1955.

Nevins, Allan, ed., *Polk*. Capricorn Books, 1968.

Nichols, Edward J., *Zach Taylor's Little Army*, Doubleday & Company, Inc., 1963.

Ramsey, Albert C., *The Other Side*. Burt Franklin, 1970 (Reprint).

Rankin, Col. Robert, *Uniforms of the Sea Services*. U.S. Naval Institute, 1962.

Ripley, Roswell Sabine, *War with Mexico*, Vols. 1 & 2. Harper & Brothers, Publishers, 1849.

Royce, Josiah, *California*. Alfred A. Knopf, 1948.

Schroeder, John H., *Mr. Polk's War*. The University of Wisconsin Press, 1973.

Scott, Winfield, *Memoirs of Lieut.-General Scott, LL.D.*, Vols. I & II, Books For Libraries Press, 1970 (Reprint).

Sedgwick, John, *Correspondence of John Sedgwick Major-General*, Vol. I, 1902.

Smith, E. Kirby, *To Mexico with Scott*. Emma Jerome Blackwood, ed. Harvard University Press, 1917.

Smith, George Winston and Charles Judah, *Chronicles of the Gringos*. The University of New Mexico Press, 1968.

Smith, Justin H., *The War with Mexico*, Vols. I & II. Peter Smith, 1963 (Reprint).

Tyler, Ronnie C., *The Mexican War*. Texas State Historical Association, 1973.

Wallace, Edward S., *General William Jenkins Worth*. Southern Methodist University Press, 1953.

Webb, Walter Prescott, *The Story of the Texas Rangers*. Encino Press, 1971.

Weems, John Edward, *To Conquer a Peace*. Doubleday & Company, Inc., 1974.

Williams, T. Harry, ed., *With Beauregard in Mexico*. Da Capo Press, 1969.

ACKNOWLEDGMENTS

The index for this book was prepared by Gale Partoyan. The editors give special thanks to K. Jack Bauer, Professor of History, Rensselaer Polytechnic Institute, Troy, New York; and Carl Dentzel, Director, The Southwest Museum, Highland Park, Los Angeles, California, who commented on the text. The editors also thank: William G. Allman, Clement Conger, Office of the Curator, The White House, Washington, D. C.; James Biddle, National Trust for Historic Preservation, Washington, D. C.; Patricia Carr Black, Mississippi State Historical Museum, Jackson; Michael Bremer, Wood-Ridge, New Jersey; Anne S. K. Brown, Providence, Rhode Island; Sidney B. Brinckerhoff, Donald H. Bufkin, Arizona Historical Society, Tucson; R. LeGette Burris, Division of Numismatics, Craddock R. Goins, Harry Hunter, Donald Kloster, Daniel Stanton, Division of Military History, National Museum of History and Technology, Smithsonian Institution, Washington, D. C.; Pierce Butler, Nashville, Tennessee; Peter Buxtun, San Francisco, California; Henry Cadwalader, York Harbor, Maine; John M. Cahoon, William Mason, Los Angeles County Museum of Natural History, Los Angeles, California; Mr. and Mrs. Archibald Campbell, Cold Spring-on-Hudson, New York; J. Duncan Campbell, Pennsylvania Historical and Museum Commission, Harrisburg; Colonel Moreau Chambers, Detmar Finke, Janice McKenny, Marion McNaughton, United States Army Center of Military History, Washington, D. C.; Stephen D. Cox, Tennessee State Museum, Nashville; John W. Crain, M. Susie Stephenson, Dallas Historical Society, Dallas, Texas; Colonel Leslie Cross, National Guard Association of the United States, Washington, D. C.; Philip H. Dunbar, Connecticut Historical Society, Hartford; Colonel John Elting, Cornwall-on-Hudson, New York; William R. Emerson, Franklin D. Roosevelt Library, Hyde Park, New York; Linda Faucheux, The Historic New Orleans Collection, New Orleans, Louisiana; Stanley Flink, Archibald Hanna, Dale Roylance, Yale University, New Haven, Connecticut; Suzanne Gallup, The Bancroft Library, Berkeley, California; Donna-Belle Garvin, New Hampshire Historical Society, Concord; Vaughn L. Glasgow, J. B. Harter, Robert R. MacDonald, Mary Louise Tucker, Louisiana State Museum, New Orleans; Edward Green, John Langellier, Presidio Army Museum, San Francisco, California; Barry A. Greenlaw, The Bayou Bend Collection, Houston, Texas; Gail Guidry, John H. Lindenbusch, Patience P. Taylor, Missouri Historical Society, St. Louis; Randy W. Hackenburg, U.S. Army Military History Institute, Carlisle Barracks, Pennsylvania; Richard B. Harrington, The Anne S. K. Brown Military Collection, Providence, Rhode Island; James J. Heslin, New-York Historical Society, New York; J. B. Hilliard, Kenneth Smith-Christmas, United States Marine Corps Museum, Washington, D. C.; Paul P. Hoffman, State of North Carolina Department of Cultural Resources, Raleigh; Joseph G. Hooper Jr., San Francisco, California; Catherine Hoover, Garry Kurutz, Maude Swingle, California Historical Society, San Francisco; Milo B. Howard Jr., Alabama Department of Archives and History, Montgomery; Commander John C. Hunt, Washington, D. C.; Inventory of American Paintings, Smithsonian Institution, Washington, D. C.; Florence Jacobson, David M. Mayfield, Church of Jesus Christ of Latter-Day Saints, Salt Lake City, Utah; Myra Ellen Jenkins, Historical Services Division, State Record Center and Archives, Santa Fe, New Mexico; Lt. Colonel Carl O. Johnson, Brigadier General John R. Phipps, State of Illinois Military and Naval Department, Springfield; Colonel Robert J. T. Joy, Uniformed Services University of the Health Sciences, Bethesda, Maryland; Jerry L. Kearns, Prints and Photographs, Library of Congress, Washington, D. C.; Richard E. Keuhne, Michael McAfee, Michael E. Moss, Walter Nock, West Point Museum, West Point, New York; Clifford Krainik, Graphic Antiquity, Arlington Heights, Illinois; Dorothy W. Knepper, San Jacinto Museum of History Association, Deer Park, Texas; Felipe La Couture, National Museum of History, Mexico City, Mexico; Robert M. Lunny, New Jersey Historical Society, Newark; Greg Martin, San Francisco, California; James R. Mitchell, William Penn Memorial Museum, Harrisburg, Pennsylvania; Weston Naef, Metropolitan Museum of Art, New York, New York; Lieutenant Craig Nannos, Broomall, Pennsylvania; Mark E. Nelly Jr., Lincoln National Life Foundation, Fort Wayne, Indiana; Arthur Olivas, Museum of New Mexico, Santa Fe; Herb Peck Jr., Nashville, Tennessee; Cecilia Steinfeldt, Witte Memorial Museum, San Antonio, Texas; Keith D. Strawn, North Carolina Museum of History, Raleigh; Joseph M. Thatcher, Conservation and Collection Care Center, New York State Parks and Recreation Department, Waterford; The late Colonel Frederick P. Todd, Cornwall-on-Hudson, New York; Jesse H. Travis, U.S. Army Quartermaster Museum, Fort Lee, Virginia; John Triss, Larry Viskochil, Chicago Historical Society, Chicago, Illinois; Ron Tyler, Amon Carter Museum of Western Art, Fort Worth, Texas; Samuel J. Wagstaff Jr., New York, New York; Joyce White, James K. Polk Birthplace State Historic Site, Pineville, North Carolina; Mary Van Zandt, University of Texas at Arlington, Arlington; Michael L. Vice, U.S. Cavalry Museum, Fort Riley, Kansas.

PICTURE CREDITS

The sources for the illustrations in this book are shown below. Credits from left to right are separated by semicolons and from top to bottom by dashes.

Cover—Charles Phillips, courtesy Library of Congress. 2—Henry Groskinsky, courtesy National Museum of History and Technology, Smithsonian Institution (2). 6 through 11—Derek Bayes, courtesy Victoria & Albert Museum, London. 12—Bob Rice, courtesy Dallas Historical Society. 15 through 17—Courtesy Library of Congress. 18—Courtesy National Portrait Gallery, Smithsonian Institution. 19 through 23—Courtesy Library of Congress. 24, 25—Courtesy The Bancroft Library; courtesy Art of the Book Collection, Sterling Library, Yale University (2). 26, 27—Courtesy Library of Congress. 29—Ed Frank. 30 through 34—Courtesy Library of Congress. 36—Courtesy Beinecke Rare Book and Manuscript Library, Yale University; courtesy Missouri Historical Society—courtesy Dr. Carl S. Dentzel Collection. 37—Courtesy Chicago Historical Society—courtesy Library of Congress. 38—Courtesy Art of the Book Collection, Sterling Library, Yale University. 40, 41—Courtesy Library of Congress. 42—Joel Snyder, courtesy Graphic Antiquity Collection, Arlington Heights, Illinois. 44—Henry Groskinsky, courtesy West Point Museum Collections, United States Military Academy (2)—Tom Tracy, courtesy the Greg Martin Collection; Henry Beville, courtesy North Carolina Museum of History, Raleigh. 45—Henry Groskinsky, courtesy West Point Museum Collections, United States Military Academy; Henry Groskinsky, courtesy National Museum of History and Technology, Smithsonian Institution. 46—Henry Groskinsky, courtesy Washington's Headquarters State Historic Site, Palisades Interstate Park and Recreation Region, New York State Office of Parks and Recreation (2)—Tom Tracy, courtesy Presidio Army Museum Collection, San Francisco; Henry Beville, courtesy Louisiana State Museum. 47—Henry Beville, Missouri Historical Society; Henry Beville, courtesy North Carolina Museum of History, Raleigh—Henry Beville, courtesy Louisiana State Museum. 48—Henry Beville, courtesy United States Marine Corps Museum; Henry Groskinsky, courtesy National Museum of History and Technology, Smithsonian Institution (2). 49—Henry Groskinsky, courtesy National Museum of History and Technology, Smithsonian Institution. 50—Henry Groskinsky, courtesy National Museum of History, Mexico City (2). 51—Henry Groskinsky, courtesy National Museum of History and Technology; Smithsonian Institution; Henry Beville, courtesy Missouri Historical Society (2)—Ed Stewart & Associates Photography, courtesy San Jacinto Museum of History Association (2). 52—Henry Groskinsky, courtesy National Museum of History, Mexico City; Henry Groskinsky, courtesy National Museum of History and Technology, Smithsonian Institution (2). 53—Henry Groskinsky, courtesy National Museum of History, Mexico City—Henry Groskinsky, courtesy National Museum of History and Technology, Smithsonian Institution—Henry Groskinsky, courtesy National Museum of History and Technology, Smithsonian Institution; Ed Stewart & Associates Photography, courtesy San

Printed in U.S.A.